**DO NOT REMOVE
CARDS FROM POCKET**

AFRICA
Apostolic Pilgrimage

AFRICA
Apostolic Pilgrimage

JOHN PAUL II

Compiled and Indexed
by the Daughters of St. Paul

ST. PAUL EDITIONS

Reprinted with permission from *L'Osservatore Romano*, English Edition.

ISBN 0-8198-0708-7 cloth
ISBN 0-8198-0709-5 paper

Photo Credits:
Felici cover, 55, 71, 87, 103, 109, 131, 138,
    143, 164, 175, 178, 217, 236, 270, 299,
    313, 331, 336, 343, 358, 381, 399, 407,
    417
Wide World Photos 25, 31, 117, 141, 193,
    227, 249, 288, 368, 391, 405

Printed in U.S.A. by the Daughters of St. Paul
50 St. Paul's Ave., Boston, MA 02130

The Daughters of St. Paul are an international congregation of
religious women serving the Church with the communications
media.

CONTENTS

FROM THE MATERIAL TO A SPIRITUAL EDIFICE

On Saturday, April 26, the Holy Father for the first time consecrated a parish church in Rome. The church in question, in the Ardeatine district of Poggio Ameno, is dedicated to the Holy Martyrs of Uganda. John Paul II delivered the following homily.

Venerable brothers and beloved sons!

1. It seems to me almost superfluous to express my satisfaction at celebrating this solemn liturgy, so evident are the reasons for pleasure and joy. Today for the first time since, by disposition of divine Providence, I assumed responsibility for Peter's See, I have the privilege of presiding over the rite of the consecration of a church here in Rome. It is a new church, a parish church, which joins the splendid crown of sacred buildings that mark the Christian face of the city, and it will receive within it the People of God, which will be able to draw from the table of the word, from the table of the Eucharist, and the other sacramental sources, that multiform nourishment necessary for its supernatural growth.

Furthermore, a public monument is erected in honor of the Ugandan martyrs and, also from this point of view, it can be said that a new host of witnesses to Christ takes its place at the side of the *candidatus exercitus,* to which the Church has so often dedicated a special place of worship on Roman soil.

From Uganda, in fact, there came to us a stupendous testimony of faith last century! Today, therefore, it can be said that Christian Rome looks once more to Christian Africa for the modern and heroic page it has added to its martyrology and its history.

A LIVING CORNERSTONE

2. Addressing my affectionate greeting to all those gathered here—the Cardinal Vicar Ugo Poletti and the Cardinal Archbishop of Kampala, Emanuele Nsubuga, the civil authorities, the parish priest with his collaborators and all the faithful of the parish—I wish to draw the attention of all, on the occasion of the consecration, to the liturgical readings which have been chosen for it. I would like to stress, in particular, the second reading, and then the Gospel text.

In the first place, mention should be made of what St. Peter said to us, because not only is it perfectly adapted to the present occasion, but it makes it possible to pass, according to a line of symmetrical consistency, from the idea of a material edifice to that of a spiritual edifice, from the Church-temple to the Church-communion of souls. At the base of the whole work—the Prince of the Apostles reminds us—there is Christ the Lord, a living cornerstone, a stone chosen and precious before God. But also our souls are living stones, and as such they are used to be constructed on the foundation of that same stone, so as to form a spiritual house, a holy priesthood, and therefore made fit to offer spiritual sacrifices, pleasing to God (cf. 1 Pt. 2:4-5).

The deep meaning of this apostolic teaching can never be stressed too much: I mean the mystery of

our being built upon Christ, that is, of becoming a
Church with Him, in Him, for Him! Remember in this
connection, beloved brothers and sons, what the Second Vatican Council proposed to us again in the
Dogmatic Constitution *Lumen gentium*, which, among
the various images of the Church, did not forget that
of a building (cf. no. 6). We must be built upon Christ,
because this and nothing else is the foundation that
gives our life stability and safety. St. Paul, in fact, explains, echoing perfectly his co-apostle Peter: in the
Church "no other foundation can anyone lay than
that which is laid, which is Jesus Christ (...). Do you
not know that you are God's temple and that God's
spirit dwells in you?" (1 Cor. 3:11, 16).

Here there is, again, the idea of the building
developed to its terminal point, of a temple complete
in all its parts. Each of us in this temple is a living
stone, but not isolated, not independent, not self-
sufficient. Each of us can build himself up only in
Christ, while without Him the whole construction
would be destined to collapse: this is the superstruc-
ture. Each of us must build himself up together with
other brothers, by virtue of the law of ecclesial communion, which is, as it were, the "cement" that
amalgamates us all in Christ: this is the being built
together. Only on these conditions does the temple of
God rise majestically.

We all form the Church of God, because we are
solidly founded on Christ, His Son, and we are closely
linked with our brothers in the faith. Precisely this
awareness is among the qualifying points of the Christian profession: *Credo unam, sanctam, cathólicam et
apostólicam Ecclésiam!* We often recite this article of
our faith, but we must also merit it, asking the Spirit

to enlighten us interiorly, in order that He may shed His divine light in the mystical temple of our soul, in which He Himself dwells.

DYNAMIC CENTER OF COMMUNITY LIFE

3. It is beyond doubt, moreover, that also the material temple is necessary. We all know the difficulties that the construction of new sacred buildings presents. It is sometimes a serious problem, not easy to solve. But the building of stone is not everything; it has a clearly instrumental and symbolic function in relation to the other superior edifice, of which I have spoken to you so far.

What then—we may ask ourselves—is the connection between the two edifices? Jesus explains it to us in the Gospel, in a passage of His talk with the Samaritan woman. "Woman, believe me, the hour is coming when neither on this mountain nor in Jerusalem will you worship the Father (...). The hour is coming, and now is, when the true worshippers will worship the Father in spirit and truth, for such the Father seeks to worship him. God is spirit..." (Jn. 4:21-23). We find in this text a revelation which enlightens us about what religious life must really be. It is "truth," because it must adapt itself to what God is. Since God is pure spirit, worship, as the supreme act of the cult we offer Him, cannot but be in spirit. To the ontological reality of God-spirit there corresponds the psychological reality of man who worships Him in spirit: here is the truth, as the dimension of the worship willed by Christ.

I express, therefore, the wish that the temple, which is publicly inaugurated today, as the dynamic center of the community life of this parish, may gather and welcome in ever larger numbers worshippers such as the Father seeks (cf. *ibid.*). Integrated as living stones in the ecclesial edifice, they will be able, without hesitation and without deviations, to follow Christ, who is the sure way to go to the Father (cf. Jn. 14:6). In this way there will begin already here below the liturgy which enables us to participate in, and have a foretaste of, the heavenly liturgy which is celebrated up above, in the holy city of Jerusalem, in a full and perfect form (cf. Const. *Sacrosanctum concilium*, no. 8). It will be up above that we will sing to the Lord our hymn of glory, with all the angels and with the saints.

MARTYRS OF UGANDA

4. The last thought that I wish to propose to you, beloved sons, is inspired by this vision of heaven, where the twenty-two martyrs of Uganda are living in God. I turn all the more willingly to these brothers of ours, as also to their African land, since I will be going there towards the end of next week. Just as Paul VI, after having canonized them (October 18, 1964), went on pilgrimage to Kampala for the consecration of the altar of their sanctuary and to conclude an important symposium of the African Episcopate, so his humble successor, for a similar pastoral reason, has decided to make a new pilgrimage to various other countries of that same continent. Now it seems to me that it is necessary to take into account the connection between the celebration this evening and both pilgrimages. It is always the Church of Rome

which, as in the past, now moves to visit chosen portions of its organic and undivided body, in order to establish, as then, a closer contact with the living stones of its uniform edifice and promote, furthermore, mutual edification in charity and peace.

My journey is intended as a joyful recognition of Paul VI's statement: *Africa est nova patria Christi* (Homily at the canonization of the Ugandan Martyrs: *AAS* LVI [1964], pp. 907-908), and it is likewise a celebration of ecclesial unity; so that the fact of being gathered here this afternoon, surrounded by the brotherly presence of Ugandan faithful, is a happy auspice for my now imminent departure. I ask you, beloved sons, to include among the intentions of your prayer also a thought for this visit of mine to Africa, in order that it may be the Lord, only the Lord, who will guide my steps and that He will help me in the ministry of strengthening my brothers, which falls upon me as Peter's successor (cf. Lk. 22:32). And I thank you already for this charity.

5. And now I address a special greeting to the pilgrimage from Uganda.

Dear pilgrims from Uganda:

I have already welcomed, in the course of last Wednesday's general audience, the pilgrims from Uganda who have come for this celebration. It is a joy to have you here today. You are the heirs of the martyrs in whose honor this church has been built. They have handed down to you the treasure of the Christian faith. It is a treasure whose value is all the more evident because of their witness to it. They were prepared to die rather than be robbed of it. They knew that it is worth more than all earthly wealth, because it gives access to riches that are infinitely superior and that last forever, because it is the gateway to a life with which the life of the body cannot be compared.

Prove yourselves worthy of the heritage that you have received. Show that you value your Christian faith as highly as did St. Charles Lwanga and his holy companions. Live in accordance with the program that my predecessor Paul VI put before you when he visited your country: "First, have great love for Jesus Christ; try to know Him well, remain united to Him, have great faith and great trust in Him. Second, be faithful to the Church; pray with her, love her, make her known, and always be ready, as your martyrs were, to bear frank witness to her. Third, be strong and courageous; be content; be happy and joyful always. Because, remember this always, the Christian life is a most beautiful thing!"

"HAPPY TO SHARE IN THE JOY OF THE YOUNG CHURCHES"

On Friday, May 2, 1980, the Holy Father left Fiumicino Airport on his journey to Africa. To the ecclesiastical dignitaries who were present for his departure he delivered the following address.

At the moment when I am about to begin my apostolic journey in Africa, I wish to thank with deep esteem and sincere cordiality those present: Their Eminences the Cardinals, the members of the Diplomatic Corps accredited to the Holy See, the representatives of the Italian government and all those who have wished to express to me their affection and their encouragement for this long new journey of mine.

The historical context of this initiative is that of participating in the celebrations of the centenary of evangelization in Ghana and in Zaire. I am going to the heart of an immense continent, Africa, which received the light of the Christian faith from the missionaries. At the same time I am happy to be able to participate intensely, with my personal presence, in the joy of those young Churches, in which native bishops have now succeeded the missionary bishops.

I also wished to extend this first visit to other nations in the center of the African continent, that is, the People's Republic of the Congo, Kenya, Upper Volta and the Ivory Coast.

I am going to the Africa of the Ugandan martyrs, and therefore, right from this moment, I cannot but express to the nations I will visit, as well as to all the other nations of that continent, the affection and the hope that the Pope and the Church cherish for them.

It was not possible, unfortunately, to include also all those African countries from which I received pressing and affectionate invitations. I thank them for this cordial gesture, and I trust I will be able to meet their desire one day.

Like my preceding journeys, this one, too, has *an eminently religious and missionary purpose:* the Bishop of Rome, the Pastor of the universal Church is going to Africa to strengthen (cf. Lk. 22:32) his brothers in the episcopate, the priests, deacons, men and women religious, missionaries, men and women, all united in the same faith in Christ who died for our sins and rose again for our justification (cf. Rom. 4:25); to pray with them and express to those local Churches, pulsating with youthful life and enthusiastic dynamism, the admiration and satisfaction of the whole Church with regard to them; and also to manifest to all the inhabitants of Africa sincere sentiments of esteem and respect for their traditions and their culture, and cordially to wish them prosperity and peace.

I am going to the Africa of the Ugandan martyrs and therefore, right from this moment, I cannot but express to the nations I will visit, as well as to all the other nations of that continent, the affection and the hope that the Pope and the Church cherish for them. Modern Africa has unquestioned importance and an original role in the context of present-day international life, owing to its problems of a political, social and economic character; of its dynamism, inherent in the fresh and vital forces of its inhabitants. That great continent is constructing its own history, though in the midst of so many tensions. African Catholics, like all believers in Christ, together with all believers in God, will certainly be able to offer a powerful and precious contribution of ideas and activity for the construction of an Africa which, in respect of ancient cultural values, will know how to live in solidarity, order and justice.

May the Lord, in these days, give strength to my steps, which proclaim peace (cf. Is. 52:7).

May the Virgin Mary, in whose motherly heart I have placed the attainment of the spiritual aims of my journey, assist me, Africa and the whole Church.

NOBLE HERITAGE OF HUMAN AND SPIRITUAL VALUES

On arrival at N'djili Airport at Kinshasa on the afternoon of May 2, 1980, the Holy Father was welcomed by President Mobutu, and in reply to a speech by the latter, His Holiness gave the following address.

Excellencies, ladies and gentlemen, Mr. President, Lord Cardinal, you dear brothers and sisters,

God bless Zaire! God bless the whole of Africa!

1. It is a very great joy for me to reach the African continent for the first time. Yes, as I kiss this soil, my heart overflows with emotion, joy and hope. It is the emotion of discovering the African reality and of meeting in it this considerable part of humanity, which merits esteem and love, and which is also called to salvation in Jesus Christ. It is the paschal joy that dwells in me and that I would like to share with you. It is the hope that a new life, a better life, a more free and brotherly life is possible on this earth, and that the Church which I represent can greatly contribute to it. This visit and the meetings it will make possible are graces for which I want first of all to thank the Lord. God be blessed!

28

CORDIAL AND FERVENT
GOOD WISHES

2. To all the inhabitants of Africa, whatever may be their country and their origin, I express my warm and friendly greetings, and my feelings of trust. I greet first of all my Catholic brothers and sons, and other Christians. I greet all those who, deeply animated with religious sentiments, are bent on submitting their lives to God or seeking His presence. I greet the families, fathers and mothers, children and old people. I greet especially those who are suffering in body and soul. I greet those who are working for the common good of their fellow-citizens, for their education, their prosperity, their health, their safety. I greet each of the African nations. I rejoice with them that they have taken their destiny into their own hands. I am thinking at the same time of the noble heritage of their human and spiritual values, their meritorious efforts, and all their present needs. Each nation has still a long way to go in order to forge its unity; deepen its personality and its culture; carry out the development that is necessary in so many fields, and do so in justice, with concern for the participation and interest of everyone; to take its place actively in the concert of nations. For this purpose Africa needs independence and disinterested aid; it needs peace. To one and all, I express cordial and fervent wishes.

A SPIRITUAL MISSION

3. I come here as a spiritual leader, the servant of Jesus Christ in the line of the apostle Peter and of all his successors, the Bishops of Rome. I have the mis-

sion, with my brothers the bishops of the local Churches, to strengthen the sons of the whole Church in true faith, and in love according to Jesus Christ, to watch over their unity and increase their witness. A large number of Africans now belong to the Christian Faith and I would like my visit to be a consolation for them, at this significant stage of their history. Two of these Churches have invited me especially for the centenary of evangelization, which others are also preparing to celebrate.

I come here as a man of religion. I appreciate the religious sense so deeply rooted in the African soul and which requires, not to be set aside, but on the contrary, purified, elevated and strengthened. I esteem those who are anxious to lead their existence and construct their city in a vital relationship with God, taking into account the moral requirements He has inscribed on the conscience of each one, and likewise the fundamental human rights, which He guarantees. I share with those who have this spiritual view of man the conviction that materialism, wherever it may come from, is a form of slavery from which man must be defended.

I come here as a messenger of peace, anxious to encourage the peacemakers, like Jesus. True love seeks peace, and peace is absolutely necessary in order that Africa may be able to dedicate itself completely to the great tasks that await it. With all my African friends, I would like every child of this continent to be able tomorrow to find nourishment for the body and nourishment for the spirit, in a climate of justice, safety and concord.

I come here as a man of hope.

I come here as a messenger of peace, anxious to encourage the peacemakers, like Jesus. True love seeks peace, and peace is absolutely necessary in order that Africa may be able to dedicate itself completely to the great tasks that await it.

DESIRE TO RETURN

4. Without waiting any longer, I thank Africa for its welcome. I was profoundly touched by the hospitality that so many countries of this continent have so generously offered me in the last few months. It was really impossible for me to accept all the invitations, during this first ten-day journey. I deeply regretted this, and I am thinking particularly of the expectation of certain countries that are particularly meritorious and rich in Christian vitality, which I would have liked so much to visit. But these are visits postponed until later. I hope that Providence will give the Pope the opportunity to carry them out in the future. I have the firm hope that I will return to this continent. Let all these countries be assured straightaway of my esteem and good wishes! I will think of them, moreover, of their merits, their joys and their human and spiritual concerns when I tackle the different themes of my journey and address the various categories of interlocutors. My message is for the whole of Africa.

PROMISING COUNTRY

5. And now, I turn specially to this country of Zaire which is in the heart of Africa and which is the first to receive me. This great promising country, which I am so happy to visit, this country called to great tasks, tasks which are difficult. My first word is to thank Mr. President and his government, and to thank the bishops, for their pressing invitation.

I know the attachment of a large number of Zaireans to the Christian Faith and to the Catholic Church, thanks to an evangelization which has progressed very rapidly.

It is now the centenary of this evangelization that I have come to celebrate with you, dear friends. It is good to look at the road traveled, along which God has not been sparing of His graces for Zaire. A host of workers of the Gospel came from far away, and dedicated their lives so that you, too, might have access to salvation in Jesus Christ. And the sons and daughters of this country accepted the Faith. It has yielded abundant fruit in a large number of baptized. Priests, sisters, bishops, a Cardinal, have sprung from the Zairean people, to animate, with their brothers, this local Church and give it its true face, fully African and fully Christian, linked with the universal Church which I represent among you. During the days that follow, we will speak of all this again. The prospect of all these meetings fills me with deep delight. Let all these brothers and sons, all the inhabitants of this country, receive my warm greeting straightaway and the friendly wishes that my heart forms for them.

God bless Zaire! God bless Africa!

"MAY THE CENTENARY OF EVANGELIZATION GIVE A NEW IMPULSE TO YOUR FAITH"

On May 2, after the official welcoming ceremonies at N'djili Airport, the Holy Father drove in a motorcade to Kinshasa Cathedral of "Notre Dame du Zaire." There he was awaited by about one thousand five hundred priests, religious and seminarians. After an address of homage by Cardinal Malula, Pope John Paul II spoke as follows.

Blessed be Jesus Christ!

May God our Father and Jesus Christ our Lord grant you grace and peace!

May the Holy Spirit be your joy!

1. Dear brothers and sisters in Christ,

Your Archbishop, dear Cardinal Joseph Malula, has just now welcomed me on behalf of you all, bishops, priests, men and women religious, seminarians and laity of the archdiocese of Kinshasa and other Catholic communities of Zaire. I thank him heartily. He recalled the vitality of the Church in Zaire, a vitality that the Church of Rome knows and appreciates. And I, Bishop of Rome, had a great desire to come to you.

I come as servant of Jesus Christ, the invisible Head of the Church. I come as the successor of the apostle Peter, to whom Jesus said: "Strengthen your brothers"; then, three times: "Feed my lambs...tend my sheep" (Jn. 21:15-17), that is, the whole flock of my disciples. By the will of God, in spite of my unworthiness, I have inherited in my turn this task, which is that of the Pope, that is of the Father, that of the Vicar of Christ on earth, who presides over the unity in faith and charity.

CENTENARY CELEBRATION

2. In the very first place, I thank God with you for all that He has carried out in Zaire in a hundred years. Today I come to celebrate with you the centenary of evangelization, to look with you at the way traveled, a way that has known difficulties and sorrows, joys and hopes. A way of grace! The centenary enables us to assess better, in a way, the blessings of the Lord and the merits of your predecessors. And, supported by this Christian history, to start off again with new impetus.

Just a century ago, in fact, some missionaries, burning with love for Christ and for you, came to share with you the faith they had themselves received; they wished, right from the beginning, to implant the Church, set up a local Church with the Africans. The harvest was a large one. Your fathers accepted the Word of God with generosity and enthusiasm. Today the tree of the Church is firmly rooted in this country; its branches spread all over the country. Faith has become the lot of a considerable number of citizens of Zaire. From your Zairean families have come bishops, priests, sisters, catechists, committed lay people, who guide or support your communities. The Gospel has left its mark in life and in morals. God be praised!

And blessed be all those who made this Church flourish, those who came from far away and those who were born in this country! Blessed be they who lead it today!

NEW STAGE OPENS

3. Dear friends, you have lived a first great stage, an irreversible stage. *A new stage* is open to you, a no less exalting one, even if it necessarily involves new trials, and perhaps temptations of discouragement. It is the stage of perseverance, that in which it is necessary to pursue the *strengthening of faith,* the conversion, in depth, of souls and ways of life, so that they will correspond better and better to your sublime Christian vocation; not to mention evangelization which you must yourselves continue in sectors or environments where the Gospel is still unknown. As St. Peter wrote to the first generations of converts in the Diaspora, I say to you: "Gird up your minds...as he who called you is holy, be holy yourselves in all your conduct" (1 Pt. 1:13-16). The task of being a Christian never ends.

In this way the Church that is in Zaire will reach its full Christian and African maturity.

TO ENCOURAGE YOU

4. I know that *your bishops*—who are your pastors and your fathers—guide you clear-sightedly and courageously along these ways of the kingdom of God, as the exhortations, letters or appeals that they have addressed to you personally or collegially, bear witness. I come tò strengthen and encourage the ministry of

these bishops who are my brothers. But at the same time, I come to encourage all Christian men and women of Kinshasa and Zaire.

I am happy that my first meeting, in this cathedral, is with the priests, men and women religious and seminarians. You have a very special place in the building up of the Church. Your ordination, your religious consecration, your call to the priesthood, are priceless graces. Give thanks to the Lord! Serve Him in joy, simplicity and purity of heart. You are destined, more than the other disciples of Christ, to be the salt that gives flavor, and the light that shines; I desired to have a long talk with priests, then with sisters, in the course of the coming days. But this very evening, I greet you with all my affection. My first word is a word of comfort, in the note of thanksgiving that is fitting for a centenary.

Priests, be happy to be ministers of Christ, proclaimers of His Word and dispensers of His mysteries: "Imitamini quod tractatis," "Practice what you preach." Be educators to faith, men of prayer, have the zeal and humility of servants, live your complete consecration to the kingdom of God of which your celibacy is the sign

Men and women religious, be happy to have given all your love to Christ; and to serve the Church, your brothers and sisters in complete availability. With all the consecrated persons of Zaire, let Christ seize your lives, in order to become transparent witnesses for the People of God and for men of good will. I am thinking of your sister, a Zairean, who preceded you, leaving a luminous example of purity and courage in faith, the Servant of God, Sister Anwarite, whom, I hope, the Church will soon be able to beatify.

And you, priests, men and women religious and laity who have come from other countries as *missionaries*, and who continue to cooperate in the various services of the Church in this country, be happy to be here where your help is precious and necessary, and where you are witnesses to the universal Church. Continue this friendly and disinterested service, under the guidance of Zairean pastors who will know how to welcome all priests fully in their presbyterium.

Seminarians, be happy to answer the call of the Master, who never disappoints. Accept the pedagogy of Christ which formed so many of your elders. Qualify yourselves, by assimilating thoroughly the solid doctrine and the discipline of life that will enable you to be spiritual guides in your turn. I hope that many will follow in your footsteps. Priestly vocations are a proof of the vitality and maturity of a local Church, which thus becomes capable of taking over responsibility for the work of the Gospel, giving the evangelical message and the mission of the Church their full Christian and African authenticity.

I cannot forget the *Christian laity* whom I will also meet: fathers and mothers of families, animators of little communities, catechists, educators, committed lay people, students and young people of Kinshasa or other cities or villages. May they be happy and proud of their faith! Wherever they work, may they be witnesses to the love of Christ who loved them first! And may they continue an apostolate in which they are irreplaceable!

THAT ALL MAY BE ONE

5. I must recommend to you all that the Apostle St. Paul expressed in all his letters, he who visited so many of the first Christian communities. It is the recommendation that inspired the last prayer of Jesus after the Last Supper: *"that they may all be one."* Yes, banish all division, live in the unity which pleases God and which is your strength, around your priests. And may the priests be united in their presbyterium around their bishops. Offer a kind welcome and real collaboration to one another, Zairean men and women, and to the foreigners who have come to share your life. The Church is a family from which no one is excluded.

Receiving your witness, I will bring you in my turn that of the Church which is in Rome, and that of the universal Church which has its center in Rome. It is one family. No community lives withdrawn within itself: it is connected with the great Church, the one Church. Your Church has been grafted onto the great tree of the Church, whence, for a hundred years, it has drawn its sap, which now enables it to give its fruits to her and to become a missionary to others itself. Your Church will have to deepen its local, African dimension, without ever forgetting its universal dimension. I know how fervently attached you are to the Pope. So I say to you: through him, remain united with the whole Church.

Now, I call upon you to turn, with me, your eyes and your hearts to the Virgin Mary.

ACT OF CONSECRATION

6. Allow me, in fact, in this year in which you are giving thanks to God for the centenary of evangeliza-

tion and the baptism of your country, to refer to the
tradition that we find at the beginning of this century,
at the beginning of evangelization in the land of
Africa.

The missionaries who came to proclaim the Gospel began their missionary service with an act of consecration to the Mother of Christ.

They addressed her as follows:

"Here we are, among those who are our brothers
and our sisters, and whom your Son, O Virgin Mary,
loved to the end. Out of love, He offered His life for
them on the cross; out of love, He remains in the
Eucharist to be the nourishment of souls; out of love,
He founded the Church to be the unshakable community in which salvation is found. All this is still
unknown to these brothers and these sisters among
whom we arrive; they do not know yet the Good
News of the Gospel. But we believe deeply that their
hearts and their consciences are prepared to accept
the Gospel of salvation thanks to the sacrifice of
Christ, and also to your motherly intercession and
mediation.

"We believe that, when Christ from the cross
gave you every man as your son, in the person of His
disciple St. John, you also accepted as sons and daughters these brothers and these sisters to whom His holy
Church sends us now, as missionaries.

"Help us to carry out the missionary mandate of
your Son in this land; help us to carry out here the
salvific mission of the Gospel and of the Church. We
consecrate to you all those whom the Spirit of Jesus
Christ wishes to illuminate with the light of faith and
in whom He wishes to light the fire of His love. We
consecrate to you their families, their tribes, the com-

munities and societies they form, their work, their joys and their sufferings, their villages and their cities. We consecrate everything, we consecrate everyone to you. Accept them in this eternal love whose first servant you were, and deign to guide, however unworthy it may be, the apostolic service that we are beginning."

FAITH AND TRUST

7. Today, a hundred years have passed since these beginnings. At the moment when the Church, in this country of Zaire, thanks God in the Holy Trinity for the waters of holy baptism that gave salvation to so many of its sons and daughters, permit me, O Mother of Christ and Mother of the Church, permit me, Pope John Paul II, who has the privilege of taking part in this jubilee, to recall and at the same time renew this missionary consecration which took place in this land at the beginning of its evangelization.

To consecrate itself to Christ through you!

To consecrate itself to you for Christ!

Permit me also, O Mother of divine grace, while expressing my thanks for all the light that the Church has received and for all the fruit she has yielded in this country of Zaire in the course of this century, to entrust this Church to you again, to place it in your hands again for the years and the centuries to come, to the end of time!

And at the same time, I entrust to you also the whole nation, which is living its own independent life today. I do so in the same spirit of faith and with the same trust as the first missionaries, and I do so at the same time with all the greater joy since the act of consecration and abandonment that I make now, is made with me at the same time by all the pastors of this Church and also by the whole People of God: this People of God that wishes to assume and continue with its pastors, in love and apostolic courage, the work of the construction of the Body of Christ and the approach of the kingdom of God on this earth.

Accept, O Mother, this act of trust of ours. Open hearts, and give strength to souls to listen to the word of life and to do what your Son constantly orders and urges us.

May grace and peace, justice and love be the lot of this people; giving thanks for the centenary of its faith and its baptism, may it look confidently towards its temporal and eternal future! Amen!

THE WORLD MUST LEARN TO RECEIVE FROM THE PEOPLE OF AFRICA

After leaving the cathedral the Holy Father drove to the Nunciature. Later he paid an official visit to the President Mobutu Sese Seko on May 2. After the President's address, the Pope replied as follows:

Mr. President,

1. In the evening of this first day on Zairean soil, so many thoughts already crowd into my mind that words jostle with one another to express what I feel. Is it the emotion of the contact, so greatly desired, and at last come true, with the peoples of Africa, first of all with the people of Zaire? Is it the welcome I was given at my arrival as well as in the city of Kinshasa itself? Is it the enthusiasm of the population and particularly of the Catholic population which was able to find a place, just now, in the cathedral and around it?

I do not really know what memory will mark most the one who is beginning today a visit from which he expects a great deal, and who would like to attain fully his twofold aim, that of a brotherly and cordial greeting from the spiritual Head of the Catholic Church to the African nations, and that of very sincere encouragement to the local Churches.

2. This is to stress, and I will not fail to recall it on the occasions that may arise, the essentially religious

character of this journey that is beginning, I am happy to say, with Zaire. Each stage will offer, however, possibilities of meeting the civil authorities. This is more than the observance of a courtesy practice, which makes it possible to thank one's hosts, as they deserve, for their generous hospitality or for the detailed and extremely absorbing organization of this stay. In this connection, Mr. President, I appreciate perfectly the quality of what Your Excellency and your collaborators have done to facilitate, and finally ensure—I do not doubt—the success of my visit. Allow me to say so before the high personalities gathered here, some of whom have not spared themselves in making their contribution in accordance with their personal responsibilities.

But I also attach great importance to *conversations* with those who hold civil power. They are so many opportunities for exchanging views, in a constructive way, on the most fundamental problems for man, his spiritual dimension, his dignity and his future, on peace also and harmony among peoples, on the freedom that the Church requests to proclaim the Gospel in the name of the respect of consciences that is contained in most constitutions or organic laws of states. The Second Vatican Council seemed to call for the multiplication of conversations of this type when it expressed itself as follows: ''The political community and the Church are autonomous and independent of each other in their own fields. Nevertheless, both are devoted to the personal vocation of man, though under different titles. This service will redound the more effectively to the welfare of all insofar as both institutions practice better cooperation.... For man's horizons are not bounded only by the temporal order;

living on the level of human history he preserves the integrity of his eternal destiny" *(Gaudium et spes,* no. 76).

3. Having already had the happiness of receiving Your Excellency in the Vatican last year, I express satisfaction at our new dialogue, which should foster understanding and prove to be particularly fruitful. This tells you with what attention I listened to your reflections. I am convinced myself that, while African questions must be the business of Africans, and not be subjected to pressure or interference from any bloc or interested group whatsoever, their successful solution cannot fail to have a beneficial influence on other continents.

But for this purpose it would also be necessary for other peoples to *learn to receive* from African peoples. It is not just material and technical aid that the latter need. They need also to give: their heart, their wisdom, their culture, their sense of man, their sense of God, which are keener than in many others. Before the world, I would like to make a solemn appeal on this occasion, not only for aid, but for international *mutual aid,* that is, this *exchange* in which each of the partners makes its constructive contribution to the progress of mankind.

4. I would also like everyone to know, from the first day of this journey, the sentiments that the Pope feels as he looks at Africa as a friend, as a brother. While sharing the concern of many people with regard to peace, the problems raised by growth and poverty and, in a word, the problems of man, he feels deep joy. The source of his joy is to see that numerous populations have been able, in the course of recent

years, to accede to national sovereignty, at the end of a process that was sometimes delicate, but which was able to lead to the choice of their future.

This is a phenomenon which I understand very well, were it only through my personal origins. I know, I have experienced the efforts made by my people for their sovereignty. I know what it means to claim the right to self-determination, in the name of justice and national dignity. Certainly, this is only one stage, for it is also necessary for self-determination to remain effective, and to be accompanied by the real participation of citizens in the direction of their own destiny: in this way, likewise, progress will bring benefit to everyone, in a fairer way. Certainly, freedom should come into play at all levels in political and social life. The unity of a people also calls for persevering action, respectful of legitimate peculiarities and at the same time carried out in a harmonious way. But so many hopes are permitted today, so many possibilities are offered, that my heart is filled with immense joy, in proportion to the trust I put in men of good will who have the common good at heart.

5. I would now like to turn my gaze, beyond this assembly, towards the whole Zairean people, and tell them how satisfied I am to be in their midst. The limitations of the program exist, it it true, and it will not be possible to go to all regions to visit populations equally dear to my heart. Let my passage, at least, at some points of the country be a concrete testimony of Christ's message of love, which I would like to bring to every family, every inhabitant, to Catholics as well as to those who do not share the same faith. Zaireans represent a hope for the Church and for Africa. It is

up to them, as good citizens, to continue their action for the progress of their country in a spirit of justice and honesty, opening up to the true values of man (cf. Encyclical *Redemptor Hominis,* no. 18). I ask God to help them in this noble task and to bless their efforts.

Thank you, Mr. President, for everything you have undertaken for me since the moment when, like the episcopate of the country, you invited me so warmly to Zaire. I will not forget the noble terms of your address, and I present to you, as well as to the members of the government and to all those who honor me with their presence, my greetings and my best wishes.

CHRISTIAN MARRIAGE— THE LEAVEN OF MORAL PROGRESS

On May 3, the Holy Father's second day in Zaire, his first engagement was a Mass for the family at 8:30 a.m. in the Church of St. Pierre, the oldest church in the city of Kinshasa. The following is the text of the Pope's homily.

Dear Christian spouses, fathers and mothers of families,

1. Emotion and joy fill my heart as the universal pastor of the Church, because I have been granted the grace of meditating for the first time with African married couples—and for them—on their particular vocation: Christian marriage. May God—who revealed Himself as being "One in Three Persons"— assist us throughout this meditation! The subject is a marvelous one, but the reality is difficult! If Christian marriage is comparable to a very high mountain which places spouses in the immediate vicinity of God, it must be recognized that its ascent calls for a great deal of time and effort. But is that a reason for suppressing or lowering this summit? Is it not through moral and spiritual ascents that the human person realizes himself fully and dominates the universe, even more than through technical and even space records, however admirable they may be?

Together, we will make a pilgrimage to the sources of marriage, then we will try to gauge better its dynamism in the service of spouses, the children, society and the Church. Finally, we will gather our energies to promote a more and more effective family apostolate.

SPLENDOR OF HUMAN LOVE

2. Everyone knows the famous narrative of creation with which the Bible begins. It is said there that God made man in His likeness, creating him man and woman. This is surprising at first sight. Mankind, to resemble God, must be a couple, two persons moving one towards the other, two persons whom perfect love will gather into unity. This movement and this love make them resemble God, who is love itself, the absolute unity of the three Persons. The splendor of human love has never been sung so beautifully as in the first pages of the Bible: "This at last," Adam says contemplating his wife, "is bone of my bones and flesh of my flesh. Therefore a man leaves his father and his mother and cleaves to his wife, and they become one flesh" (Gn. 2:23-24). Paraphrasing Pope St. Leo, I cannot help saying to you: "O Christian spouses, recognize your eminent dignity!"

This pilgrimage to the sources also reveals to us that the initial couple, in God's plan, is monogamous. This is again surprising for civilization—at the time when the Bible narratives take shape—is generally far from this cultural model. This monogamy, which is not of Western but Semitic origin, appears as the expression of the interpersonal relationship, the one in which each of the partners is recognized by the other in an equal value and in the totality of his person. This monogamous and personalistic conception of the human couple is an absolutely original revelation, which bears the mark of God, and which deserves to be studied more and more deeply.

CHRISTIAN MARRIAGE

3. But this story which began so well in the luminous dawn of mankind, experiences the drama of the rupture between this new couple and the Creator. It is original sin. This rupture, however, will be the occasion of another manifestation of God's love. Compared very often to an infinitely faithful husband, for example, in the texts of the psalmists and prophets, God constantly renews His covenant with this capricious and sinful humanity. These repeated covenants will culminate in the definitive covenant that God sealed in His own Son, sacrificing Himself freely for the Church and for the world. St. Paul is not afraid to present this covenant of Christ with the Church as the symbol and model of every covenant between man and woman (cf. Eph. 5:25), united as spouses indissolubly.

Such are the letters patent of nobility of Christian marriage. They produce light and strength for the everyday fulfillment of the conjugal and family vocation, for the benefit of the spouses themselves, their children, the society in which they live, and the Church of Christ. African traditions, judiciously utilized, may have their place in the construction of Christian homes in Africa. I am thinking in particular of all the positive values of the family feeling, so deeply rooted in the African soul and which takes on multiple aspects, which can certainly give so-called advanced civilizations food for thought: the seriousness of the matrimonial commitment at the end of a long process, priority given to the transmission of life and therefore the importance attached to the mother and children, the law of solidarity among families related by marriage, which is exercised especially in favor of old persons, widows and orphans, a kind of co-responsibility in taking charge and bringing up the children, which is capable of relieving many psychological tensions, the cult of ancestors and of the dead which promotes faithfulness to traditions.

Certainly, the delicate problem is to assume all this family dynamism, inherited from ancestral customs, while transforming it and purifying it in the perspectives of the society which is springing up in Africa. But in any case the conjugal life of Christians is lived—through different ages and situations—in the footsteps of Christ, the Liberator and Redeemer of all men and of all the realities that make up men's lives. "Do everything in the name of the Lord Jesus," as St. Paul said to us (Col. 3:17).

UNION OF HEARTS

4. It is, therefore, by conforming to Christ who gave Himself up for love of His Church that spouses have access, day after day, to the love of which the Gospel speaks to us: "Love one another, as I loved you," and more precisely to the perfection of indissoluble union on all planes. Christian spouses have promised to share with each other all they are and all they have. It is the most audacious contract that exists, the most marvelous one too!

The union of their bodies, willed by God Himself as the expression of the even deeper communion of their minds and their hearts, carried out with equal respect and tenderness, renews the dynamism and the youth of their solemn commitment, of their first "yes."

The union of their characters: to love a being is to love him such as he is, it is to love him to the extent of cultivating in oneself the antidote of his weaknesses or his faults, for example, calm and patience, if the other manifestly lacks them.

The union of hearts! There are innumerable fine shades of difference between the love of man and that of woman. Neither of the partners can demand to be loved in the same way as he or she loves. It is important—on both sides—to renounce the secret reproaches that separate hearts and to free oneself of this sorrow at the most favorable moment. To share the joys and, even more so, the sufferings of the heart, is a strong bond of unity. But it is just as much in common love of the children that the union of hearts is strengthened.

The union of intelligences and wills! Spouses are also two forces different but united for their mutual service, for the service of their home, their social environment, and the service of God. Essential agreement must be manifested in the determination and pursuit of common aims. The more energetic partner must support the will of the other, replace it sometimes, and act on it skillfully—in an instructive way—as a lever.

Finally the union of souls, themselves united with God! Each of the spouses must reserve moments of solitude with God, for "heart-to-heart" communication in which the partner is not the first concern. This indispensable personal life of the soul with God is far from excluding the sharing of all conjugal and family life. On the contrary it stimulates the Christian couple to look for God together, to discover His will together and to carry it out in practice with the light and the energies drawn from God Himself.

LOVE FOR CHILDREN

5. This view and this realization of the covenant between man and woman go far beyond the spontaneous desire that unites them. Marriage is really for them a way of advancement and sanctification. And a source of life! Do not Africans have an admirable respect for life about to be born? They love children deeply. They welcome them with great joy. Christian parents will be able to put their children on the way of an existence related to human and Christian values. By showing them through a whole lifestyle, courageously revised and perfected, the meaning of respect for every person, disinterested service of others, renunciation of caprice, forgiveness often repeated, loyalty in everything, conscientious work, the meeting of faith with the Lord, Christian spouses introduce their own children into the secret of a successful existence which goes far beyond the discovery of a "good position."

MORAL PROGRESS

6. Christian marriage is also called to be a leaven of moral progress for society. Realism makes us recognize the threats that weigh on the family as a natural and Christian institution, in Africa as elsewhere, as a result of certain customs, and also of generalized cultural changes. Does it never happen to

you to compare the modern family to a canoe on the river, pursuing its course in the midst of rough waters and obstacles? You know as well as I do how much the concepts of faithfulness and indissolubility are attacked by opinion. You know too that the frailty and break-up of homes lead to a series of miseries, even if African family solidarity tries to put things right as regards the taking over of the children. Christian couples—thoroughly prepared and duly accompanied—have to work without losing heart at the restoration of the family which is the first cell of society and must remain a school of social virtues. The State must not fear such homes but protect them.

MANIFESTING GOD

7. A leaven of society, the Christian family is also a presence, a manifestation of God in the world. The pastoral constitution *Gaudium et spes* (no. 48) contains luminous pages on the influence of this "intimate partnership of life and love" which is at the same time the very first grass-roots ecclesial community. "The Christian family springs from marriage, which is an image and a sharing in the partnership of love between Christ and the Church; it will show forth to all men Christ's living presence in the world and the authentic nature of the Church by the love and generous fruitfulness of the spouses, by their unity and fidelity, and by the loving way in which all members of the family cooperate with each other." What dignity and what responsibility!

Yes, this sacrament is a great one! And let spouses have confidence: their faith assures them that they receive, with this sacrament, the strength of God, a

The view and the realization of the covenant between man and woman go far beyond the spontaneous desire that unites them. Marriage is really for them a way of advancement and sanctification. And a source of life! Do not Africans have an admirable respect for life about to be born? They love children deeply. They welcome them with great joy. Christian parents will be able to put their children on the way of an existence related to human and Christian values.

grace that will accompany them throughout their life. May they never neglect to draw upon this gushing source which is in them!

FAMILY APOSTOLATE

8. I would not like to end this meditation without warmly encouraging African bishops to continue—despite the well-known difficulties—their efforts of "apostolate of Christian homes," with renewed dynamism and unfailing hope. I know that this is already the constant concern of many and I admire them. I likewise congratulate the many African families who already realize the Christian ideal of which I have spoken, with specifically African qualities, and who are an example and an attraction for so many others. But I take the liberty of insisting.

Without abandoning any of their concerns for the human and religious formation of children and adolescents, and taking into account African sensibility and customs, dioceses must gradually set up an apostolate aimed at the two spouses together and not just at one of the partners. Let preparation of the young for marriage be intensified, encouraging them to follow a real preparation for married life, which will reveal to them the meaning of the Christian identity of the couple, and make them mature for interpersonal relations and for their family and social responsibilities. These centers of preparation for marriage need the united support of dioceses and the generous and competent help of chaplains, experts and married couples able to bear witness of high quality. I stress above all the mutual help that each Christian couple can give to another.

DAYS OF RETREAT

9. This family apostolate must also accompany young married couples, as they set up their home. Days of spiritual renewal, retreats, meetings of married couples will support young couples in their human and Christian progress. Let care be taken on all these occasions that there is a good balance between doctrinal formation and spiritual animation. The part of meditation, conversation with God who is faithful is of essential importance. It is near Him that spouses draw the grace of faithfulness, understand and accept the necessity of asceticism, which generates true freedom, resume or decide their family and social commitments which will make their homes centers of influence. It would certainly be very useful for married couples of a parish and a diocese to form groups in order to create a vast family movement, not only to help Christian couples to live according to the Gospel, but to contribute to the restoration of the family by defending its values against attacks of all kinds, and in the name of the rights of man and of the citizen. On this vital plane of the family apostolate, more and more adapted to the needs of our time and your regions, I have full confidence in your bishops, my beloved brothers in the episcopate.

10. May you find in this talk the sign of the great interest that the Pope takes in the serious problems of the family, the testimony of his trust and his hope in your Christian homes and the courage to work, you yourselves, more than ever, in this African land, for the greater good of your nations and for the honor of

the Church of Christ, at the solid construction of family communities "of life and love" according to the Gospel! I promise you that this great intention will always have a place in my heart and my prayer. May God, who revealed Himself as a family in the unity of the Father, the Son and the Spirit, bless you, and may His blessing remain upon you forever!

BRING THE AUTHENTIC GOSPEL TO THE AFRICAN CULTURES

After the Mass for the family on Saturday morning, May 3, John Paul II blessed the foundation stone of the Kinshasa Faculty of Theology. He then went to the Nunciature and continued on foot to the Interdiocesan Center where he met the Zairean bishops to whom he gave the following address.

Beloved brothers in Christ,

1. What a joy for me to meet you all together! What a comfort! A century ago, it can be said that real evangelization was just beginning; and now today the Christian faith is implanted nearly everywhere in this country, the ecclesiastical hierarchy is organized, sons of this country, *ex hominibus assumpti*, have taken over the guidance of the Church, in union with the Church in Rome. The springing up of your Christian communities, the vitality of this People of God, is a miracle of grace which renews in our time what it did at the time of the Apostles Peter and Paul.

There have been stages, dates which no one can forget:

—the ordination of the first Zairean priest, Stefano Kaoze (1917);

—the consecration of the first Zairean bishop, Most Rev. Pierre Kimbondo (1956);

—the establishment of the hierarchy in Zaire (1959);

—the call of the first Zairean bishop to enter the Sacred College of Cardinals, Cardinal Joseph Malula (1969).

I have come to thank God with you, to celebrate the centenary of evangelization!

I have come to recognize with you the apostolic toil, patient and sagacious, of the many missionaries, bishops, priests, men and women religious. They loved you to the extent of dedicating their lives to initiating your fathers to the Gospel, a Gospel which they themselves had received through grace, and they had enough confidence in your forebears to consider them, too, capable of setting up a local Church, and to prepare its pastors. I have come to recognize the good work that you yourselves have undertaken, following them, or with them, to the extent to which they still offer you an indispensable service today. I have come to tell you of my respect, my esteem, my affection, for your persons, for your episcopal body, for the Church that gathers in your country. And I have come to strengthen your holy ministry, as Jesus asked Peter to do.

EVANGELIZATION CONTINUES

2. The aim of this ministry is still evangelization. It is the same for all countries, for old Christian communities as for the young Churches. For evangelization consists of stages and ever deeper levels, and it is a work to be resumed constantly. Certainly, about half of your fellow-citizens have joined the Church through baptism; others are preparing to do so. But there is still a wide field of apostolate, in order that the light of the Gospel may also shine in the eyes of

the others. Above all, it is necessary to bring about the penetration in depth of this Gospel in minds, in morals, in the daily faith and charity of persons, families and communities, and perseverance must be ensured. It was the problem that the Apostle Paul met with, in the communities he visited, and the Apostle John, in the communities that he sustained with his letters, to the third generation of Christians (cf. Rev. 1-3), or again my predecessor St. Clement of Rome. It was the problem known, too, to the courageous bishops of my nation, such as St. Stanislaus.

DOCUMENTS ON FAITH

3. In this connection, I have noticed the zeal, courage and cohesion that you have shown, to enlighten and guide your Christian people, when circumstances demanded it. For you have not been spared trials! For example, you drew up and published documents on faith in Jesus Christ in 1974, then "on the present situation." In 1977, you stimulated your faithful, "all jointly liable and responsible," to overcome discouragement and immorality. In the same year, you exhorted your priests, and men and women religious, to conversion. You even called your fellow-countrymen as a whole to bring about "the recovery of the nation." These acts of the Episcopal Conference, without counting those of bishops in their dioceses, show your sense of pastoral responsibility.

I hope with you that these appeals, together with the assiduous reading of the Word of God, will be taken up again, meditated upon and above all put into practice, in their consequences and with perseverance, by those whose conscience you wished to form or awaken. For, you know as I do, this education to faith calls not only for clear texts, but for closeness, a pedagogy which exploits this teaching, which convinces and sustains, with a patience and love inseparable from pastoral authority, thanks to priests and educators who themselves set an example. I wanted, with these simple words, to express to you appreciation and encouragement for your work of evangelization.

IMPORTANT ASPECTS

4. One of the aspects of this evangelization is the *inculturation* of the Gospel, the *Africanization* of the Church. Several people have told me that you set great store by it, and rightly so. That is part of the indispensable efforts to incarnate the message of Christ. The Gospel, certainly, is not identified with cultures, and transcends them all. But the kingdom that the Gospel proclaims is lived by men deeply tied to a culture; the construction of the kingdom cannot dispense with borrowing elements of human cultures (cf. *Evangelii nuntiandi,* no. 20). Indeed, evangelization must help the latter to bring forth out of their own living tradition original expressions of Christian life, celebration and thought (cf. Exhortation *Catechesi tradendae,* no. 53). You wish to be at once fully Christians and fully Africans. The Holy Spirit asks us to believe, in fact, that the leaven of the Gospel, in its authenticity, has the power to bring forth Christians in the different cultures, with all the riches of their heritage, purified and transfigured.

In this connection, the Second Vatican Council had expressed very well some principles which always throw light on the way to follow in this field: "The Church...fosters and takes to herself, insofar as they are good, the abilities, the resources and customs of peoples. In so taking them to herself, she purifies, strengthens and elevates them....

"In virtue of this catholicity each part contributes its own gifts to others parts and to the whole Church, so that the whole and each of the parts are strengthened by the common sharing of all things and by the common effort to attain to fullness in unity....

"The Chair of Peter...presides over the whole assembly of charity, and protects their legitimate variety while at the same time taking care that these differences do not hinder unity, but rather contribute to it" (*Lumen gentium*, no. 13).

Africanization covers wide and deep fields, which have not yet been sufficiently explored, whether it is a question of the language to present the Christian message in a way that will reach the spirit and the heart of Zaireans, of catechesis, theological reflection, the most suitable expression in liturgy or sacred art, or community forms of Christian life.

WISDOM AND ALSO TIME

5. It is up to you, bishops, to promote and harmonize the advance in this field, after mature reflection, in concerted action among yourselves, in union also with the universal Church and with the Holy See. Inculturation, for the people as a whole, cannot be, moreover, but the fruit of gradual maturity in faith. For you are convinced as I am that this work, for

which I am anxious to express to you all my confidence, requires a great deal of theological lucidity, spiritual discernment, wisdom and prudence, and also time.

Allow me to recall, among other examples, the experience of my own country. In Poland, a deep union has been established between the ways of thinking and living that characterize the nation and Catholicism; this impregnation took centuries. Here, taking into consideration a different situation, it should be possible for Christianity to unite with what is deepest in the Zairean soul for an original culture, at the same time African and Christian.

As regards faith and theology, everyone sees that important problems are at stake: the content of faith, the search for its best expression, the connection between theology and faith, the unity of faith. My venerated predecessor Paul VI had referred to this matter at the end of the 1974 Synod (cf. *AAS* 66 [1974], pp. 636-637). And he had himself recalled certain rules to the delegates of SCEAM in September 1975:

"a) When it is a question of the Christian faith, it is necessary to abide by the 'identical, essential, constitutional heritage of Christ's own doctrine, professed by authentic tradition and authorized by the one, true Church';

"b) it is important to carry out a thorough investigation of the cultural traditions of the various populations, and of the philosophical ideas that underlie them, in order to detect elements that are not in contradiction with the Christian religion and the contributions that can enrich theological reflection" (*AAS* 67 [1975], p. 572).

Last year, in the exhortation on catechesis, I myself drew attention to the fact that the evangelical message cannot be isolated purely and simply from the biblical culture in which it took its place to begin with, nor even, without serious loss, from the cultures in which it was expressed throughout the centuries; and that on the other hand the power of the Gospel transforms and regenerates everywhere (cf. *Catechesi tradendae*, no. 53).

In the field of *catechesis*, presentations better suited to the African soul can and must be made, while at the same time taking into account the more and more frequent cultural exchanges with the rest of the world. Care must be taken simply that the work is carried out in a team and controlled by the episcopate, so that the expression may be correct and the whole doctrine may be presented.

In the field of sacred arts and the *liturgy*, a whole enrichment is possible (cf. *Sacrosanctum concilium*, nos. 37-38), provided the meaning of the Christian rite is always preserved and that the universal, catholic element of the Church is clearly seen ("the substantial unity of the Roman rite"), in union with other local churches and in agreement with the Holy See.

In the *ethical* field, all the resources of the African soul, which are, as it were, toothing stones of Christianity, must be highlighted. Paul VI had already recalled them in his message to Africa on October 29, 1967, and you know them better than anyone, as regards the spiritual view of life, the sense of the family and children, of community life, etc. As in all civilizations, there are other less favorable aspects.

Anyhow, as you recalled so well, there is always a conversion to be effected, in regard to the person of

Christ, the only Savior, and His teaching, such as the Church transmits it to us: it is then that the liberation, the purification, the transfiguration, the elevation that He came to bring and that He realized in His Paschal Mystery of death and resurrection takes place. It is necessary to consider both the Incarnation of Christ and His Redemption. You yourselves made a point of specifying that recourse to authenticity does not permit "opposing the principles of Christian morality to those of traditional morality" [Letter of February 27, 1977]. In a way, the Gospel satisfies human aspirations to the full, but by challenging man's depths in order to make him open to the call of grace and in particular to a more trusting approach to God, to a widened, universal human authenticity it does not turn the African man away from his duty of conversion. In short, it is a question of becoming authentic Christians, authentically African.

MARRIAGE PROBLEMS

6. In this work of inculturation and the pursuit of indigenousness, already well begun, as in the work of evangelization as a whole, many particular questions will arise on the way, concerning such and such a custom—I am thinking in particular of the difficult problems of marriage—such and such a religious act, such and such a method. Difficult questions, the attempt to solve which is entrusted to your pastoral responsibility, to you bishops, in dialogue with Rome: you cannot abandon it. It calls in the first place for *perfect cohesion among you.* Each Church has its problems, but everywhere, I am not afraid of repeating, as I said to the Polish bishops: "It is this unity which is the

source of spiritual strength.'' This solidarity applies to all fields: research, great pastoral decisions, and also mutual esteem, whatever your origin may be, without forgetting mutual support, in the exemplary life which is asked of you and which may call for brotherly admonitions.

TRUSTING COMMUNION

7. It will not have escaped your notice either to what extent *solidarity with the universal Church* in things that must be common, and in particular *trusting communion with the Holy See*, are necessary for the Catholic authenticity of the Church in Zaire, for its strength and for its harmonious advance. But they are also necessary for the vitality of the universal Church, to which you will bring the testimony of your pastoral solicitude and the contribution of your evangelizing zeal, on important points for the whole Church. These are the requirements, or rather, the grace of our catholicity (cf. *Lumen gentium*, no. 13, quoted above). God be praised for allowing His Church this vital exchange and this communion between all the members of the same Body, the Body of Christ! The Holy See will not release you from any responsibility; on the contrary it will drive home to you your responsibility; and it will help you to find the solutions most in keeping with your vocation. Personally, I am sure that your concerns will meet with understanding there.

CONCRETE PROBLEMS

8. Now, I would like to say a word also about some concrete pastoral problems: I recall them to show the share I take in your responsibility.

I have spoken of your unity among bishops, of your collegial co-responsibility which has stood the test of experience in particularly difficult moments. I also encourage you to stimulate as much as you can, in each of your dioceses, the unity of the living forces of evangelization, and in the first place of your priests. Some of them are Zaireans and it is very lucky for the future of your Church. Many others, secular and often religious priests, have come as "missionaries" or have stayed to help you, while they are aware that they must, as opportunities arise, yield the first place to indigenous pastors. You all recognize that their service was essential for the evangelization the centenary of which we are celebrating, and that it remains important and indispensable today, in view of the large number of the faithful and the complexity of apostolic needs. They remain among you, the expression of the universality and of necessary exchanges among Churches. Let them all, Zaireans or not, form only one presbyterium around you! Let everything be done to smooth and multiply the ways of mutual esteem, brotherhood and collaboration! Let everything be banished that would be the cause of suffering or exclusion, on both sides! Let everyone be penetrated with sentiments of humility and mutual service! For Christ! For the witness of the Church! Let everyone be able to say: "See how they love one another!" For the advance of evangelization! Progress has already been made. I am sure that you will do everything to create this atmosphere.

Furthermore, you have called all your priests and sisters several times to great dignity of life. I have noted a passage that you quoted in its poetic form: "You yourselves, be the first to reform. Be clad in virtues, not silk. Be chaste in body, simple in conscience. Both by night and by day, apply yourselves to study. Keep a humble dignity for the people and combine sweetness with earnestness" (Exhortation of June 10, 1977). Yes, the radical love that consecrated souls have dedicated to the Lord, for Himself and for a more available service for all their brothers and the proclamation of the world to come, with the discipline of life it demands, must shine forth like light, be like salt, maintain "within the People of God the indispensable 'tonus' which helps it to raise the human dough" (ibid.). In particular, priests, religious men—and also sisters—must have strong convictions about the positive and essential values of chastity in celibacy, and be very vigilant in their behavior in order to be faithful without any ambiguity to this commitment that they have undertaken—for the Lord and for the Church—and which is essential, in Africa as elsewhere, as witness and to carry along the Christian people in the laborious march towards holiness. All that is possible with the grace of God, and particularly by taking to heart spiritual means and the multiple needs which call for pastoral zeal. Priests are certainly in great need of your brotherly help, your closeness, your personal example, your affection.

PRIESTLY VOCATIONS

9. The holiness and zeal of your priests will also greatly facilitate the awakening of priestly vocations, and I think I am touching here on one of your major concerns. How will the Church in Zaire face the future if it does not have more of its own priests, secular or religious? We must pray and get people to

pray for that. We must "call" to the Lord's service, make families and young people understand the beauty of this service. But the problem is also that of the formation of these seminarians or novices: may they always be able to benefit from the presence, the dialogue and the example of spiritual directors, expert in the guidance of souls.

I believe, moreover, that many religious *vocations* have flourished among you, in the framework either of the missionary congregations, or now of institutes born on your soil. May they, thanks to a thorough formation, thanks to their dedication to apostolic works, thanks to their transparent witness, write a new page in the life of sisters in the Church! I do not forget the one who has left such a luminous trail that there has been talk of her beatification, Sister Anwarite.

ROLE OF CATECHISTS

10. I rejoice, too, at everything that has been done in this country to endow the Church with *lay catechists* and leaders of little communities, who are the mainsprings of evangelization, in constant and direct contact with families, children, and the different categories of the People of God. It is certainly necessary to promote all this deployment of the indispensable action of the laity, in close communion with the pastors. I will have the opportunity to deal with this subject at greater length in the course of my journey.

As regards *family life*, I spoke about it at length this morning. How to make the young and married couples progress towards the full realization of God's plan for spouses and parents, in spite of the difficulties that certainly exist, but relying at the same

Yes, the radical love that consecrated souls have dedicated to the Lord, for Himself and for a more available service for all their brothers and the proclamation of the world to come, with the discipline of life it demands, must shine forth like light, be like salt, maintain "within the People of God the indispensable 'tonus' which helps it to raise the human dough."

time on the resources of the African soul, on the centuries-old experience of the Church and on grace—that is a pastoral aim of prime importance. It will be a blessing for the Church and an outstanding step forward for the country.

One thing that parents, pastors and all workers of evangelization must take to heart, is *the religious education of children,* whatever the position of schools may be and particularly because of the present position: family initiation to the Gospel, continued by a systematic catechesis, as I set forth, following upon the Synod of bishops, in the exhortation *Catechesi tradendae.*

FOR THE COMMON GOOD

11. I am also thinking of the whole participation that the Church brings to the development of the country, not only by forming the conscience of citizens to the sense of loyalty, gratuitous service, work well done, brotherhood—which is directly her role—but by providing *on many planes* for the multiple needs of the populations, which are often aggravated by trials, on the plane of schools, medical care, means of subsistence, etc. Making good what is lacking in this way is a duty imposed by charity on the Church—*caritas urget nos*—which the sense of the common good of your country makes you accept as natural.

LOVE OF COUNTRY

12.   You love this country deeply. I understand these feelings. You know the love I bear for the land

in which I have my roots. The unity of a country is forged, furthermore, through trials and efforts in which Christians have their share, especially when they form a considerable part of the nation. Your service of God includes this love of your country. It contributes to the good of the country, just as the civil power is ordained to this on its own plane. But it is distinguished from the latter and, while respecting its competence and responsibility, it must be able to exercise itself in full freedom, in its sphere which is the education to faith, the formation of consciences, religious practice, the life of Christian communities, and the defense of the human person, of his freedoms and his rights, and of his dignity. I know that this has been your concern. And I hope that the result will be a peace beneficial to all.

RESEARCH AND TEACHING

13. A last point: to help the Christian elite to cope according to faith with the problems that a rapid evolution and the contact with other civilizations, other systems of thought, will not fail to raise, it is essential, on the theological plane, that research and teaching should be promoted, in your country, in the right way, that is, by combining with deep-rootedness in the tradition of the whole Church, which has given your community its sap, the reflection required by your African roots and the new problems that arise. This is to say, that I form fervent good wishes for your theology faculty at Kinshasa, for its high intellectual level, its ecclesial faithfulness and its influence in your country and beyond.

DIALOGUE TO CONTINUE

14. I will stop here today. But it is a dialogue that will always have to be continued with the successor of Peter, with the authorities of the Holy See, and with other local Churches, which have only one concern: to enable the impetus of your Church to continue on its way under the best conditions, "quite openly and unhindered" (Acts 28:31). And I hope that this impetus will be of advantage not only to yourselves, but that it will be more and more *missionary*. "You are your own missionaries," Paul VI said at Kampala, eleven years ago. It is partly realized. But I add: aim at being missionaries in your turn, not only in this country where the Gospel is still awaited, but outside, and in particular in other African countries. A Church that gives, even from its limited resources, will be blessed by the Lord, for one can always find someone poorer than oneself.

The Holy Spirit has made you pastors of your people at this important hour of the Christian history of Zaire. May He strengthen the faith and charity of all those entrusted to you! And may Mary, the Mother of the Church, intercede for you all. Be assured of my prayer, as I count on yours. With my affectionate apostolic blessing.

POPE'S GREETING TO BISHOPS FROM OTHER COUNTRIES

On Saturday, May 3, after his address to the Zairean bishops, the Holy Father subsequently met a group of visiting bishops from various African countries, who had come to the Inter-diocesan Center at Kinshasa to meet him. He spoke to them briefly as follows.

I now add a word for bishops who have come from other African countries.

Beloved brothers in Christ, this meeting with you gives me great joy. I long to get to know, too, each of your countries, each of your Churches, on the spot. I would have liked to widen the circle of my visits. Perhaps you are some of those who invited me insistently? It did not seem possible this time to go beyond the program which was fixed for converging and well-pondered reasons. I deeply regret it, all the more so in that your Christian communities are very fervently and spontaneously attached to the Pope, and deserved particular encouragement, either because of their vitality, or because of their trials. I regret it also for my own sake, for I would have appreciated this new witness. But I consider myself bound by each of these invitations, which I will try to honor with the help of God in due time. In the meantime, tell your confreres, your priests, your men and women religious, your laity, that the Pope loves them and blesses them with great affection.

I know that Africa is far from being uniform, that the peoples and races are different, the traditions special, and also the implantation of the Catholic Church is varied. It sometimes happens that you find yourselves in the situation of the little flock which must preserve its Christian identity and at the same time bear witness to it.

However, a part of the pastoral problems that I have tackled with your confreres of Zaire apply also to you: the continuation of evangelization, the deepening of the Christian spirit, Africanization, the solidarity of the bishops, with one another, with the other local Churches and with the Holy See, the dignity of the life of priests and religious, your presence in their life, the question of vocations, family problems, human advancement, etc. A magnificent role is entrusted to you all, with the grace of God: to contribute to build up a civilization in which God has His place and in which man is consequently respected. If it were necessary to leave an order to all members of your Churches, I would say: keep united. Thank you for your visit! May the peace of Christ be with you all!

FULLY INVOLVED
IN THE CHURCH'S
PROPHETIC MISSION

The Holy Father's first engagement on Saturday afternoon, May 3, was at the Carmel of Kinshasa where he met 1,250 sisters of the diocese of Kinshasa and more than 2,500 from the other dioceses of Zaire, and from Burundi, Zambia and Uganda. After an address of homage by the President of the Union of Major Superiors of Zaire, he spoke to them as follows:

Dear sisters,

Let us give thanks to God our Father, through His Son Jesus, our Lord, in the Spirit who dwells in our hearts, for the great happiness of this meeting and for the fruits that will spring from it in your respective communities and in the life of the Church in Africa!

1. At these very special moments, forget your legitimate particular characteristics in order to feel deeply your unique belonging to the same God and Father, recalled in a striking way by the Apostle Paul in his letter to the Ephesians: "one Lord, one faith, one baptism, one God and Father of us all" (Eph. 4:5-6). Let me encourage you to celebrate deeply and fervently the anniversary of your birth to divine life by the grace of baptism, as the most important event of your existence, and the most significant one of your Christian vocation to brotherhood.

Having come to religious life from very different social environments, countries and even continents, you live in communities to bear witness—contrary to nationalistic feelings, prejudices, sometimes hatred—to the possibility and the reality of this universal brotherhood, to which all peoples aspire vaguely. You are sisters also because you have all heard the same evangelical call: "If you would be perfect, go, sell what you possess and give to the poor, and you will have treasure in heaven; and come, follow me" (cf. Mt. 19:21). This unique call in its divine source is another requirement—whether you are dedicated to contemplation or engaged in the direct tasks of evangelization—to be on extremely fraternal terms among yourselves and among congregations, and to help one another better and better on three planes which seem to me essential: to see your consecration in the right way and carry it out courageously, to be eager to take part in the mission of the Church, to pursue a solid spiritual formation and judicious openness to the realities of your age and your environments.

A ROYAL OFFERING TO CHRIST

2. In a few words, the Second Vatican Council describes consecrated life as "a gift of God which the Church has received from her Lord and which by His grace she always safeguards" (*Lumen gentium*, no. 43). Without ignoring the shadows of the bimillenary history of the People of God, it can be stated that woman—on her side—has responded magnificently to Christ's calls to the evangelical fullness of the gift of oneself.

There is, it seems, in woman's body and heart, an extraordinary disposition to make her life a royal offering to Christ as the one Bridegroom. This femininity—often considered by a certain public opinion as sacrificed in a crazy way in religious life—is, as a matter of fact, refound and expanded on a higher plane: that of the kingdom of God. For example, physical *fecundity,* which has such a great place in African tradition, as well as attachment to the family, are values that can be lived by the African sister within a far wider and ever renewed community, and to the benefit of an absolutely astonishing spiritual fecundity. It is in this perspective that religious chastity, very faithfully observed, stands out clearly as preferential love of the Lord and complete availability for others.

In the same way many African women who have entered religion are trying to give the vow of poverty a new face, more in keeping with the environments from which they have come. They are anxious to live on the fruit of their work and to share this fruit constantly with others.

While remaining strictly faithful to the authentic conception of religious obedience—which is always the sacrifice of one's own will—many sisters are endeavoring to live it in trusting dialogue with their leaders in whom they see a presence of Christ. This new aspect is in keeping with the dignity and the advancement of woman in our time.

Speaking to you in this way, dear sisters, I would like to help you to grasp, or to grasp again, the essential characteristic of your religious state: the complete consecration, forever, of your innermost self and your feminine capacities to Christ and His kingdom. We have reached here the very heart of the mystery of your life, which is difficult to understand outside of the Faith. A mystery which goes beyond all the rest: the acquisition of qualifications and diplomas, the distribution of duties and responsibilities, cares of administration or implantation, problems of structures and observances. In a word, your consecration, lived radically, is the essential feature of your religious state, the permanent rock, which enables congregations and their subjects to cope with the adaptation required by circumstances without running the risk of weakening or betraying the charism with which Christ endowed His Church.

PROPHETIC MISSION

3. Solidly rooted in the prior requirements of your complete gift, authenticated by the Church, your life cannot but be consumed in the service of this Church for which Christ gave Himself up (cf. Eph. 5:25).

The mission of the Church is in the first place prophetic. She proclaims Christ to all nations (cf. Mt. 28:19-20) and transmits to them His message of salvation. This involves your personal and community lifestyle in the first place (cf. *Evangelii nuntiandi,* no. 14). Is it really luminous (cf Mt. 5:16), prophetic? The present-day world is awaiting everywhere, perhaps vaguely, consecrated lives which tell, in acts more than words, of Christ and the Gospel. The Epiphany of the Lord, which you like to celebrate in Africa, depends on you! The prophetic Church also relies on you, here as in other continents, to take part eagerly in her immense catechetical work.

Sisters who are catechists and sisters devoted to the formation of lay catechists, are awaited everywhere. Are religious women who—for reasons of personal fulfillment—abandon too easily this important ecclesial task, always certain that they are faithful to their consecration? I know that the efforts and the results of catechetical teaching in Africa are remarkable. But they must be continued and expanded. Christians of all ages and from all walks of life need to be accompanied in order to cope with the social and cultural changes of our times. I ask you, my sisters, to contribute even more to the prophetic mission of the Church.

Evangelization, of oneself and of others, leads to divine worship. The Church has also a priestly vocation with which you are closely associated. Following in the steps of St. Benedict or St. Bernard, St. Clare of Assisi or St. Teresa of Avila, enclosed nuns assume full time, on behalf of the Church, this service of divine praise and intercession. This form of life is also an apostolate of very great ecclesial and redeeming value, which St. Thérèse of the Child Jesus illustrated magnificently in the course of her short life in the Carmelite convent at Lisieux. Let us not forget that Pope Pius XI proclaimed her "Patron saint of the missions." So I express my deepest encouragement to contemplatives on African soil and I ask God that their convents may be filled with seriously motivated vocations.

How could I forget sick sisters, infirm and old? Throughout the day and often at night, when sleep is difficult, they present to the Lord the silent offering of their almost uninterrupted prayers, their physical or moral sufferings, their *fiat* to divine will. They, too, are the priestly people that Christ won with His blood on the cross. With Him, they save the world.

As for sisters who exercise a direct apostolate in towns and villages, the Church, in the person of bishops and priests, expects a great deal of their talents and their zeal for the animation of Christian assemblies. Initiation to the deep meaning of the liturgy, to the celebration of the sacraments, especially the Holy Eucharist, as well as the formation of children and adults to personal prayer, to the generous offering of their daily life, in union with that of Christ (cf. 1 Pt. 2:4-10), is an extremely important field in which you are capable of excelling, owing to your pedagogical qualities, your innate sense of the mystery of God, and your own generosity in prayer. The fervor of the People of God, honoring their Lord, depends a great deal on you.

Finally, the mission of the Church is a *royal* one. It is in the first place the bishop who must watch over the growth and unity of faith, as well as the brotherhood of love, in his diocese. It is he who directs and stimulates apostolic activities. But in the People of God, who are all urged to devote their forces and their specific talents in the various pastoral sectors of the life of dioceses and parishes, sisters certainly have their place (cf. *Evangelii nuntiandi*, no. 69). I leave it to African bishops to discern with wisdom the signs of the times in their own dioceses and to see concretely, with the various congregations, how sisters can be more effectively integrated in the pastoral activities of the diocesan Church today. Allow me, however, to stress here that your feminine gifts predispose you to exercise among African girls and women the very precious role of "counselors," in a similar way to the service carried out by "village mothers."

HUMAN FORMATION

4. Dear Sisters, I do not want to conclude this fatherly talk without encouraging you warmly to remain always in search of *spiritual deepening and human formation,* in order to be, to an increasing extent, "more a woman" and "more a sister."

Help one another, among religious houses, among congregations, to organize times and places of silence and meditation, in order to benefit from sessions of spirituality, theology and apostolate. Encourage one another to take part in them. Contribute by mutual aid to cover the expenses caused by these retreats and sessions. With your diocesan leaders, take care always to appeal to reliable and competent guides. Jesus Himself used the proverb "a tree is judged by its fruits"! With calmness and common sense, always see where these retreats and sessions are taking you. To more intimacy with the Lord? To more courage and evangelical transparency? To more brotherly love? To more personal and community poverty? To more sharing of what you are and what you have with the underprivileged? To more zeal for the mission of the Church? If so, the means chosen were reliable and have been utilized seriously. If not, it is important to change them before it is too late.

PROBLEMS OF TODAY

5. Because you are sisters today, it is indispensable, even if you are contemplatives, to watch over your human formation, to know sufficiently *the life and the problems of people* today, especially if you have the mission of proclaiming the Gospel to them. Young

people and adults are sensitive to the humanity of those who have "lost everything and gained everything" to follow Christ! On this plane of the obligation to seek formation and information, take stock fairly of how far you have gotten: the golden rule is the constant subordination of your human acquisitions to the very special mission that Christ has entrusted to you in His Church, for the salvation of your human brothers.

Dear Sisters, I know that you pray for me a lot, and I thank you with all my heart. In exchange, I wish to assure you that sisters of the whole world have a very great place in my everyday life and prayer. You are, all of you, my concern and my joy, my support and my hope! May the Lord strengthen you in your consecration and your mission, for His glory and for the greater good of your African dioceses and the whole Church!

TO HEADS OF OTHER CHRISTIAN DENOMINATIONS

After leaving the Carmel on Saturday afternoon, May 3, the Holy Father visited the leprosarium, called Hôpital de la Rive, and comforted the patients there. Later in the evening he met the heads of the other Christian denominations in the Nunciature and delivered the following address.

Dear friends in Christ,

1. I am happy to be able to meet you this evening and to greet you all in the name of our Lord Jesus Christ. Thank you for your presence. We have the joy of being together, united by our love for the Lord, for Him who prayed, on the evening of Holy Thursday, that all those who believed in Him should be one. We will ask Him, therefore, to bring it about that all those who lay claim to His name may be fully faithful to the calls of grace and will find themselves again, one day, in His one Church.

2. We must thank the Lord that the conflicts of the past have made way for an effort of meeting based on mutual esteem, and pursuit of truth and charity. Our meeting this evening is a sign of this. However, as we know, the magnificent aim that we are pursu-

ing to obey the Lord's command is not attained. To reach it, there is required, with the grace of God, "change of heart and holiness of life" which constitute, with prayer for unity, as the Second Vatican Council pointed out, "the soul of the ecumenical movement" (Decree *Unitatis redintegratio,* no. 8). All initiatives in view of unity would be vain if they were deprived of this foundation, if they were not based on the constant and sometimes painful pursuit of the full truth and of holiness. This pursuit, in fact, brings us closer to Christ and, through Him, really brings us nearer to one another.

I know, and it makes me very happy, that various forms of collaboration in the service of the Gospel already exist between the different Christian churches and communities in your country. This commitment is a sign of the witness that all those who act in Christ's name wish to bear to God's salvific action at work in the world; it is also a real step towards the unity that we ask for in our prayer.

3. Since my election as Bishop of Rome, I have reaffirmed several times, as you know, my ardent desire to see the Catholic Church fully enter the holy work which has as its aim the restoration of unity. I hope that my presence among you today will be considered a sign of this commitment. Certainly, the different countries and the different regions each have their religious history—that is why the methods of the ecumenical movement may differ—but its essential imperative always remains identical: the search for the truth in its very center, Christ. It is He whom we seek above all, in order to find real unity in Him.

Dear friends in the Lord, I again thank you heartily for having been present with me today. May our

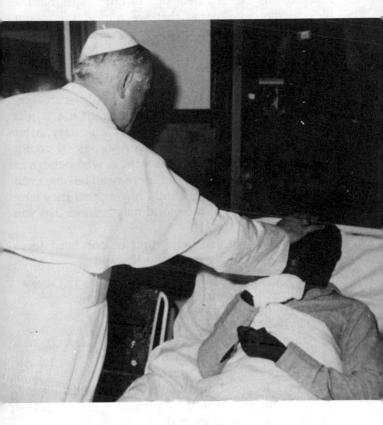

**Pope John Paul II blessing a leper as he
visited the Kinshasa River Hospital.**

meeting this evening be a sign of our desire that the blessed day may come that we appeal for in our prayer, the day when, through the work of the Holy Spirit, we will really be one "so that the world may believe" (Jn. 17:21)!

Praying this evening for unity, for the reunion in His one Church of all those who act in Christ's name, we cannot do better than take up again the Lord's own words, on the evening of Holy Thursday, after He had prayed especially for His Apostles: "I do not pray for these only, but also for those who believe in me through their word, that they may all be one; even as you, Father, are in me, and I in you, that they may also be in us, so that the world may believe that you sent me" (Jn. 17:20-21).

Together, we ask the Father of our Lord Jesus Christ to grant that we may do His will:

Our Father, who art in heaven,
Hallowed be thy name.
Thy kingdom come,
Thy will be done,
On earth as it is in heaven.
Give us this day our daily bread,
And forgive us our trespasses,
As we forgive those who trespass against us,
And lead us not into temptation,
But deliver us from evil.
Amen.

MEN HAVE A RIGHT TO PEACE AND SECURITY

The Pope's last engagement on Saturday evening, May 3, was in the Nunciature with the Diplomatic Corps accredited to Zaire. After an address by the Doyen of the Corps, Ambassador Fiankan of the Ivory Coast, John Paul II replied as follows:

Your Excellencies,
Ladies and Gentlemen,

1. In the framework of the visit I am paying, as spiritual leader, to Zaire and to the Catholic communities that live in this territory, I am happy at the possibility I am given of meeting and greeting the Diplomatic Corps accredited to the Kinshasa government. I would like to begin by thanking your Doyen who has succeeded, with so much courtesy, in becoming your interpreter, addressing to me words which I greatly appreciated.

The Holy See itself, anxious to promote a climate of dialogue with the civil authorities responsible for society, is happy to establish—with the States that so desire—stable relations, as an instrument based on mutual understanding and trust, in the service of the future and of the progress of man in all his dimensions. Such has been and such is the case of Zaire, and I rejoice in the contacts made possible with its rulers through the presence of a Pontifical Representative in this country. The latter has a special role among the pastors of the various dioceses, but, like you, he must also try to get to know better the inner reality of this

country which has so many human and natural poten-
tialities, to discover better the aspirations of its
citizens, and to promote a spirit of understanding and
cooperation on the international plane.

2. Invested, in this great capital, with a mission
inspired by the noblest ideals of human brotherhood,
it seems to me that you are all aware, ladies and
gentlemen, of the importance of the stake, which goes
beyond the immediate setting. You find yourselves,
we find ourselves, in the heart of Africa. It is for me
an opportunity to inform you of a very strong conviction, and at the same time an imperious necessity.
The conviction that no local situation is without re-
percussions on a far vaster scale today; I see as proof
of this the events that mark, sometimes painfully, one
part or other of the continent, and cannot but wound
the dignity of the African soul and even the conscience
of humanity.

3. Is it necessary to recall the problems linked
with racism, which so many voices have denounced
throughout the world, and which the Catholic
Church, on its part, condemns most firmly? My
predecessors in the See of the Apostle Peter, the Second Vatican Council and the bishops directly concerned have had many opportunities to proclaim the
anti-evangelical character of this practice (cf. among
others Pius XI: the Encyclical *Mit brennender sorge*,
nos. 2-3; John XXIII: Encyclical *Pacem in terris*,
no. 86; Paul VI: message *Affricae terrarum*, no. 17, October 29, 1967; allocution to the Kampala Parliament,
August 1, 1969). Certain commentators have also
stressed my concern to defend on all points *human
rights*, according to God; I can tell you that, in my
opinion, it is by struggling against this scourge of

racism that I intend to act also to promote respect for those rights. Very fortunately, there are signs, such as in Zimbabwe, that patient efforts can be a good foundation of realistic hopes.

4. Is it necessary to recall, furthermore, the right of peoples to decide for themselves, without denying, however—for wisdom must not be lacking—what has emerged from the vicissitudes of history? How could one fail to desire, in strict justice, to have access to real mastery, and in all fields, of one's own destiny? In the last twenty years particularly, Africa has undergone undeniable changes in its political and social structure. Reasons for serious preoccupation remain, however, either because young nations have felt some difficulty in reaching an interior balance in such a short period; or because, in spite of the initiatives of international authorities, the process towards sovereignty turns out to be too long or to lack sufficient guarantees.

5. Among many subjects, I wanted to talk to you explicitly about these because of their prime importance, but it is time, in order not to overtax your benevolence, to come to the urgent necessity to which I referred above. It springs from an overall view of the world. Formulating it, I do not claim to compete with the strategists of the international community. It is not my mission, nor my intention, nor my sphere of competence. I come here, to Africa, in possession only of the power of the Gospel, that of God (cf. 1 Cor. 1:26, 2:9). I would like to bring forth in man, my brother, who is listening to me, perhaps, a sense of real respect for and of the dignity of his African brother.

It is with astonishment mingled with sadness that we see that this continent, too, is marked by influences directed from inside and outside, often under cover of economic aid, actually in the perspective of an interest that has nothing really humanitarian about it but its label. If only the different nations that compose it can live and grow in peace, without becoming involved in ideological or political conflicts that are alien to its deep mentality! If only they are not led to devote to armaments, for example, an excessive part of the means at their disposal, sometimes restricted (cf. my address to the XXXIV General Assembly of the United Nations Organization, no. 10), and if only the assistance they receive has not any strings attached to it!

6. Such factors cannot lead to anything but violence, or even give the latter an endemic character: an open violence, which sets nations or ethnical groups in opposition to one another, and a more subtle— because less visible—violence, which affects even morals, by becoming—it is terrible to say!—a practically normal means of asserting oneself with regard to others. That is not worthy of man, and it is not worthy in particular of the African. who has a keen sense of what is called, I think, palaver—that is to say, fair confrontation through conversation and negotiation.

People should begin by discussing in order to get to know one another, and not to clash. They should begin by loving before judging. They should seek tirelessly all paths that may lead to peace and agreement, and, if the way seems still a long one, undertake new efforts. Struggles and conflicts have never solved any problem in depth.

On the occasion of my journey in Ireland last year, I said insistently and I repeat here "that violence is evil, that violence is unacceptable as a solution to problems, that violence is unworthy of man" (at Drogheda, September 29, 1979, no. 9). Here as elsewhere, I will become an indefatigable messenger of an ideal excluding violence, an ideal based on brotherhood which has its origin in God.

7. Yes, a more real observance and "practice" of human rights as a whole are the aims that lead me to pick up frequently the pilgrim's stick, in order to awaken or reawaken the conscience of mankind. Man's greatness is at stake. Man will affirm himself in this way, and not by the race towards an illusory and fragile power. Man has the right, is entitled in particular, to peace and security. He has the right that the State, responsible for the common good, should educate him to practice the means of peace. The Church has always taught, I wrote in my encyclical *Redemptor hominis,* that "the fundamental duty of power is solicitude for the common good of society.... Precisely in the name of these premises of the objective ethical order, the rights of power can only be understood on the basis of respect for the objective and inviolable rights of man.... The lack of this leads to the dissolution of society, opposition by citizens to authority, or a situation of oppression, intimidation, violence, and terrorism, of which many examples have been provided by the totalitarianisms of this century" (no. 17).

8. All that, with a fairer distribution of the fruits of progress, seems to me to constitute as many conditions to accelerate a more harmonious development of this land which I am so happy to tread in these days. May God sustain the efforts of leaders, at the

national levels as well as at the international one, in particular in the framework of the Organization of African Unity, in order that Africa may mature in serenity, and find, in the concert of nations, the role and the weight that it should have. In this way it will be better able to let other peoples benefit from its specific genius and its particular heritage.

Ladies and gentlemen, I express to you again my deep satisfaction at having been able to greet you and to tell you some of the thoughts that are closest to my heart; and offering you my fervent wishes for the high duties you assume, I ask the Almighty to assist you and all your dear ones.

A DISTRESSING ACCIDENT

A distressing note shed gloom on the joyful atmosphere of the Holy Father's meeting with the African people on Sunday, May 4. Nine persons were killed and many others injured at dawn, in a crush caused by the pressure of the crowd which had already been waiting for a long time to enter the area in which the ordination of eight bishops by the Pope was to take place later. According to information received, the persons who, at that moment, were near an entrance gate, were trodden on by the enormous multitude pressing from outside. The tragic event occurred some hours before the Holy Mass began, which, in spite of the presence of a multitude far larger than all expectations, took place without any difficulties, in an atmosphere of deep and reverent participation.

The news of the tragic event in the morning took a long time to spread, and it was known in detail only in the afternoon. It came to the knowledge of the Holy Father after his meetings with the young and with the priests, and was confirmed during the talk with President Mobutu. The Holy Father was deeply grieved and moved and at once expressed the desire to go in the evening to the hospital, where it was thought that the bodies would be laid out, also to comfort the members of their families. Having recognized, unfortunately, the practical impossibility of satisfying this wish, the Holy Father, who had prayed for the victims, entrusted to Cardinal Malula the task of going on his behalf to the families to bring them the apostolic blessing and to express his heartfelt solidarity.

The Holy Father's Sympathy

To Cardinal Joseph Malula
Archbishop of Kinshasa

As soon as I was informed this evening of the tragic accident that took place today before the beginning of the ceremony at the Palace of the People, in which several persons lost their lives and others were injured, I at once expressed the desire to go with my collaborators to pray beside the mortal remains of the victims and to express personally my consolation to the families of the deceased.

As this proved to be absolutely impossible, I hasten to express my deep emotion and sorrow to you who are the pastor of this city, and I charge you with expressing to the sorely tried families my heartfelt condolences for the death of these victims.

Imploring for them eternal rest in the peace of the Lord, I entrust their souls to the divine mercy and I pray to God to grant the families in this hour of such tragic loss the comfort of His promises. I express my best wishes for the speedy recovery of the injured, and I bless them with all my heart.

Kinshasa, May 4, 1980.

LOVING PRESENCE
OF CHRIST
IN THE MINISTRY
OF THE COMMUNITY

On Sunday, May 4, the Holy Father's first engagement was the ordination of eight bishops: four for Zaire, two for Burundi, one for the Sudan and one for Djibouti. The ordination ceremony took place, in the presence of an estimated one and a half million people, at an altar erected in front of the People's Palace. The following is the text of the Pope's homily during the Mass at which he was assisted by Cardinals Agnelo Rossi and Joseph Malula.

Dear brothers in Christ,

On this day of great joy, on this solemn occasion, I address first of all you who are going to receive the grace of the episcopate: "No longer do I call you servants,...but I have called you friends" (Jn. 15:15). That is what Christ says to the Apostles, that is what He says to you.

LIKE THE APOSTLES

1. For a long time already, you have been closely associated with Christ's life. Your faith developed on this African soil, in your family or in your Christian community, and it yielded its fruits. Then you followed Christ who beckoned to you to dedicate yourselves entirely to His mission. You received the

ministerial priesthood of priests in order to be dispensers of the mysteries of God. You endeavored to exercise it with wisdom and courage.

Now you have been chosen to "feed the flock of which the Holy Spirit has made you guardians," as St. Paul said to the elders of Ephesus, bishops to preside over it in the name and in the place of God, and to walk at its head. You receive, as St. Ignatius of Antioch said, "the ministry of the community." For this purpose, like the Apostles, you are enriched by Christ with a special outpouring of the Holy Spirit which will make your ministry fruitful (cf. prayer of the anointing of bishops). You are invested with the fullness of the priesthood, a sacrament which impresses its sacred character upon you; thus, in an eminent and visible way, you will hold the place of Christ Himself, Doctor, Priest and Pastor (cf. *Lumen gentium,* nos. 20-21). Give thanks to the Lord! And sing: alleluia!

It is a great joy and an honor for the communities in which you have your roots or which receive you as pastors, for Zaire, Burundi, the Sudan, Djibouti, and also for the religious communities that formed you. You have been "chosen from among men...appointed to act on behalf of men in relation to God" (Heb. 5:1). When young Churches see their sons assume the work of evangelization and become bishops of their brothers, it is a particularly eloquent sign of the maturity and autonomy of these Churches! On this day, let us take care not to forget also the merits of all the pioneers who have prepared, remotely or closely, these new leaders, and in particular the missionary priests and bishops. For them, too, let us give thanks to the Lord!

OVER FIFTY ZAIREAN BISHOPS

2. It is the Risen Christ, glorified by the hand of God and put by His Father in possession of the promised Holy Spirit (cf. Acts 2:33), this Christ whom we contemplate with particular joy in this paschal time—it is He who acts through our ministry. For He is the Beginning, He is the Head of the Body which is the Church (cf. Col. 1:18). In the Holy Spirit, Christ continues His work through those whom He has established as pastors and who constantly transmit this spiritual gift through the laying on of hands. They are the "vineshoots through which the apostolic seed is transmitted" (cf. *Lumen gentium,* no. 20, quoting Tertullian). Thus the line of the episcopate continues unbroken from the origins. So you enter the episcopal college which succeeds the college of the Apostles. You will work beside your elders, with your elders.

Over fifty Zaireans have already been aggregated to the episcopal body since the first episcopal ordination in 1956, and the situation is similar in the other countries represented here. You will work in communion with your brothers scattered all over the universe, who form only one whole in Christ, united around the bishop of Rome, Peter's successor. You will be all the more attached to this indispensable communion because you are ordained by the one to whom the Holy Spirit has entrusted, as to Peter, the task of presiding over unity. Yes, give thanks to the Lord! And sing: alleluia!

TO PREACH AND SANCTIFY

3. You receive a great grace to exercise a demanding pastoral task. You know its three aspects which

are usually designated as ''teaching of doctrine, ministry of sacred worship and holding of office in government'' (cf. *Lumen gentium,* no. 20). The conciliar constitution *Lumen gentium* (nos. 18-27) and the decree *Christus Dominus* (nos. 11-19) remain the charter of your ministry on which you must often meditate.

You are responsible in the first place for the preaching of the Gospel, the book of which will be laid on your head during the consecrating prayer, and then placed in your hands. Here, in Africa, the first thing asked of ecclesiastics is: give us the Word of God. Yes, it is a marvelous thing to see the thirst of your fellow-countrymen for the Gospel: they know, they feel, that it is a message of life.

To do so, you will not be alone. Your priests, your deacons, your women and men religious, your catechists, your lay people are also very meritorious, daily and tenacious evangelizers, very close to the people, and sometimes even pioneers, in places or environments where the Gospel has not yet fully penetrated. Your role will be to sustain their zeal, harmonize their apostolate, see to it that the proclamation, preaching and catechesis are faithful to the authentic meaning of the Gospel and to the whole doctrine, dogmatic and ethical, that the Church has set forth in the course of these twenty centuries on the basis of the Gospel.

You will have to try at the same time to see to it that the message really reaches hearts and transforms behavior, using a language adapted to your African faithful. As the liturgy will tell you: in season and out of season, ''preach the word of God yourselves with great patience and with a care to instruct." You are essentially witnesses to the divine and Catholic truth.

You receive the charge of *sanctifying* the People of God. In this sense, you are fathers and you transmit Christ's life through the sacraments, which you celebrate, or entrust to your priests for regular, worthy and fruitful celebration. You will have to prepare your faithful for these sacraments, and encourage them to live by them perseveringly. Your prayer will constantly accompany your people along the ways to holiness. You will contribute to preparing, with the grace of the Lord, a Church without a spot or a wrinkle, which proclaims the new Jerusalem, of which Revelation speaks to us, "prepared as a bride adorned for her husband" (Rv. 21:2).

SPECIAL AUTHORITY

4. Finally, you receive the *pastoral government* of a diocese, or you take part in it as auxiliary bishop. Christ gives you authority to exhort, to distribute ministries and services, according to needs and capacities, to see to it that they are carried out, to reprove mercifully, if need be, those who go astray, to watch over the whole flock and defend it, as St. Paul said (Acts 20:29-31), and to arouse an increasingly missionary spirit. In all things seek the communion and the building up of the Body of Christ.

You rightly bear on your head the emblem of the leader and in your hand the shepherd's crook. Remember that your authority, according to Jesus, is that of the Good Shepherd, who knows His sheep and is very attentive to each one; that of the Father who reveals Himself through His spirit of love and dedication; that of the steward, ready to give an account to his Master; that of the "minister," who is in the midst of his people "as he who serves" and is ready to give his life. The Church has always urged the head of the Christian community to care particularly for the poor, the weak, those who are suffering, and the under-privileged of every kind. She asks you to give special support to your companions in service, the priests and the deacons: they are brothers, sons and friends for you (cf. *Christus Dominus*, no. 16).

The strict administration which is entrusted to you requires of you, together with authority, the prudence and wisdom of "elders"; the spirit of fairness and peace; faithfulness to the Church, of which your ring is the symbol; exemplary purity of doctrine and life. It is a question, in a word, of leading ecclesiastics, religious and laity to the holiness of our Lord; of leading them to live the new commandment of brotherly love, which Jesus left us as His testament (Jn. 13:34). That is why the recent Council reminds all bishops of the fundamental duty of "giving an example of sanctity in charity, humility and simplicity of life" (cf. *Christus Dominus*, no. 15). St. Peter wrote to the "elders": "Tend the flock of God that is your charge...being examples to the flock" (1 Pt. 5:2-3).

ACCORDING TO GOD'S LAW

5. In this way you will provide for the good of souls, for their salvation. In this way you will continue the building of the Church already so well implanted in the heart of Africa and particularly in each of your countries. In this way you will contribute a

Beloved brothers, by humbly submitting your whole person to Christ, who calls you to represent Him, you are sure of His grace, His strength, His peace. Like St. Paul, "I commend you to God and to the word of his grace" (Acts 20:32). May God be glorified in you!

precious share to the vitality of the universal Church, bearing with me and with the bishops as a whole the solicitude for all the Churches.

Moreover, by forming consciences according to the law of God and by educating them to responsibilities and to communion in the Church, you will contribute to form honest and courageous citizens whom the country needs, enemies of corruption, lies and injustice, architects of concord and of brotherly love without frontiers, concerned about harmonious development, especially of the poorest categories. By doing so, you exercise your mission which is of the spiritual and moral order: it enables you to speak out on ethical aspects of society, whenever the fundamental rights of persons, fundamental freedoms and the common good require it. All that in respect of the civil authorities which, on the political plane, and in the pursuit of means to promote the common good, have their specific spheres of competence and responsibilities. In this way you will prepare in depth social progress, the welfare and peace of your dear country, and you will merit the esteem of your fellow-citizens. You are here the pioneers of the Gospel and of the Church, and at the same time the pioneers of the history of your people.

SUBMITTING TO CHRIST

6. Beloved brothers, this ideal must not overwhelm you. On the contrary, it must attract you, and serve you as a springboard and hope. Certainly, we all have this treasure in earthen vessels (cf. 2 Cor. 4:7), including the one who is speaking to you, to whom the name of "Holiness" is given. A great deal of hu-

mility is necessary to bear this name! But by humbly submitting your whole person to Christ, who calls you to represent Him, you are sure of His grace, His strength, His peace. Like St. Paul, "I commend you to God and to the word of his grace" (Acts 20:32). May God be glorified in you!

WELCOME TO NEIGHBORS

7. And now, I turn more directly towards all those who surround you with their sympathy and their prayer. Dear brothers and sisters of Kinshasa, Zaire, Burundi, the Sudan and Djibouti, welcome with joy our brothers who become your fathers and pastors. Have for them the respect, affection and obedience that you owe to the ministers of Christ who is Truth, Life and the Way. Listen to their testimony, for they come to you as the first witnesses of the Gospel. Their message is the message of Jesus Christ. Open your souls to the blessings of Christ, to the life of Christ which they bring you. Follow them along the ways they trace out for you, in order that your conduct may be worthy of the disciples of Christ. Pray for them. With them, you are going to build the Church in Africa; you are going to develop Christian communities, in close communion with the universal Church whose sap you have received and continue to receive, in a trusting relationship with Peter's See, the principle of unity, but with the vigor and the spiritual and moral riches that the Gospel will have caused to spring from your African souls.

By the providence of God, this great hour touches also English-speaking Africa, and in particular the Sudan. In the person of the new auxiliary bishop of

Juba, I greet the entire Archdiocese and all the sons and daughters of the Church in that land: grace and peace to all of you in Jesus Christ, the Son of God, in Jesus Christ, the Good Shepherd who, through the ministry of bishops, continues the pastoral care of His entire Church. May the love of the Savior be in your hearts today and always!

And you, dear friends who do not share the Christian faith but wished to accompany Catholics at this liturgical celebration, I thank you and I invite you, too, to welcome these new bishops as religious leaders and defenders of man and as peacemakers.

Now we prepare for the Rite of Ordination. Like the Apostle Paul beside the elders of Ephesus to whom he had just made his pressing recommendations, we are going to pray. Blessed be the Lord who prolongs in this way His work among us! May all the Apostles intercede for us! May the Virgin Mary, the Mother of the Savior, the Mother of the Church, the Queen of Apostles, intercede for us! We dedicate to her these new servants of the Church. Let us give thanks to the Lord, in faith, charity and hope! Amen. Alleluia!

"WE PRAY TO MARY FOR AFRICA"

At the conclusion of the Mass on May 4, during which he ordained eight bishops at Kinshasa, John Paul II recited the Regina Caeli *prayer with the huge congregation. Before doing so he gave the following address which was transmitted to Saint Peter's Square in Rome by Vatican Radio.*

Dear brothers and sisters of Kinshasa, Zaire and Africa, present here or connected with us by radio, I call upon you to pause in the middle of this splendid day, in order to turn to the Virgin Mary, our Mother. It is a beautiful custom, an ancient custom of the Catholic Church, to mark the day by a pause for prayer, in the morning, at midday or in the evening, repeating to Mary the first greeting of the Angel Gabriel and her own answer in the Angelus, or else, during the Easter period, singing our praise to the Queen of Heaven, *Regina Caeli.*

The Son of God became flesh in her; it is the Incarnation, and He rose again; these are the joyful and glorious mysteries that are at the center of our Faith. We must constantly contemplate them with Mary. Yes, it is with Mary, the Mother of Jesus, that we become real disciples of her Son, like the Apostles at Cana.

It is with Mary that we open our heart to the Holy Spirit, like the Apostles at Pentecost. It is with Mary, with this Mother, that we have recourse to God's fatherly tenderness, for all our human and spiritual needs. The Africans understand so well, in their families, the role of woman, the bearer of life and the guardian of the home. How I wish, dear friends, that they would have a spontaneous and frequent devotion for Mary, the Woman blessed among all women, the Woman glorified at the side of the Lord Jesus, the Mother whom God gives us!

We pray to her for the great intentions of Africa. That God may always have there the place that is due to Him. That every man may be respected in his dignity as a man and as a son of God. That the poor, the sick, the old, prisoners, strangers may find comfort and hope. That the African peoples, who show such a fine sense of hospitality, may benefit from the respectful solidarity of other peoples. That they may safeguard, purifying them constantly, the real values of the African soul, and that they may enrich the heritage of mankind with them. That peace may reign in nations and among nations. And that the leaders of the peoples may guide them, in a spirit of service, in justice and with wisdom.

We pray especially to Mary in order that the Gospel of Jesus may always be received in Africa as a light, as a greeting, for it is light and salvation in our eyes. That Christian communities may grow and be strengthened in unity and holiness. That the laity may live according to their Baptism. That God may bring forth numerous vocations of priests, brothers and sisters, and lead them to their fulfillment. Let us pray especially for these new bishops on whom we laid our hands to communicate the fullness of the gifts of the Holy Spirit. The choice of these pastors is a sign of the maturity of your Churches. They are now going to join their brothers, my brothers, to walk at the head of the flock, as Jesus asked the Apostles, and particularly Peter, to do.

May Mary watch over these Churches, over the one Church of her Son!

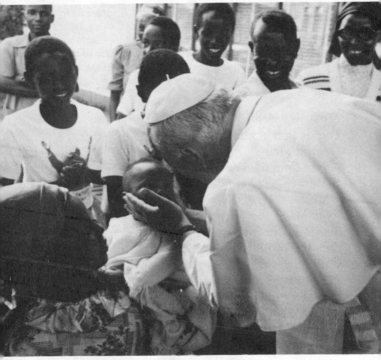

The Africans understand so well, in their families, the role of woman, the bearer of life and the guardian of the home. How I wish that they would have a spontaneous and frequent devotion for Mary, the woman blessed among all women.

"PROCLAIM MAN RENEWED IN CHRIST"

On Sunday afternoon, May 4, John Paul II returned to the vast square in front of the People's Palace and there he met thousands of university students and a group of intellectuals. He was welcomed by Msgr. Tshibangu Tshishiku, Rector of the National University of Zaire and Auxiliary Bishop of Kinshasa, and also by the Minister of Education. The Holy Father gave the following address.

Most Reverend Rector,
Ladies and gentlemen of the teaching staff,
Dear students,

1. I am deeply touched by the words of welcome that have just been addressed to me, and I thank you warmly. Is it necessary to tell you my joy at being able to contact the African university world this afternoon? In the tribute you have paid to me, I see not only the honor done to the first pastor of the Catholic Church; I also perceive an expression of gratitude to the Church, for the role she has played in the course of history and which she still plays in the promotion of knowledge and science.

CONCEPT OF UNIVERSITY

2. Historically, the universities had their origin in the Church.

For centuries, she developed a conception of the world in which the knowledge of the period was set in the wider view of a world created by God and redeemed by our Lord Jesus Christ. Thus, a great many of her sons dedicated themselves to teaching and research, to initiate generations of students into the different stages of knowledge in a complete view of man, integrating, in particular, consideration of the ultimate reasons of his existence.

However, the very concept of university, universal by definition in its project, does not imply that it is set, in a way, outside the realities of the country in which it is implanted. On the contrary, history shows how universities have been instruments of formation and dissemination of a culture peculiar to their country, contributing a great deal to forging awareness of national identity. Thereby, the university is naturally part of the cultural heritage of a people. In this sense, it could be said that it belongs to the people.

This way of seeing the university in its essential aim, to reach as much knowledge as possible, and in its concrete roots within a nation, is of great importance. It manifests in particular the legitimacy of the plurality of cultures, recognized by the Second Vatican Council (cf. *Gaudium et spes*, no. 53), and it makes it possible to discern the criteria of true cultural pluralism, connected with the way in which each people moves toward the one truth. It shows, too, that a university faithful to the ideal of complete truth about man cannot ignore, even on the pretext of realism or the autonomy of sciences, the study of the superior realities of ethics, metaphysics and religion. It was from this standpoint that the Church took a special interest in the world of culture, and made important contributions to it. For her, the divine revelation about man, about the meaning of his life and his effort for the construction of the world, is essential for complete knowledge of man and in order that progress may always be completely human. Such is the aim of the missionary activity of the Church: to bring it about, as the Council again recalls, that everything that is good in the hearts of men, in their thought, and in their culture, may be raised and reach its completion for the glory of God and the happiness of man (cf. *Lumen gentium,* no. 17).

TWENTY-FIFTH ANNIVERSARY

3. The University of Kinshasa takes its place in a remarkable way in this historical collaboration between the Church and the world of culture. The centenary of the evangelization of Zaire coincides, in fact, with the twenty-fifth anniversary of the national university of the country. How could we fail to rejoice together at the clear-sightedness of those who founded this university? It shows plainly the place that man's cultural and spiritual advancement has in evangelization. It is the proof that the Church, and particularly the famous Catholic University of Louvain, had been right in their view and had confidence in the future of your people and your country! Even now, the importance of the Catholic community in your country makes it desirable that the university should remain open to trusting relations with the Church!

Thus, paying tribute, today, in your presence, to the national university of Zaire and to the Zairean university community, I do so looking towards the whole African university world. It plays and will play to an ever increasing extent an outstanding role, irreplaceable and essential, in order that your continent may fully develop all the promise it bears for itself and for the world as a whole.

UNIVERSITY'S ROLE

4. You will allow me, I am sure, a former university professor, who dedicated long and happy years to university teaching in his native land, to talk to you for a few moments of what I consider are the two essential aims of all complete and authentic university formation: *knowledge* and *conscience*, in other words, access to knowledge and the formation of conscience, as is clearly expressed in the very motto of the National University of Zaire: *Scientia splendet et conscientia.*

The first role of a university is the teaching of knowledge and scientific research. Of this vast field, I will deal here only with one point: knowledge means truth. So there would be no true university spirit if there were not the joy of seeking and knowing, inspired by ardent love of truth. This pursuit of truth is the grandeur of scientific knowledge, as I recalled on last November 10, addressing the Pontifical Academy of Sciences: "Pure science is a good, worthy of being loved for it is knowledge and therefore perfection of man in his intelligence. Even before its technical applications, it must be honored for its own sake, as an integral part of culture. Basic science is a universal good, which every people must be able to cultivate in full freedom from any form of international constraint or intellectual colonialism" (*L'Osservatore Romano*, French edition, November 20, 1979).

Those who dedicate their lives to science can, therefore, feel a legitimate pride, and also those who, like you students, may spend several years of their lives being trained in a scientific discipline, for nothing is finer, in spite of the work and the trouble it demands, than to be able to engage in the pursuit of truth about nature and about man.

TRUTH ABOUT MAN

5. How can we fail to draw your attention briefly here to love of the truth about man? Human sciences have, as I have already stressed several times, an increasing place in our knowledge. They are indispensable to arrive at a harmonious organization of life in common in a world in which exchanges are becoming more and more numerous and complex. But at the same time, it is only in a very special sense, radically different from the usual one that we can speak of "sciences" of man, precisely because there is a truth about man that transcends all attempts of reduction to any particular aspect whatever. In this field, a really complete researcher cannot disregard, in the elaboration of knowledge as in its applications, spiritual and moral realities which are essential to human existence, or the values that are derived from them. For the fundamental truth is that man's life has a meaning, on which the value of personal existence depends as well as a correct conception of life in society.

FORMATION OF CONSCIENCE

6. These rapid considerations on love of truth, which I would like to be able to develop at length dialoguing with you, will have already shown you

what I mean when I speak of the role of the university and of your studies for the formation of conscience. Certainly, the university has in the first place a pedagogical role of formation of its students, in order that they will be capable of reaching the level of knowledge required and of exercising their profession effectively in the world in which they will later be called to work. But beyond the different branches of knowledge which it has the function of transmitting, the university cannot ignore another duty: that of permitting and facilitating the integration of knowledge in a wider, fundamental context, in a fully human conception of existence. In this way, the thoughtful student will avoid succumbing to the temptation of ideologies, deceptive because they are always simplified, and will be made capable of seeking at a higher degree the truth about himself and his role in society.

7. Dear friends, teachers and students, I would like to be able to express personally to each of you and to each of those you represent, the whole student world, the world of culture and of science in Zaire and in Africa, all my encouragement to accept fully, each one of you, your responsibilities. They are heavy ones; they demand the best of oneself, for the university has not as its aim in the first place the pursuit of degrees, diplomas or well-paid posts: it has an important role for man's formation and service of the country. That is why it entails great requirements with regard to the work to be carried out, with regard to oneself and with regard to society.

If all university research calls for real freedom, without which it cannot exist, it also requires on the part of students hard work, qualities of objectivity, method and discipline, in short, competence. This, as you well know, opens onto the two other aspects. One of the characteristics of university work and of the intellectual world is that, more than elsewhere perhaps, each one is constantly referred to his own responsibility in the direction he gives to his work. On this last point, I am happy to repeat to you the greatness of your role and to encourage you to face up to it with your whole soul. You are not just working for yourselves, for your advancement. You take part, by the very fact that you are university students, in research concerning the truth about man, in pursuit of his good, with the care of cooperating in the exploitation of nature for a real service of man, in promotion of the cultural and spiritual values of mankind.

Concretely, this participation in the good of humanity is realized through the services you render and which you will be called to render for your country: for the physical and moral health of your fellow citizens, and for the improved economic and social condition of your nation. For the privileged education that the community offers you is not given to you in the first place for your personal profit. Tomorrow, it is the whole community, with its material and spiritual needs, which will have the right to turn to you, which will need you. You will be sensitive to the appeals of your fellow countrymen. A difficult but exalting task, worthy of the sentiment of solidarity, which you possess so strongly: you will have to serve man, to serve the African in his deepest and most precious aspect: his humanity.

Jesus Christ is, in all truth, man's Way—
yours. That is why evangelization, which responds to a command of the Lord, also finds its
place in your collaboration in the future of your
people, for it is collaboration in faith, in divine
plans for the world and for mankind, and, in
short, collaboration in the history of salvation.

THE PRIMACY OF TRUTH AND MAN

8. The perspectives which I merely sketch before you this afternoon, dear friends, imply a fundamental reality: that ethics, morality, spiritual realities, should be perceived as elements that make up the complete man, understood both in his personal life and in the role he must play in society, and therefore as essential elements of all society. The primacy of truth and the primacy of man, far from conflicting with each other, unite and are harmoniously coordinated for a spirit anxious to reach and respect reality in all its fullness.

It follows further that, just as there is a wrong way of conceiving technical progress by making it everything for man, by making it serve entirely the satisfaction of his most superficial desires falsely identified with success and happiness, there is also a wrong way of conceiving the progress of our thought about the truth concerning man. In this field, as you can clearly feel, progress takes place through deep investigation, through integration. Errors are corrected, but they have always been errors, whereas there is no truth about man, about the meaning of his personal and community life, that can be "outdated" or become an error. This is important for you who, in a rapidly changing society, must work at its human and social progress by integrating the truth that comes to you from the past with that which will enable you to cope with new prospects.

9. It is in accordance with the truth about man, in fact, that materialism, in all its forms, must be rejected, for it is always a source of subjection: either subjection to a soulless pursuit of material goods, or,

far worse, the subjection of man, body and soul, to atheistic ideologies, always, when all is said and done, the subjection of man to man. That is why the Catholic Church has wished to proclaim solemnly the right to religious freedom in loyal pursuit of spiritual and religious values; that is also why she prays that all men may find, in faithfulness to the religious sense that God has put in their hearts, the way to the whole truth.

10. I would like to add here a short word particularly for my brothers and sisters in our Lord Jesus Christ. You believe in the message of the Gospel, you wish to live by it. For us, the Lord Jesus Christ is our Way, our Truth, and our Life (cf. Jn. 14:6). I have already developed, especially in the first encyclical, *Redemptor hominis,* which I addressed to the world at the beginning of my pontifical ministry, and also in my message of January 1st on "truth the power of peace," how, for us Christians, Christ our Lord, through His Incarnation, that is, through the reality of our humanity which He assumed for our salvation, revealed to us the most complete truth that exists about man, about ourselves, about our existence. He is, in all truth, man's Way—yours. That is why evangelization, which responds to a command of the Lord, also finds its place in your collaboration in the future of your people, for it is collaboration in faith, in divine plans for the world and for mankind, and, in short, collaboration in the history of salvation.

PROCLAIMING GOD'S WORD

11. At the moment when the centenary of the proclamation of the Word of God is being celebrated in

Zaire, and at the moment when a new African world is being formed in the service of a richer humanity for Africa, you are called to participate fully, while being at the same time witnesses to Christ in your university and professional life. Give proof of your competence, of your African wisdom, but be at the same time men and women who bring the testimony of your Christian conception of the world and of man. Let your whole life be for those around you, and beyond them for your whole country, a proclamation of the truth about man renewed in Christ, a message of salvation in the risen Lord. I count on you, Catholic university students, dear boys and girls; I count on your faithful commitment to service of your country, of the Church, of the whole of mankind, and I thank you for it.

12. Dear friends, teachers and students, at the beginning of its existence, your university had as its motto: *Lumen requirunt lumine:* by its light, they seek the light! I hope that your studies, your researches, your wisdom will be for you all a way towards the supreme Light, the God of truth, whom I pray to bless you.

CHRISTIAN VOCATION OF AFRICANS NOURISHED BY YOUR MINISTRY

After his meeting with the university students on Sunday afternoon, May 4, the Holy Father then met the priests and men religious in the Sacred Heart Church beside the nunciature. After an enthusiastic welcome from them, he spoke to them as follows:

Dear brother priests,

1. I have deeply desired this meeting with you. Priests, as you know, have a special place in my heart and my prayer. It is natural: with you, I am a priest. He who has been constituted Pastor of the whole flock has his eyes fixed first on those who share his pastorate—which is the pastorate of Christ—on those who bear every day "the weight and heat of the day." And your mission is so important for the Church!

Last year, for Holy Thursday, I made a point of addressing a special letter to all priests in the world, through their bishops. In the name of the whole Church, I expressed to you my feelings of gratitude and trust. I reminded you of your priestly identity, in relation to Christ the Priest, the Good Shepherd: I set your ministry in its place in the Church. I also showed the meaning of the requirements attached to your priestly state. I hope that you have read this letter, and that you will reread it. I cannot take up again here all its themes, not even briefly. I shall rather give some thoughts as an extension of it. I was anxious particularly to speak personally to you, priests in Africa, priests in Zaire. It is one of my first meetings on African soil, a very special meeting with my brother priests.

PRIESTS FROM AFRICA

2. Beyond your persons, I am thinking of all the priests of the African continent. Of those who came from far away for the beginnings of evangelization and who continue to bring their precious and indispensable help. I hardly dare say "missionaries," for you must all be missionaries. I am thinking also—and quite particularly in this talk—of the priests who have come from African peoples: they already constitute an answer rich in consoling promises. They are the most convincing proof of the maturity that your young Churches have acquired; they are already, and they are called more and more, to be their animators. They are particularly numerous in this country. It is a great grace for which we thank God, in this centenary of evangelization. It is also a great responsibility.

TO BE A PRIEST

3. Among so many thoughts that crowd in on me at this moment, which will I choose as the subject of this meeting? It seems to me that the best beginning is given to us by the apostle Paul, when he exhorts his disciple Timothy to rekindle the gift of God that is within him through the laying on of his hands (cf. 2 Tim. 1:6), and to draw, from renewed awareness of

this grace, the courage to continue generously along the way undertaken, because "God did not give us a spirit of timidity but a spirit of power and love and self-control" (*ibid.*, 1:7).

Our meditation today must begin then by recalling the fundamental features of the priesthood. To be a priest means being a mediator between God and men, in the Mediator par excellence who is Christ.

Jesus was able to carry out His mission thanks to His complete union with the Father, because He was one only with Him. In His condition as a pilgrim along the ways of our earth (*viator*), He was already in possession of the end (*comprehensor*) to which He was to lead others. In order to be able to continue Christ's mission effectively, the priest must also, in a way, have already arrived at the destination to which he wishes to lead others: he does so through assiduous contemplation of the mystery of God, nourished by study of the Scripture, a study which blossoms in prayer. Faithfulness to the moments and means of personal prayer, the more official prayer of the hours, but also the worthy and generous accomplishment of the sacred acts of the ministry, help to sanctify the priest and lead him to an experience of the mysterious and fascinating presence of the living God, enabling him to act forcefully on the human environment around him.

PRIEST AS MEDIATOR

4. Christ exercised His office as Mediator mainly by offering up His life in the sacrifice of the cross, accepted out of obedience to the Father. The cross remains the "necessary" way for the meeting with God.

It is a way on which the priest first and foremost must embark courageously. As I recalled in my recent letter on the Eucharist, is he not called to renew *in persona Christi,* in the Eucharistic Celebration, the sacrifice of the cross? According to the fine expression of the African Augustine of Hippo, Christ on Calvary was "priest and sacrifice, and therefore priest because he was sacrifice" (*Confessions,* X, 43, 69). The priest who, in the radical poverty of obedience to God, to the Church, to his bishop, has been able to make his life a pure offering to offer, in union with Christ, to the heavenly Father, will experience in his ministry the victorious power of the grace of Christ who died and rose again.

As Mediator, the Lord Jesus was, in all the dimensions of His Being, the Man for God and for brothers. Likewise the priest; that is the reason why he is asked to dedicate his whole life to God and to the Church, in the depths of his being, his faculties, his feelings. The priest who, in the choice of celibacy, renounces human love in order to be open completely to love of God, becomes free to give himself to men through a gift that does not exclude anyone, but embraces them all in the flow of charity, which comes from God (cf. Rom. 5:5) and leads to God. Celibacy, by linking the priest with God, sets him free for all the work required by the care of souls.

AFRICAN AND CHRISTIAN

5. Here we have sketched in a few strokes the essential character of the priest, such as it has been handed down to us by the venerable tradition of the Church. It has a permanent value, yesterday, today,

tomorrow. It is not a question of ignoring the new problems raised by the modern world, and also by the African context, for it is important to prepare priests who are at once fully African and truly Christian. The questions raised by the culture in which the priestly ministry is integrated, call for mature reflection. But in any case it is in the light of the fundamental theology that I have recalled that they must be tackled and solved.

IMPORTANT MINISTRY
OF RECONCILIATION

6. It is not necessary for me now to dwell on the different functions of the priest. You have meditated upon, and you must often take up again, the texts of the Second Vatican Council, the constitution *Lumen gentium* (no. 28) and the whole decree *Presbyterorum ordinis.*

The proclamation of the Gospel, of the whole Gospel, to every category of Christians and also to non-Christians, must have an important place in your life. The faithful are entitled to this. Under this ministry of the Word of God there fall particularly *catechesis,* which must be able to reach the heart and the mind of your fellow countrymen, and the formation of catechists, religious and lay. Be educators to the Faith and the Christian life according to the Church, in the personal, family and professional fields.

The worthy celebration of the sacraments, the dispensation of the mysteries of God, is equally central in your lives as priests. In this field, take assiduous care to prepare the faithful to receive them, so that, for example, the sacraments of Baptism, Penance, the Eucharist, marriage, may bear all the fruit. For

Christ exercises the power of His redeeming action in the sacraments. He does so particularly in the Eucharist and in the sacrament of Penance.

The apostle Paul said: "God...gave us the ministry of reconciliation" (2 Cor. 5:18). The People of God are called to a continual conversion, to an ever-renewed reconciliation with God in Christ. This reconciliation is carried out in the sacrament of Penance, and it is there that you exercise, par excellence, your ministry of reconciliation.

Yes, the Pope knows your difficulties: you have so many pastoral tasks to carry out, and time is always lacking. But each Christian has a right, yes, a right, to a personal meeting with the crucified, forgiving Christ. As I said in my first encyclical, "It is evident that this is also a right on Christ's part with regard to every human being redeemed by him" (*Redemptor hominis*, no. 20). That is why I beg you, always consider this ministry of reconciliation in the sacrament of Penance as one of the most important of your tasks.

Finally, the "spiritual power" that has been given to you (cf. decree *Presbyterorum ordinis*, no. 6), has been given to construct the Church, to lead it like the Lord, the Good Shepherd, with humble and disinterested devotion, always welcoming, ready to assume the different ministries and services that are necessary and complementary in the unity of the presbyterium, with a great concern for collaboration among you, priests, and with your bishops. The Christian people must be carried along to unity on seeing the brotherly love and cohesion that you manifest. Your authority in the exercise of your functions is bound up with your faithfulness to the Church which entrusted them to you. Leave political responsibilities to those who are charged with them: you have another part, a magnificent part—you are "leaders" for another reason and in another way, participating in the priesthood of Christ, as His ministers. Your field of interventions, and it is a vast one, is that of faith and morals, where people expect you to preach at the same time with courageous words and with the example of your life.

DEVELOPING THE ROLE
OF THE LAITY

7. Every member of the Church has an irreplaceable role. Yours consists also in helping all those who belong to your communities to carry out theirs—religious, sisters and laity. In particular you must develop the role of the laity: it must never be forgotten, in fact, that Baptism and Confirmation confer a specific responsibility in the Church. I deeply approve, therefore, of your concern to bring forth collaborators, to train them for their responsibilities. Yes, you must know how to address them, tirelessly, direct, concrete and precise appeals. You must form them by making them become aware of the hidden riches they bear within them. Finally, you must really be able to collaborate, without monopolizing all the tasks, all the initiatives or all the decisions, when it is a question of what is in their sphere of competence and responsibility. It is in this way that living communities are formed, which really represent an image of the primitive Church, in which we see appear, around the Apostle, the names of those many helpers, men and women, whom St. Paul greets as his "fellow workers in Christ Jesus" (Rom. 16:3).

HOPE IN THE RISEN CHRIST

8. In all this pastoral work, the inevitable difficulties must not affect our confidence. *Scimus Christum surrexisse a mortuis vere.* The presence of the Risen Christ is the certain foundation of a hope "that does not disappoint us" (Rom. 5:5). That is why the priest must be always and everywhere, *a man of hope.* It is true that the world is racked by deep tensions, which very often give rise to difficulties the immediate solution of which is beyond us. Under these circumstances, and at all times, the priest must be able to offer his brothers, by word and example, convincing reasons for hope. He can do so because his certainties are not based on human opinions, but on the solid rock of the Word of God.

THE PRIEST MUST BE A MAN OF DISCERNMENT

9. Sustained by it, the priest must show himself to be *a man of discernment and a true teacher of the Faith.*

Yes, he must be a man of discernment, especially in our age. For, as we all know, if the modern world has made great progress in the field of knowledge and human advancement, it is also steeped in a large number of ideologies and pseudo-values which, through a fallacious language, too often succeed in luring and• deceiving a number of our contemporaries. Not only is it necessary not to succumb to them, this is only too evident, but the task of pastors is also to form the Christian judgment of the faithful (cf. 1 Tim. 5:21; 1 Jn. 4:1), in order that they, too, may be capable of resisting the deceptive fascination of these new "idols."

In this way, the priest will reveal himself also as a true teacher of the Faith. He will lead Christians to become mature in their Faith, by communicating to them an ever deeper knowledge of the Gospel message—"not their own wisdom but the Word of God" (decree *Presbyterorum ordinis*, no. 4)—and helping them to judge by its light the circumstances of life. Thus, thanks to your persevering efforts, today, in Africa, Catholics will be able to discover the answers which, in full faithfulness to the immutable values of Tradition, will also be able to satisfy adequately the needs and challenges of the present.

FOSTERING VOCATIONS

10. I have recalled the role of all the faithful in the Church. But, at the end of this talk, I draw your attention to the primary duty you have with regard to vocations. The meaning of every Christian vocation depends so closely on that of the priestly vocation that, in communities where the latter disappears, the very authenticity of Christian life is affected. Work tirelessly, therefore, dear brothers, to make the whole People of God understand the importance of vocations; pray and get people to pray for that. Take care that Christ's call is presented well to the young; help those that the Lord calls to the priesthood or to the religious life to discern the signs of their vocation; support them throughout their formation. You are certainly convinced that the future of the Church will depend on holy priests, because the priesthood belongs to the structure of the Church such as the Lord willed it. Finally, dear brothers, do you not think that

the Lord will use in the first place the example of our own life, generous and radiant, to bring forth other vocations?

FAITH IN THE PRIESTHOOD

11. Beloved brothers, have faith in your priesthood. It is the priesthood of always, because it is a participation in the eternal priesthood of Christ, who "is the same yesterday and today and forever" (Heb. 13:8; cf. Rev. 1:17ff.). Yes, if the demands of the priesthood are very great, and if I have not hesitated, however, to speak to you about them, it is because they are simply the consequence of the closeness of the Lord, of the confidence He shows in His priests. "No longer do I call you servants,...but I have called you friends" (Jn. 15:15). May this song of the day of our ordination remain for each of you, as for me, a permanent source of joy and trust. It is this joy that I call upon you to renew today. May the Virgin Mary always sustain you on the way, and may she introduce you more and more every day to intimacy with the Lord! With my affectionate apostolic blessing.

Work tirelessly, therefore, dear brothers, to make the whole People of God understand the importance of vocations; pray and get people to pray for that. Take care that Christ's call is presented well to the young; help those that the Lord calls to the priesthood or to the religious life to discern the signs of their vocation; support them throughout their formation.

MISSIONARY SPIRIT DEEPLY ROOTED IN POLAND'S FAITH

After his meeting with the priests in Kinshasa on Sunday, May 4, the Holy Father went to the nunciature where he met the Polish community living in Zaire, and spoke to them as follows:

Beloved brothers and sisters, missionaries,
Dear fellow-countrymen, participants in this unusual meeting in Africa!

1. With deep emotion I meet you here in Africa, where you represent our common country and the Church which carries out its mission of salvation in it. I greet you with the venerated greeting of our Fathers. It contains in it not only the whole depth of the affective content, which recalls your native land, the family, the parish, the environment in which you grew up and which you then left, seized by the invitation "Follow me," to become sowers of the Word of God; but it expresses, in a sense, the very substance of the missionary vocation, the ideal of the work of evangelization.

In the name of Jesus Christ, who was crucified and rose again, you have come here in order that all peoples may praise the Lord, that all nations may glorify Him (cf. Ps. 116 [117]).

"How beautiful upon the mountains are the feet of him who brings good tidings, who publishes peace, who brings good tidings of good, who publishes salvation" (Is. 52:7).

In the name of Jesus Christ, I have undertaken this pilgrimage of mine to the living sanctuary of man's heart in Africa, to take part in the joys of the jubilee of this young Church and, at the same time, to thank God, together with it, for the graces bestowed upon it especially in this century, and to entrust to divine mercy the promising future of this Church.

2. I meet you, dear missionaries, brothers and sisters, in the same name. I rejoice because I am able, in the course of these days, to take a place in your everyday missionary work in a special way and to share your missionary effort, carrying out this service with regard to our brothers on the African continent.

We know very well that we owe our Faith to others who, driven by the call of the divine Word, came to us and sowed among our ancestors the Good News, announced peace, revealed happiness and proclaimed salvation. They grafted them into the mysteries of divine life and made them a part of the living organism of the Church.

The living testimony of the maturity of every Church is not only its opening to the Word of God, to the good of salvation, but the capacity of giving to others what it lives itself. With this donation it not only manifests this maturity, but deepens it and consolidates it. Therefore, like the whole Church, also the local Churches wish to become missionary, to become the subject of this "missionary-mindedness" of the Church. Although we did not always have, in the course of history, the conditions to express this missionary character externally, the missionary spirit was, however, and still is, deeply rooted in the Faith of our people. And missionary problems always find a deep echo in the heart of the People of God in our country. In spite of the difficulties mentioned, the Church in our country has written a splendid missionary page; it is enough to recall Blessed Maximilian M. Kolbe, Blessed Mary Teresa Ledochowska, Father Bejzym, not to mention so many other less known and anonymous workers in the missionary field.

It continues to write this missionary page. You, present here, and all those who have not been able to come here, are the proof of it.

How much I rejoice as Pope and as a Pole whenever news reaches me of the departure of a missionary, of a sister, of lay persons from Poland, and these departures, thank God, are more and more numerous!

3. In the name of Jesus Christ I meet you, fellow countrymen present here, together with all those absent—perhaps there are not many of them—you whom destiny has directed here and who have found your second country in the African continent!

You who, carrying out your service, serve the homeland!

You, missionaries of human values, who have come here to share, on this developing continent which needs help, your knowledge, your experience and your capacity, in respect of the dignity and rights of every man!

This respect for dignity and freedom, one's own and that of others, is deeply rooted in our Christian and national tradition, because we know the price of these fundamental and inviolable human values. We know that it is not possible to bring real good to the other man if purposes contrary to it or perhaps secondary interests are hidden behind him.

4. I hope that our African brothers, among whom you work, will be able to say of you what we read in Isaiah's text:

"How beautiful upon the mountains are the feet of him who brings good tidings, who publishes peace, who brings good tidings of good, who publishes salvation."

5. I have brought with me here in Zaire the image of the Mother of God of Czestochowa, so dear to us. In this way, I refer to that splendid tradition of the first missionaries in Africa, who entrusted all their work of evangelization to the Mother of Christ, the Mother of the Church and our Mother.

I, too, entrust one and all of you to her: your labors and your cares, your crosses and your joys, your toils and your dedication. May she always remind you that you are servants of Christ, who listen to His Word and carry out what He orders.

To her, the Black Madonna, the Mother of Mercy, the Mother of life and hope, the Queen of Peace, I entrust particularly the Church in Africa, its present and its future, all the problems with which it has to cope in this black land.

6. I continue with my missionary journey, and you remain here with God!

May almighty God bless you: Father, Son and Holy Spirit.

Amen.

LOVE THE SIMPLE, FRUITFUL PRAYER OF THE ROSARY

On Sunday evening, May 4, the Holy Father presented a copy of the Black Madonna of Czestochowa to a Kinshasa church under the care of the Missionary Fathers of the Consolata. The brief ceremony took place in the nunciature after the Pope's meeting with the Polish community, and His Holiness gave the following address.

Dear brothers and sisters in Christ,

Among all the joys bestowed upon me during my pastoral visit to Africa, the one you give me at this moment has quite a special flavor. Your plan to erect a shrine dedicated to the Mother of God and to venerate her through the image of our Lady of Czestochowa, so popular in my native Poland, makes my heart glad. I congratulate all those who have contributed to work out this project and I express fervent good wishes for the fruitfulness of the ministry that the Missionaries of the Consolata will carry out in this future place of worship.

This name, "Mother of God," given to one of your churches, will always be an invitation to advance in real Marian piety, as described by my dear predecessor Paul VI in his apostolic exhortation *Marialis cultus*. Marian devotion, rightly understood, must bring Christians towards deeper and deeper knowledge of the mystery of the Trinity, following the example of Mary.

She abandoned herself to the Father's loving will in the *Fiat* of the Annunciation. She believed the Spirit who carried out the astonishing work of divine motherhood in her womb. She contemplated the Word of God living in the human condition to save mankind. Mary of Nazareth is the first believer of the new Covenant to experience the one God in three Persons, the source of all life, all light, all love. We beg her to guide those men and women who have been baptized in the name of the Father, the Son and the Holy Spirit, in their discovery of the true face of God.

And with Mary, you will love the Church. "The active love that Mary showed at Nazareth, in the house of Elizabeth, at Cana and on Golgotha...finds its extension in the Church's maternal concern that all men should come to knowledge of the truth (cf. 1 Tim. 2:4), in the Church's concern for people in lowly circumstances and for the poor and weak, and in her constant commitment to peace and social harmony, as well as in her untiring efforts to ensure that all men will share in the salvation which was merited for them by Christ's death" (*Marialis cultus*, no. 28).

The image of Mary will therefore be in your church, at the center of your parish. You will often come to greet her, to venerate her. You will come to entrust your intentions to this Mother. You will pray to her for your families: may she be, like the women of this country, the guardian of your homes! You will pray to her for the needs of your brothers and sisters, for the needs of the whole Church. You will come to draw the strength to take an active part in the numerous tasks of the Church, in your parish, in the diocese. You will pray to her also for me to whom the Lord has entrusted the duty of Pastor of the whole Church. You will love the simple and so fruitful prayer of the rosary. And I can assure you that I will pray for you too, especially in the daily recitation of my rosary.

I bless you in the name of the Father, the Son and the Holy Spirit.

"I LEAVE MY HEART IN THIS CITY"

Leaving Kinshasa for Brazzaville on Monday morning, May 5, the Holy Father improvised the following address of thanks to His Excellency, President Mobutu Sese Seko, who had come to see him off.

This is above all a repetition, because they are the words I expressed before you just now, Mr. President; but I would like to repeat them over the microphone, to give my voice greater strength. I am deeply moved by the whole of this visit. I am moved also by this solemn moment of taking leave of Kinshasa, because it is only Kinshasa that I have to leave now. I still remain on the territory of your country, on returning from Brazzaville this afternoon; so it is not so easy to send me away from Zaire so quickly! I stay on until tomorrow.

But here, in the capital, and also in the presence of Mr. President, in the presence of the authorities, the authorities of the state and above all the authorities of the city of Kinshasa, I wish to renew my cordial thanks to this city in which I have spent three days, three days full of content, and also full of work, pastoral work, meetings, experiences. It was a unique experience for me: this meeting with the Church in Kinshasa, which represents in a way the Church in Zaire, the meetings with the people of Zaire who are now living an extremely important historical moment.

I have said this several times, Mr. President, and I repeat it. I see this beginning of a historic way on which you are starting here together; and I rejoice, I am happy, I am grateful to Providence that, at the start of the historic path that your country and your people are undertaking, the Church can participate in such a fine, very effective way. I thank Providence for that.

This stay in your city has also been marked by some events that deeply grieved me. These events, these accidents, came to my knowledge only last night. I wish to express my condolences above all to the families and also to the whole community of Kinshasa, and also to the President of the Republic. We are now going to take part in an action of solidarity with those who have had to pass through this sorrow. But it is an element, an important human element. This element, of course, is part of a whole; for me personally, it is also a sorrow. But it is as in the Paschal Mystery, in which the passion mingles with the resurrection. Our faith helps us to pass through sorrows, and also to bring to souls that are sad the consolation and the hope of resurrection. I think also of this event in this way. And, all things considered, I leave this great city, the capital of modern Zaire, above all with a feeling of deep joy.

Mr. President has told me several times that Zaire deserved this visit. And I approve with my heart, with my words, with all my exterior and interior attitudes. Zaire has really deserved this visit. It is for me a great grace to have been able to pay it, to be able to carry it out in these days.

Mr. President, I was saying last night that this visit is not just something extraordinary, additional, a work of supererogation; it is a part of my duty. I must know how you live, what is your situation, the situation of your people, of your country, of your Republic, the situation of the Church in this country. That is why I have come, to carry out my duty. I have carried out this duty with great feeling, with my whole heart. In ending this address, I must tell you, Mr. President, and all of you present here, that I leave my whole heart in this city of Zaire. Thank you very much!

APOSTOLIC ZEAL AND FAITHFULNESS TO THE CHURCH

Early on Monday morning, May 5, the Holy Father left Kinshasa and crossed the Zaire river by ferryboat to Brazzaville, the capital of the People's Republic of the Congo. The crossing took about twenty minutes. On his arrival he was welcomed by the President of the State, His Excellency Denis Sassou N'Guesso. In answer to the latter's address, John Paul II replied as follows:

1. May God bless the Congolese land where I have been invited to stop in the course of my pastoral visit in Africa!

Mr. President,

It is words of peace and blessing that the Head of the Catholic Church comes, on this day, to address to the nation in which you hold the highest office. With what joy and what gratitude to God, who has permitted this longed-for journey! Having been able to go to several countries already to bring the witness of the Gospel, since Providence called me to service of the universal Church, I was eager to go and meet the African peoples in their own countries and to express to them my solicitude: "The daily pressure upon me of my anxiety for all the churches" (2 Cor. 11:28).

By kindly offering their hospitality and their assistance, the authorities of the People's Republic of the Congo certainly deserve due thanks for their welcome, and especially Your Excellency. I express to

I wish to bless all of you and encourage you in your work, in your various activities, but above all in your life, thinking of your joys and sorrows, and also of all the efforts you undertake on the personal plane or as citizens. I bring you all, without any exception, my deep affection, with good wishes for all your personal and family intentions. And good wishes also for your country and its prosperous and peaceful future.

them my respectful greeting as a portrayal of the increasingly trustful relations I would like to maintain personally with them.

2. I greet you all, dear Congolese women and men, inhabitants of Brazzaville, and you who, undeterred by a tiring journey, have flocked here from other regions of the country, and you, too, who remain in your towns and villages and are perhaps listening to me by radio. I wish to bless all of you and encourage you in your work, in your various activities, but above all in your life, thinking of your joys and sorrows, and also of all the efforts you undertake on the personal plane or as citizens. I bring you all, without any exception, my deep affection, with good wishes for all your personal and family intentions. And good wishes also for your country and its prosperous and peaceful future.

3. To the Christian communities of the country and to those dedicated to them, as well as to Catholics in neighboring countries whom I will not have the chance of visiting, I address my fervent encouragement for their apostolic zeal and their faithfulness to the Church. May God reward them for so much ardor and make it a subject of edification for their brothers in the Faith in Africa as in the world! I will have the happiness, in a moment, of meditating with the delegations gathered in the cathedral, and of addressing them, but through them the Vicar of Christ will speak to everyone.

Yes, I pray for the success of this Congolese stage of my journey, a journey of friendship, a religious journey, on which I base a great many hopes, for it is intended to serve the future of peoples according to God.

CERTAINTY OF THE FAITH—A SUPPORT OF DAILY TRIALS

After the official welcome by the president of the republic at Brazzaville on May 5, John Paul II drove in an open car to the Cathedral of the Sacred Heart where there were assembled to meet him all the bishops of the People's Republic of the Congo, and also of the Central African Republic and of the Republic of Chad. Also present were very many priests, men and women religious, and many of the laity. After the Pope's address which is published below, the Holy Father visited the tomb of Cardinal Emile Biayenda who was assassinated during the night between March 22-23, 1971. At the tomb, His Holiness knelt in prayer for a few minutes.

Dear brothers in the episcopate, and you who have dedicated your lives to the Lord, and you faithful of the Church in the Congo.

1. Receive the fatherly and affectionate greeting of the Vicar of Christ, who has come to see you as a pilgrim of the Gospel, to say to you like the apostle Paul: (I am) "thankful for your partnership in the gospel from the first day until now. And I am sure that he who began a good work in you will bring it to completion at the day of Jesus Christ.... For God is my witness, how I yearn for you all with the affection of Christ Jesus" (Phil. 1:5-6, 8).

I wanted to express to you personally this constant solicitude which I feel for you, so great was my desire to see you, to encourage you all and to bless you. You yourselves wished to be able to give the

Pope, in the course of his journey in Africa, the testimony of your Faith and your faithfulness to the Church. Answering your invitation with joy, I am aware that we are living a very special moment, on both sides, and that the Lord asks us to make it fruitful. Beyond the human and spiritual joy of this meeting among brothers in Jesus Christ, it is the very presence of Christ that seizes us in this venerable place, the first episcopal see of the Congo. Let us turn our gaze together in a prayer of thanksgiving and supplication towards Him who was sent into the world "so that we might live through him" (1 Jn. 4:9).

CHURCH IN AFRICA
REACHES MATURITY

2. A prayer of thanksgiving for everything He has already realized in you and with you, all of you whom He called to go and bear fruit. Was it not as a result of your persevering efforts that the seed sown by the first missionaries had such a large yield? that the formation of catechists, undertaken systematically, offers a remarkable tool for evangelization today? I know, moreover, that a number of young people are available to cooperate in the religious instruction of school children, and to transmit to them their own reasons for hope. I know too that everywhere, in parishes as in distant stations, people are not afraid of difficulties, and are working courageously to proclaim the Good News. That is, it seems to me, a proof, as it were, of maturity. The disciples of Jesus will drink His cup (cf. Mk. 10:39). They were chosen for that reason. He made them acquainted with that, too,

and that is why He now calls them His friends (cf. Jn. 15:15). When I see all these courageous Christians here in Africa, I cannot help thinking that, nowadays, Christ has many friends in Africa, and that the Church in Africa has the maturity to face up to all vexations and all trials.

Courage, loyalty, enthusiasm about possessing a treasure, and the desire to share it, such are the qualities of the apostle, and you have to cultivate them. In the eyes of men this treasure is intangible; it cannot but be mysterious. But you know yourselves, and, in a way, you are living these words, such profound ones, that the Scriptures put in Peter's mouth: "I have no silver and gold, but I give you what I have; in the name of Jesus Christ of Nazareth, walk" (Acts 3:16).

In the history of the Congo faithful witnesses have already arisen, faithful to their God, faithful to the Gospel message, faithful to the universal Church and to the teaching of the Pope. I want to give thanks also for all of them, and especially for the example left by dear and venerated Cardinal Emile Biayenda. His tragic death made you mourn a father. I myself mourned a beloved brother. I come to mourn him and pray here, on his tomb, in your midst, with you, certain that if Christ wanted him beside Him, it was because his place was ready for eternity (cf. Jn. 14:2-3), and because in this way he can intercede even better for you and for his country. In this sense, his pastoral ministry is continuing in your service. The Lord be thanked for having given us this Pastor, this son of the Congolese nation and of the Church, Cardinal Biayenda!

PRAYER FOR CATHOLICS
IN THE CONGO

3. And now, Lord, I beseech You for my brothers and sisters, the Catholics of the Congo. I entrust them to You, since You have permitted me to visit them in their country. I commend to You their faith, young but now full of vitality, that it may grow, that it may be pure and beautiful, and communicative, that it may continue to express itself and to be freely proclaimed, for eternal life is that they know the only true God and Jesus Christ, whom He sent (cf. Jn. 17:3). I entrust them also to Your holy Mother, the Blessed Virgin Mary, Mother of the Church and our Mother. May she take them under her motherly protection and watch over them in their difficulties! May she teach them to stand at the foot of Your cross and to gather around her while waiting for Your coming, at the end of time!

With them, I pray to You for their unity, which has its source in You, and without which their testimony would be weakened: unity of the episcopal body, unity in the clergy and in the dioceses, capacity of collaborating beyond all ethnical or social differences, unity also with Peter's See and the Church as a whole. You cannot close Your ears to this prayer, You who gave Yourself up to gather the children of God.

Listen further to the invocation we address to You on this day for the sanctification of priests, men and women religious, and all those who, in the various formation centers, are preparing to consecrate their lives to You. Answering Your call, may they be able to renounce for You things of this world, and all pursuit of material or human glory, and be available for the urgent needs of the Church in some mission that will be entrusted to them (cf. *Ad gentes*, no. 20). Rejoicing in their total gift, rejoicing in their celibacy, may they experience more and more deeply, they for whom the Eucharist marks the peak point of all their days, what it means to offer one's life as a sacrifice for the salvation of men.

THE SACRIFICES OF MISSIONARIES

In Your goodness, I know that You will remember particularly the sacrifice of missionaries, who, out of love for You, left their country of origin, their families, everything they had, to come and live in the midst of their Congolese brothers, to love this people, become theirs, and to serve them. Reward such generosity, Lord! Let it be recognized, let it bring forth other vocations, let it awaken a real missionary spirit in everyone.

Surround with Your benevolence also and particularly Your humble servants, the bishops, to whom You have entrusted these local Churches. I am beside them, this morning, to strengthen them in Your name. They are there, the three pastors of the Congo, and most of their confreres of the neighboring episcopal conferences with whom they usually meet under the presidency, today, of Archbishop N'Dayen of Bangui. There are even some bishops from other nearby countries. They have brought their pastoral concerns and all the intentions with which their communities have charged them. Yes, as You asked of Peter and his successors, I wish to bring them the calm strength and the certainty of Your help in their daily toil, which is so meritorious. And I wish to assure those who have not been able to join us of my brotherly and spiritual closeness, to take a part of their burden on my shoulders, while some of them are suffering so cruelly from the sufferings of their people. Dear confreres of Chad, I am thinking of you in the first place, and of the flock entrusted to you. May God help you to dress wounds and to cure hearts! May He give you peace!

BE PIOUS AND YOU WILL UNDERSTAND

4. Brothers and sisters, I cannot continue any longer. So many thoughts fill my mind of which I would have liked to talk to you. It seemed to me that, limited by the program, the Pope could at least dedicate this meeting to a common prayer, inviting you implicitly in this way to do the same on every occasion, so that you will really proclaim what you have contemplated of the Word of Life (cf. 1 Jn. 1:1). That is what is expected of God's ministers. All the rest can be given by others. If you wish to be zealous, be pious in the first place, and you will understand everything. Live in union with God. He will help you to bear human tribulations, because you will learn to connect them with the cross, with Redemption. But, more than that, He will come within you and make His dwelling there.

Pray for me too, my beloved in the Lord. Have I your promise? I promise you on my part that this new tie that has just been established with this part of Africa will have a concrete expression, at the memory of your faces, your persons, those who benefit from your pastoral care or whom you represent here in some way. To all, my blessing and very fervent wishes. And may God bless your country too and all the surrounding nations.

THE STATE AND THE CHURCH AT THE SERVICE OF MANKIND

After meeting the bishops in the cathedral of Brazzaville on Monday morning, May 5, John Paul II paid a courtesy visit to the President of the People's Republic of the Congo, His Excellency, Denis Sassou N'Guesso. In reply to an address by the latter, the Holy Father spoke as follows.

Mr. President,

1. On my arrival at Brazzaville, I was very happy, in reply to Your Excellency's kind words, to express my very great joy at this visit to the Congolese people, its leaders, and the Catholic Church existing in this country. Since the possibility is offered to me again, I would like to utter my feelings of gratitude once more, and take the opportunity to express some thoughts in the framework of this meeting, a meeting on which I am basing a great many hopes.

2. Is it not the first time, in fact, that the Pope is able to talk to the Head of the Congolese state, and tell him simply what is closest to his heart? It is true that, desiring to strengthen their friendly relations, the Holy See and the People's Republic of the Congo have established diplomatic relations, and now have accredited representatives whose mission is, precisely, to promote a permanent dialogue, useful in order to understand each other better, and beneficial because it springs from a spirit of loyal cooperation. It is a personal pleasure for me to have received your ambas-

sador in the Vatican last week; from now on, he will become the spokesman of the government and will be able, in return, to set forth to it the views of the Holy See.

3. But in addition to this habitual means of conversing, which we all hope will be effective, it seems that a direct contact such as this one brings with it a special inclination to develop the serene and constructive climate that must reign between us.

This contact invites mutual respect. It takes place between the heads of two different entities. The Church is a spiritual institution, even if her expression is also a social one; she is set beyond temporal countries, as a community of believers. The state is an expression of the sovereign self-determination of peoples and nations, and constitutes a normal realization of the social order; that is what its moral authority consists of (cf. my address to the Diplomatic Corps to the Holy See, January 12, 1979). To become aware of this difference of nature will avoid all confusion and make it possible to proceed in clarity.

It is to recognize the specific character of the Church, which is not dependent on a civil or political structure. It is to recognize the state as having the right to exercise its authority sovereignly in its territory, and its rulers as having the responsibility of working for the common good of the peoples whose mandatories they are. The very idea of sovereignty, made up of rights and duties, implies political independence and the possibility of deciding the country's destiny autonomously (cf. *ibid.*). Where better than in Africa was it fitting to recall it? In a score of years, this continent has seen a large number of nations accede to sovereignty. The fact of a country taking over its destiny is a matter both of dignity and of justice. The process was sometimes a difficult one. It is not yet completed everywhere; it also presupposes that the populations can really take part in it.

4. Here, then, is the foundation of mutual esteem between the Church and the state. It will be expressed by respect of the specific field of each, in accordance with their different natures. The state can rely on the loyal collaboration of the Church, seeing that it is a question of serving man and contributing to his integral progress. And the Church, in the name of her spiritual mission, asks on her part for the freedom of addressing consciences as well as the possibility for believers of professing their Faith publicly, nourishing it and proclaiming it. I know, Mr. President, that you have understood this aspiration, which cannot harm in any way the sovereignty of the state whose guardian you are. Religious freedom is, in fact, at the center of respect for all freedom and for all the inalienable rights of the person. It greatly helps to safeguard, for the good of everyone, what is the essential part of a people as of a man, that is, its soul. It is fortunate that Africans set great store by it.

5. I was speaking a moment ago of service to man. That is an aim about which dialogue is permitted. That is an ideal that could be described as common to the Church and to the state. It deserves ever new attention on our side. My wish is that the conversations that have already taken place on this point, both at the local level with the pastors responsible for the Church in the Congo and between the authorities of the Republic and the Holy See, will continue more

frequently and at a deeper level. There is no doubt that they would turn out to be profitable and useful for this great cause.

I greet you respectfully, and I ask the Almighty to assist Your Excellency and the high personalities present here in their service of the Congolese human community.

FROM EVANGELIZATION TO A SOLID CATECHESIS

At midday, May 5, John Paul II concelebrated Mass with thirteen bishops from the Congo, the Central African Republic and Chad. The altar was erected in the middle of the Boulevard de l'Armêe, in order to accommodate the hundreds of thousands who were present. The following is the text of the Holy Father's homily.

Dear brothers and sisters in Christ,

"Sing...with thankfulness in your hearts to God" (Col. 3:16).

1. Today, it is the Bishop of Rome who comes to you, as successor of the apostle Peter to whom Jesus said: "Strengthen your brethren" (Lk. 22:31). I come, therefore, to strengthen you in faith, charity and hope.

I come to strengthen you in the Faith that you already possess, thanks to an evangelization that has borne fruit. I will speak to you of this evangelization to encourage you to continue it.

I come to stimulate your charity for one another and for everyone, "love which makes unity in perfection." For this purpose, I recall to you the words of the apostle Paul: "Put on...compassion, kindness, lowliness, meekness, and patience, forbearing one another and...forgiving each other" (Col. 3:12-13). Had not Jesus said: "Love your enemies...so that you may be sons of your Father?" (Mt. 5:44-45)

155

I come to strengthen your hope in order that no trial may turn you off the path along which you have started or away from the purpose of your Christian life: the salvation of your souls, the building up of the Church.

I do so while binding your Catholic community to the universal Church, which is one in the diversity of her members.

INTREPID MISSIONARIES

2. But in the very first place, the Pope would not have had the opportunity to come to your country if he had not been preceded, just a century ago, by intrepid missionaries, who, on their part, had no concern but for your spiritual good. They came to your country, burning with love for Christ and for you, to propose to you the Gospel that they had themselves received. For all Faith comes from Christ, through the apostles. "But how are men to call upon him in whom they have not believed? And how are they to believe in him of whom they have never heard? And how are they to hear without a preacher? And how can men preach unless they are sent?" (Rom. 10:1-15)

These missionaries were welcomed in your country. They had to begin by living with you, by praying in your midst, by bearing witness to their love—for this love is the heart of our message—in the form of friendship, hospitality, mutual help and also care and instruction. They proclaimed the Gospel, for they knew your hunger for the Word of God. Some of your fathers accepted the Faith. They prepared for a long time for Baptism. The Church in the Congo was born from that time. But the concern of the missionaries was also to prepare among the sons of this nation evangelizers, catechists, and soon priests, and men and women religious. In your country, the Church developed rapidly, to the extent that a large number of your fellow countrymen entered her family. We will not forget, however, the sum of patience, trials, sorrows, joys and hope of the missionaries and the merits of your fathers.

Today the Church is led by Congolese bishops, who have been constituted your pastors, through the laying on of hands of their elders. It is a sign of the maturity of your Church. Your community had even given the universal Church a Cardinal, that is, a collaborator more specially bound to the Pope and to the Church of Rome, whom we all mourn. Your communities are called to become stronger and to grow. Live in thanksgiving!

MEANING OF GOOD NEWS

3. Let us reflect for a moment, brothers and sisters, about this evangelization which must be continued. The Gospel means "Good News." What *Good News?*

The Gospel does not promise wealth, or easy conditions of life, or even daily bread, although it lays upon us the duty of working for them, in solidarity, with courage and a sense of justice; without neglecting, moreover, to ask God for them at the same time and to thank Him who is the Author of all good.

Perhaps you identify the Good News, then, with peace? In fact, it is a marvelous thing—peace in society, peace in families, the peace of a free life, and above all peace in the heart of each one, the peace of an upright conscience which lives in serenity and trust, before God and before men. "Let the peace of Christ rule in your hearts," St. Paul says (Col. 3:15).

But this peace itself comes from the Good News of God's love who loved us first, and forgave us. "For God so loved the world that he gave his only Son, that whoever believes in him should not perish but have eternal life...that the world might be saved through him" (Jn. 3:16-17). As my venerated predecessor Paul VI pointed out in the Apostolic Exhortation *Evangelii nuntiandi,* "Perhaps this attestation of God will be for many people the unknown God whom they adore without giving him a name." For us, "the Creator is not an anonymous and remote power; He is the Father. '...That we should be called children of God, and so we are.' And thus we are one another's brothers and sisters in God" (no. 26).

CHRIST WHO LIVES

4. This truth was revealed by God, in Jesus Christ, He who died and rose again for us, the "First and the Last," "the living one," "the faithful and true witness" (Rev. 1:17-18; cf. 2:14), who gathers His disciples in a deeply united family, as the members of His Body, the Church. This truth is attested by twenty centuries of Christian history. It has been lived by millions of disciples of Jesus Christ in all countries, often to the point of holiness, sometimes to martyrdom. Have you not already experienced how it illuminates your lives? It shows you their meaning and their purpose. It assures you that God the Father and His Son make their dwelling in you. It assures you of the presence of the

Holy Spirit, the Counsellor, who frees you from your sins, from everything within you and outside you that threatens to turn you aside from integrity, purity of life, justice, peace, reconciliation, sharing and brotherly love. This means that education in Faith lays the moral foundations of a better, really renewed life in society. Christians initiated into the sacraments have the joy of uniting here below around the Lord, to participate in His sacrifice and in His banquet—Holy Mass—while waiting for eternal life with Him. To evangelize is to bring this Good News to all environments, to propose it by peaceful means to free consent, and, through its impact, to transform from within, and make humanity itself new (cf. *Evangelii nuntiandi*, no. 18).

TRUE CHRISTIAN LIFE

5. Certainly, adherence in Faith to this Good News requires a conversion, not just before Baptism, but throughout one's life. The idols that must be renounced are always springing up again, even if they sometimes bear new names, in the old Churches of the West as in the young Churches of Africa. There are obstacles at the level of the human mind—and materialism, ideological or practical, is not one of the least—which can turn people away from the message of salvation, making them think that it is useless or illusory. There are obstacles, even more perhaps, at the level of our personal or family habits, the morals of society, which tend to relegate the Gospel as an ideal that is too difficult. It is true that Jesus said: "You must be perfect, as your heavenly Father is perfect" (Mt. 5:48).

It must be remembered then that God is also the God of mercy, as the Church is a merciful mother. In spite of the sinful, weak and hesitant character of her sons, she invites them to hope, she proposes to them a Christian ideal, holiness, not as a burden, but as a light that draws and elevates hearts. Even if evangelization experiences, here or there, progressive and laborious stages—the task of becoming a Christian never ends! The Church knows that the sons of this country are capable of a true Christian life. They have already proved it abundantly. And she counts on them a great deal.

WORK OF EVANGELIZATION

6. This evangelization of the personal and collective conscience of men must, therefore, be continued according to the ways which are similar in the whole Church (cf. Decree *Ad gentes,* nos. 11-18; Exhortation *Evangelii nuntiandi,* nos. 21-24; 40-47), but the concrete application of which you must find here, in accordance with your African culture and your present situation. The first place goes to the witness of your lives as Christians, that of families, adults and the young, and of consecrated persons: your Christian way of living may show, in itself, and in full respect for others, the attraction of the Gospel. An explicit and precise proclamation of the Gospel, which nourishes the mind and the heart, is also necessary: this is the role of preaching, the Liturgy of the Word, but also of catechesis. Yes, today you all need a solid catechesis, which will deepen your personal attachment to Jesus Christ and enable you to account for the hope that is in you. I know that your apostolate dedi-

cates much effort to this catechesis, and to the formation of catechists. I congratulate you on this. Families and parishes must give priority to this formation, not only of children, but of the young, students, future spouses, in the framework also of preparation for the sacraments. Finally I hope that your Christian communities know the fervor of prayer and the power of brotherly cohesion.

GRATITUDE TO WORKERS

7. In this work, there is room for all the workers of evangelization. I thank the priests, brothers, sisters and the laity who have come from afar, who continue to work here, under the guidance of Congolese bishops. Not only do they still bring you precious support, but they help to link you with the universal Church, and I am sure that this experience is beneficial for their own Churches. These priests form one presbyterium with the priests of this country, to whom I would like to express especially my affection and my trust. Dear friends, the Lord has called you to serve Him, in a complete dedication of your lives of which celibacy is one of the signs, making you available for everyone. Be holy priests, the devoted and competent spiritual guides that your people need. It is a great grace! I also hope that priestly and religious vocations may arise in large numbers and be strengthened in a thorough formation. I hope, finally, that many Christian lay people will also bring their irreplaceable help for evangelization, as catechists, and in an apostolate from person to person, from family to family, from the elder to the younger.

PERIOD OF TRIALS

8. I know that you are continuing evangelization under conditions that are not easy, with means that are often poor. You have gone through great trials. I would like to strengthen your hope. Entrust your needs to the Lord, who is faithful, and help one another. You know in whom you have put your trust. With St. Peter I say to you: be firm in the faith, knowing that your brothers throughout the world are enduring similar ordeals (cf. 1 Pt. 5:9). And again: "Have unity of spirit, sympathy, love of the brethren, a tender heart and a humble mind" (*ibid.* 3:8). The power of God is in you, according to your degree of faith and love, and according to your cohesion. Yes, let your unity be without a flaw: it is your strength.

A BROTHERLY LIFE

9. In this way you will likewise be, in the midst of your fellow countrymen who do not share your faith, peacemakers, and even the "salt" and the "leaven" of which Jesus speaks, for the brotherly life to which they aspire. I have already let it be understood: evangelization normally involves care for human development and social progress. You, too, are attached to the independence and honor of your nation; you desire an increase of the means of subsistence, a just order for everyone, a peaceful life. You wish to serve your country. You are concerned about the poor. You know that a soulless civilization would not bring happiness. You are ready to dedicate your work and your honesty to this work, in respect for everyone, banishing hatred, violence and lies. Those

who are in charge of the common good cannot ignore that your Christian contribution is beneficial for the country. I do not doubt that they will continue to grant you the rightful religious freedom which you are recognized as having and the possibility of working, as good citizens, for the advancement of the nation. May God bless the Congo!

LIFE IN THE CHURCH

10. Finally, dear friends, I am thinking of your integration in the universal Church. It is a great and beautiful mystery. The tree of the Church, planted by Jesus in the Holy Land, has not ceased to develop. All the countries of the old Roman Empire have been grafted onto it. My own country, Poland, had its hour of evangelization, and the Church of Poland has been grafted onto the tree of the Church, to make it produce new fruit. Now your community of Congolese believers has been grafted, in its turn, onto the tree of the Church. The graft lives on the sap that circulates in the tree; it cannot survive unless closely united with the tree. But as soon as it is grafted, it brings to the tree its heritage and produces its own fruit. It is only a metaphor. The Church causes the new peoples that have come to her to live by her life. No new community grafted onto the tree of the Church can live its life independently. It lives only by participating in the great vital current that makes the whole tree live. Then the Church receives new treasures of vitality and can thus manifest a greater variety of fruits in the world. Such are my wishes for the Church in the Congo. May its attachment to the universal Church and to

Peter's successor, who is the principle and the founda-
tion of the unity of all, be strengthened! May its own
vitality, unity and holiness grow! And may it let the
Church benefit from them! In the breath of the Holy
Spirit! With Mary, the Star of Evangelization! Amen!
Alleluia!

JUSTICE, PEACE, PROSPERITY TO ALL!

Before leaving Brazzaville on May 5, to fly to Kisangani in Zaire, Pope John Paul II bade farewell to the Congolese people in the following short address.

Dear Congolese,

It is time, unfortunately, to leave you. I must go also to other regions where my coming is awaited and continue this pastoral visit which has been so successful with you. You were happy to see me. I can tell you that my joy was even greater. I would have liked to shake all your hands, bless you all, have for each one, especially for the children, the sick, the poor, a word of comfort and encouragement. It would have been necessary to remain too long, and I have not the right to impose upon your hospitality, even though you offered it willingly.

I owe this hospitality also, and in particular, to your President and to all the leaders of the state. You will want me to tell them, in your presence, how grateful I am to them. And you will allow me to present to them, since they have the heavy task of guiding the country, my very sincere wishes for its future, in justice, peace and prosperity for all.

My fervent thanks again to you, my brother bishops and priests, and to all Congolese Catholics. I have seen your faith, your courage, your apostolic zeal. I have heard you sing your love of Christ and His Mother, the Blessed Virgin Mary. I have seen you pray, and I have prayed with you and for you. We have remembered together the deceased pastors of these dioceses, whose ministry remains an example for everyone. In particular, we prayed together at the tomb of the late Cardinal Biayenda, a faithful pastor and great servant of his country. Continue, progress further and further on the road that leads to God. Today I leave you a little of myself, and I take with me all your generosity, your ardor, and the proofs of your deep attachment to the Church.

Farewell, land of the Congo! May you yield lasting fruit, and give the Church and the world the testimony of your vitality!

GOD IS CLOSE TO YOU!

On arrival at Kisangani Airport (Zaire) from Brazzaville on Monday afternoon, May 5, John Paul II was met by Archbishop Fataki, and by the Minister for the administration of the territory, representing President Mobutu. The papal motorcade then drove to the Cathedral of Kisangani where Archbishop Fataki delivered a speech of homage. In the course of his speech the Archbishop expressed the hope that the day would not be far distant when the Servant of God, Sister Marie-Clementine Nengapeta Anwarite, of the ecclesiastical province of Kisangani, would be beatified. In reply the Holy Father spoke as follows:

1. I greet you, dear inhabitants of Kisangani, and tell you of my very great joy to be among you. Through you, I greet affectionately all my Catholic sons and daughters and all the inhabitants of the region.

2. In particular I thank your Archbishop, Most Reverend Fataki, for the kind words he has just addressed to me. I am returning, in a way, the good visit he had paid me in Krakow. With him, I greet cordially all your bishops who welcome me here this evening. With them, I greet all those who have heard the word of God and are trying to put it into practice. I would not like to forget anyone, but I wish to express straightway, in a few words, my special affection for the priests, men and women religious and seminarians, all these men and women who wish to give themselves to God. What is the center of your lives? Is it not the call that you have heard, the Lord's call: "Come, and follow me"? I pray to Him to bless you. In spite of sacrifices, you will never feel sad and isolated if you really live with Him.

I also address my greeting to you all, fathers and mothers of families, young men and women, students and children. I have come for the joy of being with you, at least for some moments, and to tell you again, following upon your bishops and your priests, that the Lord loves us all and calls us all. I greet also with special affection the sick, the infirm, all those who feel unhappy in soul and in body: the Pope blesses you all.

3. I shall just recall to you this evening some words of the Lord which should fill us with joy and hope. As a sign that God had really come down among men, He said: "The poor receive the gospel"; the poor hear the good news of salvation! And He also said: "Come to me, all you who are crushed under the weight of your burden, and I will give you new strength." Coming to you, I wish to remind all disciples of Christ of this great message of the Gospel, on which the love that we have for one another is based, and I repeat what St. Paul taught the first Christians: "The Lord Jesus became poor for us, and he enriched us with his poverty." That is still taking place today. It is taking place in your country, in the heart of Africa.

Yes, to those who have to struggle to make a living, who till the earth laboriously to have their daily food, who feel they are helpless, frustrated, to all those who are suffering, the Lord gives the life of His grace; God is present among you. That is the essential thing. That is what makes the universal Church, which is spread all over the world, and which unites us all. That is what gives the strength to be faithful, in spite of difficulties. Be faithful, then, to the one Church of Christ. See how well they had understood

that, those who, among you, among your fellow countrymen and among the missionaries, have preferred
to sacrifice their lives to remain faithful to the divine
life they had received. I am thinking here particularly
of two persons whose names are well known to you.
These two persons are, for us all, luminous examples
of Christian life, given joyfully to God.

I am thinking—as you know—of Sister Anwarite,
whom the Church hopes to be able to beatify soon.

I am also speaking of a Zairean catechist: Isidore
Bakanja, a true Zairean, a true Christian. After having
given all his free time to the evangelization of his
brothers, as a catechist, he did not hesitate to offer his
life to his God, strong with the courage he drew from
his faith and from the faithful recitation of the rosary.

In the Lord's name, I ask you, arriving among
you, to be proud of this and above all to be able to
follow them! I give you an appointment in this very
place, tomorrow morning, for Holy Mass, and I willingly bless you.

CHRIST'S CHURCH LIVING IN THE RURAL WORLD

On May 6, John Paul II concelebrated Mass in the open space in front of the Cathedral of Our Lady of the Rosary at Kisangani. During his homily he recalled the figure of Sister Marie-Clementine Anwarite, whose process of beatification has begun in Rome. She was born on November 29, 1939, and made her religious profession in the Congregation of the Holy Family (Jamaa Takatifu) founded by Most Reverend Camillo Verfaillie, Vicar Apostolic of Stanleyville (Kisangani). All the religious of the Congregation were seized by the troops of Colonel Olombe at Bafwabaka on November 29, 1964. The sisters were all tortured, and on November 30, Sister Anwarite was killed in defense of her vow of chastity.

At the end of the Mass the Holy Father went to the cemetery of Makiso to pray at the tomb of the twenty-nine missionaries killed in 1964.

The following is the text of the homily.

Dear brothers and sisters,
Dear sons and daughters of the Church,

1. Our short meeting last night in the square of this cathedral had let me foresee that you would participate in large numbers in the Eucharist this morning. Thank you with all my heart! Thank you and all those who have asked you to represent them because distance or sickness have prevented them from being present. I pray for them and I bless them. The Lord rejoices in your multitude and I am filled with joy.

On seeing you, I think of the Revelation to Saint John that we read on the Sundays of the Easter period.

170

All nations, all races, all languages take their place in the endless procession of those who bear God's mark on their forehead. Think of your Baptism and your Confirmation. Christians of Kisangani and of this great rural region, you are part of this immense crowd that St. John was unable to count. You are the People of God, walking today on African land, and you live your belonging to the Lord through the realities of the rural world. I would like to meditate with you on these two aspects of your concrete existence and, finally, help you to contemplate her whom the Second Vatican Council so happily presented as being the Mother of the Church, and to whom we pray this morning under the name of Our Lady of the Rosary.

2. Just as the first Christian communities of Jerusalem, Antioch, Corinth and Rome, sprang from the preaching of the Good News, which is essentially the mystery of Christ, so your "mission" posts and your parishes have come into being, in the last hundred years, from the proclamation of the Gospel to your fathers in the faith. It was the work, in the beginning, of missionaries who had come from afar, burning with love for Christ and for you. They proposed to you the message they had themselves received, for no one discovers it by himself; it is received from the Church.

The Christians of this region have now become a whole people, with pastors chosen among the sons of this country. And all together, bishops, priests, sisters and faithful, you are the Church; you belong to this immense People of God that came into being at Pentecost and is destined to know the fullness of which St. John caught a glimpse. Here below it experiences trials, sometimes humiliations and persecutions. It in-

cludes martyrs, saints, such as your fellow countrymen who preferred to sacrifice their lives rather
than be unfaithful to their Baptism, such as Sister Anwarite, whom the Church is thinking of declaring
blessed. Some people, perhaps, tend too much to
reduce the Church solely to what is visible or else to
her leaders, her institutions, her organization. Actually, as the recent Council said so well, the Church-
People of God is a mystery.

3. What, then, is this *mystery?* A very strong
expression of the apostle Paul to the Christians of
Corinth helps you to grasp it: "You are the body of
Christ and individually members of it" (1 Cor. 12:27).
Or again, "Christ is the head of the body, the
Church" (Col. 1:18). We are mysteriously united and
integrated in the life of the risen Christ, who is
glorified on God's right side, as the members are to
the head. The Church is Christ living today in all continents, in all those who have been converted or are
constantly being converted to Him, to such an extent
that their life is no longer just their life, but that of
Christ in them. You receive the eucharistic body of
Christ to become, even more, the members of His
Body.

4. Christians of the region of Kisangani, have you
this mysterious and dynamic view of the Church? Of
your vital bond with Christ, and with the other
members of Christ? That must be confirmed in the
style of your eucharistic celebrations on Sundays,
which you wish to be dignified, joyful and prayerful.
That must be confirmed also in your everyday behavior, in the family, in your district, in your village. In
order to realize truly this Church, this Christian family bound to Christ, it is good to hold, and you already

do so, other meetings of prayer, reflection, sharing and mutual aid, in order to be better disciples of Christ and live His brotherhood in the environments of your life and your work.

5. Precisely, you are the Church, the Christ living in the rural world. This social background marks you, and it is your mission to make it more worthy of God and therefore more human. And there, you must feel specially close to Christ.

For Jesus, indeed, His earthly life took place mainly in an essentially agrarian civilization. He spent thirty years in one of the smallest villages of Palestine, Nazareth. During His public life, He visited a great many villages of peasants and modest fishermen. He observed at length and loved nature, flowers and trees, the seasons, work in the fields, the work of the ploughman, the harvester, the vine grower, the shepherd, the woman who goes to draw water, knead the dough, prepare meals. He knew the local customs that formed the rhythm of life. He shared the events of the village, the hospitality offered to friends, weddings, mourning. He lingered beside children playing, sick people suffering. We know this because He used all these observations marvelously to make His listeners understand the mysteries of the kingdom of God which He came to reveal, so that the Gospel is for you, inhabitants of the rural world, a book of racy language, which is very accessible to you.

6. But there is an even deeper dimension than this attractive closeness to Jesus of Nazareth. For Jesus is the Son of God, ''incarnate,'' who had come in the flesh, to live the concrete realities of our existence, at once as a man and as the Son of God. It is an extraordinary mystery! You feel the dignity that He confers

on your lives as humble workers, since He lived this life at Nazareth, in Palestine! He lived it under the eyes of God His Father, closely linked with Him, in thanksgiving. He offered God all its joys and all its sorrows. He lived it with simplicity, purity of heart, with courage, as a servant, as a welcoming friend for the sick, the afflicted, the poor of all kinds, with a love that no one will surpass and which He made His testament: love one another, as I loved you. It is that life which, through the ordeal of His sacrifice offered to free the world of its sins, is now glorified beside God.

I invite you likewise, dear friends, to become aware of the dignity of your life, which was sanctified by Christ and redeemed by Him in the mysteries of His Incarnation and His Redemption, and I call upon you, too, to make it an offering pleasing to God, by imprinting on it the mark of prayer and love. This perspective will already transform your life from within and will make you participate in Christ's holiness.

7. I think it will also be able to stimulate you to change the conditions of your rural life to the extent to which they deteriorate through negligence or sin and prevent men from living in dignity, hope and peace. For the kingdom of heaven which we are preparing must already find a rough model in this earthly life. This progress is of great importance for the kingdom of God (cf. *Gaudium et spes*, no. 39).

Yes, if you become aware of the dignity of your life and your work, you will try, with the generous love of the Christian, to make them more worthy for yourselves and for others. You will not accept that country people should be considered as second-class

Be disciples of Christ and live His brotherhood in the environments of your life and your
work. You are the Church, the Christ living in
the rural world. This social background marks
you, and it is your mission to make it more worthy of God and therefore more human. And
there, you must feel especially close to Christ.

men or women. You will not resign yourselves to the
fact that certain persons are crushed by poverty, or
are the victims of injustice. It would not be just or in
conformity with the Gospel of Christ that those who
are stronger or luckier should exploit the others;
St. James already denounced this evil (Jas. 4:13; 5:6).
You will help one another to cope with difficulties.
You will reflect together and envisage common actions, modest ones, perhaps—for alone you do not
have the means to act effectively—but realistic ones.

You who are rightly attached to your lands, you
will help to check the rural exodus, so harmful for
rural life and for the whole nation. Your country owes
it to itself to satisfy its food needs; agricultural products are more necessary than certain luxury products.
The industrial development of African countries
needs agricultural development; it is grafted upon it.
The lives of its sons are at stake.

8. Certainly, the Christian churches do not
themselves have to propose or implement technical
solutions for the management of the rural world. But
they are guardians of the evangelical meaning to be
given to the life of men and societies. Christians,
formed by them, will bring to these human solutions
a dimension that will throw light on the choice of
aims and methods. They will be, for example, concerned about respect for persons. They will look after
children and the weak. Their honesty will not tolerate
corruption. They will look for more just structures in
the field of real estate. They will advocate mutual aid
and solidarity. They will want their community to remain a brotherly one. They will be peacemakers.
They will consider themselves managers of God's
creation, which can never be wasted or ravaged at

will, for it is entrusted to men for the good of all. They will see to it that materialism does not prevail, for it would actually be slavery. In short, they want to work straightway at a world more worthy of God's sons. This is the role that the Church recognizes Christian lay people as having, with the help of their pastors. Yes, that is a testimony of the Church.

9. Dear brothers and sisters, in order to carry this out in a really Christian way, you must first be animated from within by the Spirit of God. For this purpose I would like you to turn even more to the Virgin Mary, your Mother, the Mother of the Church.

We are celebrating the Mass of Our Lady of the Rosary, before this cathedral which is dedicated to her. It is a very great joy for me. Who, better than Mary, lived a very simple life, sanctifying it? Who, better than Mary, accompanied Jesus all through His life, joyful, suffering and glorious, and entered the intimacy of His filial sentiments for the Father, and His brotherly sentiments for others? Who, better than Mary, now associated with her Son's glory, can intervene in our favor?

She must now accompany your life. We are going to entrust this life to her. The Church proposes to us for this precise purpose a very simple prayer, the rosary, which can be spread out calmly according to the rhythm of our days. The rosary, recited slowly and meditated upon, in the family, in community, or personally, will gradually let you enter the sentiments of Christ and His Mother, recalling all the events which are the key of our salvation. As you recite one *Ave Maria* after another, you will contemplate the mystery of the Incarnation of Christ, of which we have spoken, the Redemption of Christ, and also the purpose at which we are aiming, in the light and the tranquillity of God. With Mary, you will open your soul to the Holy Spirit, so that He may inspire all the great tasks that await you. With her, mothers will carry out their role as bearers of life, guardians and educators of the home.

May Mary be your guide and your support. Amen.

WITNESS OF YOUR MISSIONARIES

At the conclusion of the Mass at Kisangani the Holy Father visited the cemetery of Makiso where he prayed at the tomb of the twenty-nine missionaries who were killed in 1964, and he gave the following brief address.

Kneeling in this cemetery at the tomb of the missionaries come from afar, we pray to You, Lord.

Blessed be You, Lord, for the testimony of Your missionaries! It was You who inspired their apostles' hearts to forever their land, their family, their native country, to come to this country, unknown to them up to then, and propose the Gospel to those whom they already considered brothers.

Blessed be You, Lord, for having supported their faith and their hope, at sowing time, and throughout their apostolic labor; for having given them resistance and patience in toil, difficulties, sorrows and sufferings of every kind.

Blessed be You, Lord, for having strengthened their attachment and trust in the sons of this people, to the extent of considering them, very soon, capable of the life of the baptized and of opening to them the way to religious life, to priestly preparation, with the tenacious will of founding, with them and for them, a local church, the fruits of which we are gathering.

Blessed be You, Lord, for all the graces that have come through their word, through their hands, through their example.

They dedicated their lives to the end for the mission, and they left their mortal remains to this land; some after a life shortened by work, some even after a life risked and offered as martyrs for the Faith. The grain of wheat had to fall in the earth and die in order to yield much fruit.

Lord, bring it about that the Church watered by their sweat and their blood may reach its full maturity. Thanks to them, others can harvest today in joy what they sowed in tears. May large numbers come forth among the sons and daughters of this country, to take over from them, in order that Your name may be glorified in this African land.

Let us take care not to forget these pioneers of the Gospel, in the memory of the heart and of prayer. We hope that You have welcomed them to Your paradise, forgiving the weaknesses that may have marked their lives like those of all human beings. Give them the reward of good and faithful servants. May they enter the joy of their Master. Give them eternal rest, and may Your light shine upon them forever.

SOLIDARITY OF THE WHOLE CHURCH WITH MISSIONARIES

On Tuesday morning, May 6, the Holy Father, accompanied by Archbishop Fataki, visited St. Gabriel's Mission, in the heart of the forest about 6 km. from Kisangani. The mission is under the care of the Missionary Brothers of St. Gabriel, and the Pope went there to bring them his message of encouragement for their work of evangelization. The Holy Father spoke to them as follows.

Dear brothers and sisters in Christ,

On the occasion of this visit to St. Gabriel's Mission, I would like to address to you a word of admiration and encouragement, which will also apply to all the mission posts scattered in this country and in other African countries. I would have liked to visit more of them, in the neighborhood of large cities, as here, or in the midst of villages in the forest or the bush. The shortness of my stay does not permit it. Let everyone know at least how much the Pope appreciates this fine service of evangelization and thanks them all, in the name of the Church

1. In the first place I greet the devoted personnel of these mission posts. They are zealous priests, who have often come from far away. They are religious, called by the expressive name "brothers," whose daily dedication, humble and effective, since the dawn of evangelization, I wish to stress. Through their competence in many fields, they have greatly contributed

to the implantation and practical and pedagogical operation of these mission posts. They are sisters, whose consecrated lives are radiant with the presence of the Lord and who carry out, thanks to the ease of their contacts with families, a magnificent work of education, charity and human advancement. They are also lay people, who cooperate in all these tasks.

Some members of these missions live like an advanced detachment, as it were, in a completely new sector of evangelization. More often, today, they live as a team, and their post, with its chapel and its different facilities, is a rallying point for Christians scattered in the surrounding districts or villages. Greeting particularly those of St. Gabriel, whom I have the joy of meeting here with their parishioners, I greet and thank warmly all the others.

2. Some thoughts spring from my heart and I will express them to you simply.

In my eyes, the mission post recalls in the first place the modesty of the beginnings: the modesty of missionary forces, very often, the modesty of Christian communities, and the modesty of pedagogical and material means. In fact, the life of these evangelizers and of their first disciples is very close to the poverty of the Gospel and the simplicity of the first Christian communities, described in the Acts of the Apostles (cf. Acts 13:14ff.). Paul, Barnabas and so many other disciples arrived empty-handed, so to speak, having only the Good News to share, the fervor of their love and the assurance of the Holy Spirit. Yes, dear friends, the Faith and charity that imbue you, that is what constitutes, in the first place, your originality, your riches and your dynamism.

3. Here, I wish to address a special word to all those who, in certain difficult mission posts, experience the trial of having to persevere and even be *buried* in solitude and forgottenness. For you do not just pass through; you remain in the midst of those whose life you have adopted. You remain patiently, even if you have to sow the Gospel for a long time without witnessing its budding and flowering. The lamp of your Faith and charity then seems to burn for nothing. But nothing is lost of what is given in this way. A mysterious solidarity links all apostles. You are preparing the ground where others will reap the harvest. Remain faithful servants.

In any case, you have not spared yourselves. You have undertaken and continued this apostolic initiative at the cost of great effort, moral and also physical, sometimes to the point of exhaustion, in a climate to which you were not accustomed and under precarious conditions of life. I think of you especially when I reread the pages of St. Paul—whose name I took—on the tribulations of the apostolic ministry, of which he draws up an impressive list (cf. 2 Cor. 4:7-18; 6:1-10). I hope, dear friends, that you will also know his hope and his joy, while waiting for the Lord's reward.

4. Your *apostolic work* takes the ordinary and necessary ways of evangelization. In the first place, to establish contacts, and manifest the Lord's love for everyone, not only benevolent attention, but a concrete love which does not neglect the various forms of mutual aid, schools, dispensaries, agricultural projects, human advancement of every kind. People know, in fact, that you are there in the first place to meet the hunger for God, the need of His word which enlight-

ens and consoles hearts, raises them and brings forth a renewal of men and of society. That is the important part of your ministry: the witness and proclamation of the Gospel, the catechesis of those who ask to be initiated into the Faith, a long preparation for the sacraments, especially of Baptism and the Eucharist, encouragement to prayer, and the formation of consciences for human and Christian responsibilities.

5. You would soon be overwhelmed if you wanted to monopolize all the tasks. It would not be a real foundation of a Church. Very soon, you try to gather round you disciples, catechists, animators, who become *evangelizers* in their turn, a little like St. Paul who appointed "elders," as they were then called, trusting the Lord (cf. Acts 14:23). The vitality of the mission lies there.

The purely evangelical service that you wish to offer this people for the salvation of whom you have sacrificed everything, must aim, in fact, at enabling the sons of this people to acquire their Christian and ecclesial maturity, and to guide by themselves the work started.

6. The fine work you are accomplishing merits the solidarity of the whole local Church and that of sister Churches all over the world.

I am particularly happy to be here, and to address, from here, all members of mission posts. It is, so to speak, a moment of "rediscovery," for me, and for the whole Church which I represent. Yes, the Church rediscovers herself alongside you missionaries—whether you are Zaireans, Africans, or come from far away—because she herself must be "missionary" entirely and at every moment. In this way the action of the salt and of the yeast, of which the Gospel speaks, spreads far and wide and in depth.

7. The task I have inherited from the apostle Peter is to unite all Christians. It is at the same time to maintain missionary zeal. May the Lord bless you and bless all similar posts!

May He bless all the members of this mission: parents, children, the young, the old, and especially the suffering! I entrust your community to the Virgin Mary, our Mother, towards whom the name of the angel Gabriel, the patron saint of this parish, directs us spontaneously. May the peace of Christ always be with you! With my affectionate apostolic blessing.

LIVE IN UNITY AND
BE PEACEMAKERS!

On May 6, before boarding the plane at Kisangani for his flight to Kenya, the Holy Father was greeted by Archbishop Fataki and several other Zairean bishops, by the Apostolic Pro-Nuncio, Most Rev. Edoardo Rovida, by the official representative of President Mobuto Sese Seko, and the Commissioner of the Upper Zaire Region. From the steps of the plane he gave the following address of farewell.

Mr. State Commissioner,
Your Eminence,
Your Excellencies,
Dear brothers and sisters,
God be praised!

1. These few days spent in the land of Zaire have enabled me to establish very agreeable and rewarding contacts with the population of this country, with its religious and civil leaders, with the different categories of the People of God: bishops, priests, seminarians, men and women religious, families, laity engaged in the different movements, catechists, students, young people, with missionaries, and with citizens of the large towns and those of rural areas who had joined them. I had to limit myself to two characteristic regions, those of Kinshasa and Kisangani. I know that the immense country of Zaire contains many others. I would still have a great many things to discover in your country! I must leave, regretfully, for other African countries. But what I expressed in the course of my meetings or celebrations, I said thinking

of all the Catholics and all the inhabitants of this nation. I am anxious to greet them for the last time, with sentiments of esteem and all the warmth of my affection.

2. I thank you, Mr. State Commissioner, for your presence, and I beg you to convey my deep gratitude to His Excellency, the President of the Republic, for the kind welcome given to me and all the zeal shown to ensure that everything would proceed smoothly during my stay. I also thank the members of the government and all officials. I was happy, moreover, to have talks with the authorities who have the heavy responsibility of the common good of the whole country.

I thank dear Cardinal Joseph Malula who gave me such a warm welcome in Kinshasa and who, being a member of the Sacred College, has long woven special ties with Peter's Successor and the Church in Rome. I thank Most Reverend Fataki, the archbishop of this place, whom I was happy to meet again here, in his country. I thank all the other bishops of Zaire, my brothers, with whom I have experienced moments of deep communion which are going to be prolonged. With them I thank all the faithful of Zaire and their pastors who showed such eagerness to come and meet the Pope, to listen to him, to pray with him and give him the testimony of their religious vitality.

3. The centenary of evangelization has permitted us to give thanks to God, for everything that has been realized from the seed of the Gospel brought by intrepid missionaries. The Church has grown and flourished, like a tree well rooted in Zairean land. The sap is that of the universal Church, for there is only one faith, one baptism, one Lord, one Spirit, one God and

Father of all. But its fruits have also, and they must have, the savor of Africa and more especially of this country and the families that compose it. The Catholic community is entrusted to bishops born of this soil, in communion with Peter's successor.

4. But, as I said on my arrival, this stage calls for yet another one. I do not merely say that of perseverance, which is already meritorious. I say rather that of progress in faith and in holiness. Christ, present among you, present in you, must grasp the depths of your African soul, with its culture—thoughts, sentiments and human aspirations—in order to "save" it, in the sense in which God sent His Son to "save" the world (cf. Jn. 3:17), that is, to redeem it, elevate it and transfigure it. It is the Redeemer's work; but one and all of you have a share of responsibility in it.

5. My last instruction will be: live in unity, strengthen this unity. And to do so, banish all division. Membership in the same Body of Christ does not tolerate any exclusion, contempt or hatred. It calls for collaboration, peace and the brotherhood of love. Be peacemakers. It is they who construct the Church. It is they who will help to build up this beautiful and great country, with other Christians and other men of good will.

Union with your bishops will be the guarantee of your progress. And likewise union with the Pope. In the memory of the heart and of prayer, you will remember the exceptional closeness of the last few days; be assured also that I will pray constantly for you.

May peace be with you all!

May peace be upon Zaire!

With my affectionate apostolic blessing.

O LORD OF ALL CREATION, BLESS THIS LAND AND NATION!

About 3:00 p.m. on May 6, John Paul II arrived in Kenya, at New Embakasi Airport, Nairobi, aboard a Zairean DC-10 airliner. Among those present to welcome him were Cardinal Maurice Otunga, Archbishop of Nairobi; the President of Kenya, Daniel Arap Moi; Vice-President Kibaki and the entire Cabinet of Ministers; the Apostolic Pro-Nuncio, Archbishop Agostino Cacciavillan; the Mayor of Nairobi; the President of the Republic of Uganda, Godfrey Binaisa; all the bishops of Kenya led by the President of the Episcopal Conference, Most Reverend John Nijenga, Bishop of Eldoret, and an immense crowd of many thousands of people, especially the young.

In reply to an address of welcome by the President of Kenya, the Holy Father spoke as follows:

Your Excellency, the President
of the Republic of Kenya,
Honorable Members of the Government,
Your Eminence, Venerable Brothers
in the Episcopate,
Mr. Mayor of the city of Nairobi,

Dear brothers and sisters,

1. I am deeply grateful for the courteous and cordial words of welcome which His Excellency, the President of Kenya, has addressed to me. For it is not only a privilege but also a joy to be able to come and visit the

people of this country. Hearing these words of welcome, which are the expression of the traditional African hospitality which graces your people, I cannot but feel that I have come among friends, that I have been accepted into your great family, the family of the whole nation of Kenya.

I thank you most sincerely, Mr. President, for the invitation you extended to me some time ago. In it I have found confirmation of the esteem which you, as head of this Republic, wish to express for me, the head of the Catholic Church. In your invitation I feel again your commitment to foster mutual understanding among all peoples and nations. In it I have encountered your deep respect for all men of religion and for the valuable contribution which true believers in God can make to the future of your country and indeed of all nations.

Through Your Excellency I greet all your fellow citizens wherever they may be: in your cities and villages, on your mountains and in your plains, by your rivers and by your lakes. I greet all the men and women of this country, which has been blessed by peace and by the unanimity of its inhabitants in their endeavors to promote just progress for everyone, while preserving a rich cultural identity. I greet the parents and their children, the pride and joy of every family and of the nation as a whole. I greet your elders and all those who are entrusted with the welfare of their fellow citizens. In a very special way, my heart goes out to the sick and suffering and to all who are weighed down by heavy burdens. Know that there is a brother who has come to you from Rome, one who thinks of you, who loves you and is close to you in prayer. And finally, I wish to extend my warm greetings also to the many citizens living outside the country, for reasons of work or study or service to their homeland.

Wananchi wote, wananchi wote wapenzi—to all of you, the people who live and work in Kenya, to all of you I say: thank you for your welcome and may peace be with you!

2. My visit is also the pastoral journey of the Bishop of Rome, the Pastor of the universal Church, to the Church in Kenya. Your Eminence, Cardinal Otunga, and my dear brother bishops: allow me to tell you how much I appreciate and bless this moment of my first contact with you on your native soil. You have invited me to come, and in the name of the Lord—in the holy name of Jesus Christ—I greet you and all the people who are entrusted to your pastoral care.

Today I am in your midst because I want to heed the command which the Lord Jesus Himself gave to St. Peter and to the other Apostles: that they should be His "witnesses in Jerusalem and in all Judea and Samaria and to the ends of the earth" (Acts 1:8), because I want to testify with you that Jesus is the Lord, that He is risen from the dead so that all people may live. I come to you as the Successor of St. Peter in the See of Rome to praise the Lord together with you for all the marvels which He has wrought in the Church in Kenya.

3. And now I wish to offer a particular greeting to you, the young people present here, and through you to all the youth of this land! For I know that you carry in your hearts your dreams for the future of Kenya, and in your hands the power to make those dreams come true. May peace and joy be always in your hearts!

I have been told that you make up more than half of the population of this nation; and so, talking to Kenya means talking to you! These then are my words to you today: be yourselves, under the fatherhood of God be upright citizens of your country, worthy sons and daughters of Kenya. Be young people, and reach out to each other in generosity and fraternal service. Be young people, and do not let your hearts know selfishness or greed. Be young people, and let your songs reveal your daring and your vision for the future:

Yes, young people of Kenya, what I have told youth all over the world I now repeat to you: the Pope is your friend and he loves you, and he sees in you the hope for a better future, a better world! My special message to you, and through you to all the young people of Kenya is this: "Always treat others as you would like them to treat you" (Mt. 7:12). Believe in the power of love to uplift humanity. With courage and prayer, with determination and effort, obstacles can be overcome, problems solved. May Almighty God protect you and sustain you in this hour of challenge and destiny.

4. And to all of you, dear friends, I express once again my thanks for the warm hospitality of your land. From this first moment on Kenyan soil you have opened your hearts to me. In return I assure you of my affection, friendship and esteem. And now I would borrow from your national anthem those words which so aptly express my sentiments and my prayer at this time as I begin my pastoral visit to Kenya: "O God of all creation, bless this our land and nation"—*Ee Mungu nguvu yetu—Ilete baraka kwetu!*

Dear friends, from this first moment on Kenyan soil you have opened your hearts to me. In return I assure you of my affection, friendship and esteem. And now I would borrow from your national anthem those words which so aptly express my sentiments and my prayer at this time as I begin my pastoral visit to Kenya: "O God of all creation, bless this our land and nation."

WE ARE THE PEOPLE REDEEMED BY THE PRECIOUS BLOOD OF CHRIST

After the official welcome at Nairobi Airport, on May 6, the Holy Father drove across the city in an open car to the Cathedral of the Holy Family for his meeting with the Church of Nairobi and of all Kenya. Among those present in the Cathedral there was also Cardinal Laurean Rugambwa, Archbishop of Dar-es-Salaam in neighboring Tanzania. After an address of welcome by Cardinal Maurice Otunga, the Holy Father spoke as follows.

Your Eminence, zealous pastor
of this beloved Church of Nairobi,
Venerable brothers in the Episcopate,
Sons and daughters of Kenya,
My brothers and sisters in Christ,

1. My first desire in this house of God is to express the Church's praise for the Father of our Lord Jesus Christ, who has gathered us together in His Son, sending forth His Holy Spirit into our midst. In the words of the apostle Peter: "Blessed be the God and Father of our Lord Jesus Christ! By his great mercy we have been born anew to a living hope through the resurrection of Jesus Christ from the dead..." (1 Pt. 1:3).

2. Today in this cathedral dedicated to the Holy Family—to Jesus, Mary and Joseph—all of us realize that together we make up the Body of Christ—together we are the Church. We are a living Church, a spiritual house made up of living stones—all of us live in Christ. We are one with all our brothers and sisters here in Kenya and throughout the world; we are one in the communion of saints, one with the living and the dead—our families, our ancestors, those who brought to us the word of God and whose memory is enshrined forever in our hearts.

Today, in particular, we are a communion of faith and love, confessing Jesus Christ as the Son of God, the Lord of history, the Redeemer of man and the Savior of the whole world. We are one united community, living in the mystery of the Church, the life of the crucified and risen Christ, and therefore His praise is in our hearts and on our lips. It finds expression in our Easter *Alleluia*. We are, as it were, the extended Holy Family, called to build and enlarge the edifice of justice and peace and the civilization of love.

3. Because of this we are challenged to live a life worthy of our calling as members of Christ's Body and as brothers and sisters of Christ in accord with our Christian dignity and duty to walk humbly and peacefully together along the path of life. Jesus Himself exhorts us to be, by our lives, the salt of the earth and the light of the world. With Him I say to you: "Let your light so shine before men, that they may see your good works and give glory to your Father who is in heaven" (Mt. 5:16).

4. Each one of us has a unique place in the communion of the one universal Church throughout

Africa and the whole world. You, the laity, pursuing a vocation of holiness and love, have a particular responsibility for the consecration of the world. Through you the Gospel must reach all levels of society. In imitation of the Holy Family, you parents and children must build a community of love and understanding, where the joys and hopes and sorrows of life are shared together and offered to God in prayer. You couples must be the sign of God's faithful and unbreakable love for His people, and of Christ's love for His Church. It is you who have the great mission of giving Christ to each other and to your children, and in this way you are the first catechists of your children. I greet also all the catechists who serve the Church of God so devotedly. And you young people who are preparing for the priesthood or religious life are called to believe in the power of Christ's grace in your lives. The Lord needs you to carry on this work of redemption among your brothers and sisters.

You religious, both men and women, through the profession of the evangelical counsels of chastity, poverty and obedience, are called to give an effective witness to Christ's kingdom, the fullness of which is to be revealed only at the coming of our Lord Jesus Christ. You are called, in a life of joyful consecration and permanent commitment, to be a sign of holiness in the Church, and therefore a sign of encouragement and hope to all the People of God. You are, moreover, in a position to make a great contribution to the Church's apostolate by your activities and your life of prayer. In fulfilling this mission the measure of your effectiveness will be in the proportion that you remain united with the bishops and work in close union with them. And you, my brothers in the priesthood, yours is a mission of proclaiming salvation, of building up the Church by the Eucharistic Sacrifice; yours is a vocation of special companionship with Christ, offering your lives in celibacy in order to be like Jesus, the Good Shepherd, in the midst of your people—the people of Kenya.

And finally, my dear brother bishops, in union with the whole episcopal college that is united with the Successor of Peter, you are called to exercise the pastoral leadership of the whole flock in the name of Jesus Christ, "the chief Shepherd" (1 Pt. 5:4); yours is therefore a role of special servanthood. You are the appointed guardians of the unity that we are living and experiencing today, because you are the guardians of God's word upon which all unity is based. And, in a particular way, dear Cardinal Otunga, by reason of your eminent position, you are yourself a visible link with the See of Rome, and a special sign of Catholic unity within your local Church. I am deeply grateful for your fidelity and for your devoted collaboration.

5. And so let us all, as one redeemed people, one Body of Christ, one Church, stand firm together in the faith of our Lord Jesus Christ, acknowledging Him as "God from God, Light from Light, true God from true God." With St. Peter, let us say to Jesus: "You are the Christ, the Son of the living God" (Mt. 16:16). And again: "You have the words of eternal life" (Jn. 6:68).

And on my part, as the Successor of Peter, I have come to you today to repeat Christ's words of eternal life, to proclaim His message of salvation and hope, and to offer all of you His peace:

"Peace to all of you who are in Christ" (1 Pt. 5:14).

Peace to the living.

Peace to the dead, to all those who have gone before us with the sign of faith.

Peace to all Kenya.

Peace to all Africa—the peace of Christ Jesus our Lord.

Amen.

FUNDAMENTAL CHOICE: FOR OR AGAINST HUMANITY

The Pope's last official engagement on May 6 was in the Nunciature with the Diplomatic Corps accredited to Kenya. During his meeting with them he delivered the following address.

Your Excellencies,
Ladies and gentlemen,

1. Your visit here this evening gives me great pleasure, for it offers me an opportunity to meet so many distinguished members of the Diplomatic Community. My cordial and respectful welcome goes also to the representatives of regional and international organizations, whose activities enrich this capital city. I thank all of you for the honor you show me by your courteous presence. I am indeed grateful to the Representative of the Holy See for having taken the initiative to offer you the hospitality of this house, which is also my home during my stay in Nairobi.

I am sure that you are well acquainted with this continent, both by virtue of your office and as a result of the daily contacts that you have with the leaders and the people of Africa. You will therefore not be surprised if I address my remarks primarily to the African situation and to some of the problems which face this continent.

A NEW ERA HAS BEGUN

2. Tonight I wish to recall the prophetic words which Paul VI addressed to the Parliament of Uganda, in which he spoke of Africa as being "emancipated from its past and ripe for a new era." Standing here in Kenya eleven years later, I dare to say: this new era has begun and Africa is showing itself ready for the challenge! During these years, so much has happened, so many changes have come about, so much progress has been made; and at the same time so many new problems have arisen. Hence, it seems that this is now an appropriate occasion for me to speak about the new reality of Africa.

Many of the African situations and problems that demand our attention today are no different from those that affect other nations and continents in the world. Others, however, are typically African in the sense that the elements of the problems and the resources available for their solutions—natural and especially human resources—are unique for this continent. In this there is one paramount factor that must be kept in mind. It is the true identity of the African, the African person, the African man and woman.

SET OF MORAL VALUES

3. The path that every human community must walk in its quest to ascertain the deeper meaning of its existence is the path of truth about man in his totality. If we want to understand the situation in Africa, its past and its future, we must start from the truth of the African person—the truth of every African in his or her concrete and historical setting. If this truth is not grasped, there can exist neither any understanding

among the African peoples themselves nor any just and fraternal relations between Africa and the rest of the world, for the truth about man is a prerequisite for all human achievements.

The truth about the African individual must be seen, first and foremost, in his or her dignity as a human person. There are present in the culture of this continent many elements which help one to understand this truth. Is it not refreshing to know that the African accepts, with his whole being, the fact that there is a fundamental relationship between himself and God, the Creator? Hence he is prone to consider the reality of himself or of the material world around him within the context of this relationship, thus expressing a fundamental reference to God who "created man in the image of himself, in the image of God he created him; male and female he created them" (Gen. 1:27). The unique dignity and fundamental equality of all human persons must therefore be accepted as the starting point for a true understanding of the identity and the aspirations of the people of this continent.

African society has also—built into its life—a set of moral values, and these values shed further light on the true identity of the African. History testifies how the African continent has always known a strong sense of community in the different groups that make up its social structure; this is especially true in the family where there is strong coherence and solidarity. And what better insight can be found into the necessity for the peaceful solution of conflicts and difficulties—a way that is in keeping with human dignity—than that innate propensity for dialogue, that desire to explain differing views in conversation, to which the African turns so easily and which he accomplishes with such natural grace? A sense of celebration expressed in spontaneous joy, a reverence for life and the generous acceptance of new life, these are some more of the elements that are part of the heritage of the African and help define his identity.

ASSUMING RESPONSIBILITY

4. It is against this background that the Catholic Church, in the light of her own convictions drawn from the message of Christ, views the realities of Africa today, and proclaims her trust in this continent.

A few days before leaving on this pastoral visit, I expressed my joy in being able to visit the peoples of Africa in their own countries, in their own sovereign states, where they are "the true masters of their own land and the helmsmen of their own destiny" (Angelus Message, April 27, 1980). In Africa, most of the nations have known colonial administration in the past. While not denying the various achievements of this administration, the world rejoices in the fact that this period is now drawing to a final close. The peoples of Africa, with a few painful exceptions, are assuming full political responsibility for their own destiny, and I greet here particularly the recently achieved independence of Zimbabwe. But one cannot ignore the fact that other forms of dependence are still a reality, or at least a threat.

Political independence and national sovereignty demand, as a necessary corollary, that there be also economic independence and freedom from ideological domination. The situation of some countries can be profoundly conditioned by the decisions of other powers, among which are the major world powers. There can also be the subtle threat of interference of an ideological nature that may produce, in the area of human dignity, effects that are even more deleterious than any other form of subjugation. There are still situations and systems, within individual countries, and in the relationships between states, that are "marked by injustice and social injury" (Address to the United Nations Organization, October 2, 1979, no. 17) and that still condemn many people to hunger, disease, unemployment, lack of education and stagnation in their process of achieving development.

FOR THE COMMON GOOD

5. The state, the justification of which is the sovereignty of society, and to which is entrusted the safeguarding of the independence, must never lose sight of its first objective, which is the common good of all its citizens—all its citizens without distinction, and not just the welfare of one particular group or category. The state must reject anything unworthy of the freedom and of the human rights of its people, thus banishing all elements such as abuse of authority, corruption, domination of the weak, the denial to the people of their right share in political life and decisions, tyranny or the use of violence and terrorism. Here again, I do not hesitate to refer to the truth about man. Without the acceptance of the truth about man, of his dignity and eternal destiny, there cannot exist within the nation that fundamental trust which is a basic ingredient of all human achievements. Neither

can the public function be seen for what it truly is: a service to the people, which finds its only justification in solicitude for the good of all.

RELIGIOUS FREEDOM

6. In the same context of the respect of the dignity of its citizens by the State, I wish to draw attention to the question of religious freedom.

Because she believes that no freedom can exist, that no true fraternal love is possible without reference to God, who "created man in the image of himself" (Gn. 1:27), the Catholic Church will never cease to defend, as a fundamental right of every person, freedom of religion and freedom of conscience. "The curtailment and violation of religious freedom of individuals and communities is not only a painful experience," I stated in my encyclical, "but it is above all an attack on man's very dignity, independently of the religion professed or of the concept of the world which these individuals and communities have." And I added that, because unbelief, lack of religion and atheism can be understood only in relation to religion and faith, it is difficult to accept "a position that gives only atheism the right of citizenship in public and social life, while believers are, as though by principle, barely tolerated or are treated as second-class citizens or are even—and this has happened—entirely deprived of the rights of citizenship" (*Redemptor hominis*, no. 17). For this reason, the Church believes—without hesitation and without doubt—that an atheistic ideology cannot be the moving and guiding force for advancing the well-being of individuals or for promoting social justice when it deprives man of his God-given freedom, his spiritual inspiration and the power to love his fellowmen adequately.

RACIAL DISCRIMINATION

7. Another problem on which the truth about man, and about the African in particular, impels me to speak out, is the persistent problem of racial discrimination. The aspiration to equal dignity on the part of individuals and peoples, together with its concrete implementation in every aspect of social life, has always been strongly supported and defended by the Church. During his visit to Africa, Paul VI stated: "We deplore the fact that, in certain parts of the world, there persist social situations based upon racial discrimination and often willed and sustained by systems of thought; such situations constitute a manifest and inadmissible affront to the fundamental rights of the human person" (To the Parliament of Uganda, August 1, 1969). In his last address two years ago to the Diplomatic Corps accredited to the Holy See, he emphasized again that the Church is "concerned by the aggravation of racial and tribal rivalries which instigate division and rancor," and he denounced the "attempt to create juridical and political foundations in violation of the principles of universal suffrage and the self-determination of peoples" (January 14, 1978).

The truth about man in Africa demands from me on this occasion that I should confirm these statements. And this I do with deep and strong conviction. Progress has been made with regard to some situations, and for this we are grateful to God. But there still remain too many instances of institutionalized discrimination on the basis of racial differences, and these I cannot abstain from exposing before world opinion. Nor let us forget in this regard the need to combat racist reactions which may surface in connection with the migration of people from the countryside to the urban centers, or from one country to another. Racial discrimination is evil, no matter how it is practiced, no matter who does it or why.

MATTER OF REFUGEES

8. Still within the context of the whole African continent, I would like to draw attention to a problem that is of such urgency that it must indeed mobilize the necessary solidarity and compassion for its solution. I refer to the question of the refugees in many regions of Africa. Large numbers of people have been compelled for a variety of reasons to leave the country they love and the place where they have their roots. Sometimes this is for political reasons, at other times it is to escape from violence or war, or as a consequence of natural disasters, or because of a hostile climate. The African community and the world community must not cease to be concerned about the condition of the refugees and by the terrible sufferings to which they are subjected, many of them for a very long time. These refugees truly have a right to freedom and to lives worthy of their human dignity. They must not be deprived of the enjoyment of their rights, certainly not when factors beyond their own control have forced them to become strangers without a homeland.

I therefore appeal to all the authorities to ensure that in their own nation rightful freedom is always offered to all citizens, so that nobody will have to go looking for it elsewhere. I appeal to the authorities of the nations whose borders the refugees are compelled to cross, to receive them with cordial hospitality. I appeal to the international community not to let the burden weigh solely on the countries where the refugees temporarily settle, but to make the necessary aid available to the governments concerned and to the appropriate international bodies.

HUMAN ENVIRONMENT

9. The presence in this city of Nairobi of such organizations as the United Nations Environment Program and the United Nations Center for Human Settlements or HABITAT draws our attention to another problem area, that of the total human environment. Man, in his aspiration to satisfy his needs and to achieve better living conditions, has created an increasing number of environmental problems. Urban and industrial expansion aggravate these problems, especially when its victims are the very weak often living in "poverty belts," lacking elementary services and normal chances for improvement. I praise the efforts of all those who are trying to increase awareness that rational and honest planning are needed to avoid or redress such situations.

BETTER COLLABORATION

10. The Holy See greets with great satisfaction every effort that is being made to achieve better col-

laboration among the African countries in order to further their development, to promote their dignity and fuller independence, and to secure their rightful share in the management of the world, while at the same time strengthening their commitment to bear their share of collective responsibility for the poor and underprivileged of the planet.

The Organization of African Unity, together with all other bodies which pursue an aim of greater collaboration among the African nations, is deserving of every encouragement. The Holy See was pleased to be invited by the United Nations Economic Commission for Africa to establish closer relations, through the participation of observers at the meetings of the Commission and its subsidiary bodies. It remains ready to extend to other African organizations similar collaboration, in accordance with its own nature and universal mission, and motivated only by the demands of its evangelical message of peace, justice and service to all humanity and to every human being.

ITS RIGHTFUL PLACE

11. It is my fervent hope that the free and independent nations of Africa will always assume their rightful place in the family of nations. In the quest for international peace, justice and unity, Africa has an important role to play. Africa constitutes a real treasure house of so many authentic human values. It is called upon to share these values with other peoples and nations, and so to enrich the whole human family and all other cultures. But in order to be able to do so, Africa must remain deeply faithful to itself; day after day, it must become ever more faithful to its own

It is a very great joy for me to reach the African continent for the first time. Yes, as I kiss this soil, my heart overflows with emotion, joy and hope. It is the emotion of discovering the African reality and of meeting in it this considerable part of humanity, which merits esteem and love, and which is also called to salvation in Jesus Christ.

There is no question of adulterating the word of God, or of emptying the cross of its power, but rather of bringing Christ into the very center of African life and of lifting up all African life to Christ. Thus, not only is Christianity relevant to Africa, but Christ, in the members of His Body, is Himself African.

It is also necessary for other peoples to learn to receive from African peoples. It is not just material and technical aid that the latter need. They need also to give: their heart, their wisdom, their culture, their sense of man, their sense of God, which are keener than in many others. Before the world, I would like to make a solemn appeal on this occasion, not only for aid, but for international mutual aid, that is, this exchange in which each of the partners makes its constructive contribution to the progress of mankind.

Dear students, the privileged education that the community offers you is not given to you in the first place for your personal profit. Tomorrow, it is the whole community, with its material and spiritual needs, which will have the right to turn to you, which will need you. You will be sensitive to the appeals of your fellow countrymen. A difficult but exalting task, worthy of the sentiment of solidarity, which you possess so strongly: you will have to serve man, to serve the African in his deepest and most precious aspect: his humanity.

I would now like to turn my gaze, beyond this assembly, towards the whole people, and tell them how satisfied I am to be in their midst. The limitations of the program exist, it is true, and it will not be possible to go to all regions to visit populations equally dear to my heart. Let my passage, at least, at some points of the country be a concrete testimony of Christ's message of love, which I would like to bring to every family, every inhabitant, to Catholics as well as to those who do not share the same faith.

You love this country deeply. I understand these feelings. You know the love I bear for the land in which I have my roots. The unity of a country is forged, furthermore, through trials and efforts in which Christians have their share, especially when they form a considerable part of the nation. Your service of God includes this love of your country. It contributes to the good of the country.

May you find in this talk the sign of the great interest that the Pope takes in the serious problems of the family, the testimony of his trust and his hope in your Christian homes and the courage to work, you yourselves, more than ever, in this African land, for the greater good of your nations and for the honor of the Church of Christ, at the solid construction of family communities "of life and love" according to the Gospel! I promise you that this great intention will always have a place in my heart and my prayer.

Speaking to you in this way, dear sisters, I would like to help you to grasp, or to grasp again, the essential characteristic of your religious state: the complete consecration, forever, of your innermost self and your feminine capacities to Christ and His kingdom. We have reached here the very heart of the mystery of your life.

The Gospel, certainly, is not identified with cultures, and transcends them all. But the kingdom that the Gospel proclaims is lived by men deeply tied to a culture; the construction of the kingdom cannot dispense with borrowing elements of human cultures. You wish to be at once fully Christians and fully Africans. The Holy Spirit asks us to believe, in fact, that the leaven of the Gospel, in its authenticity, has the power to bring forth Christians in the different cultures, with all the riches of their heritage, purified and transfigured.

Prove yourselves worthy of the heritage that you have received.... Have great love for Jesus Christ; try to know Him well, remain united to Him, have great faith and great trust in Him.... Be strong and courageous; be content; be happy and joyful always. Because, remember this always, the Christian life is a most beautiful thing!

The Church, in the name of her spiritual mission, asks on her part for the freedom of addressing consciences as well as the possibility for believers of professing their Faith publicly, nourishing it and proclaiming it. Religious freedom is, in fact, at the center of respect for all freedom and for all the inalienable rights of the person. It greatly helps to safeguard, for the good of everyone, what is the essential part of a people as of a man, that is, its soul. It is fortunate that Africans set great store by it.

I greet with special affection the sick, the in-firm, all those who feel unhappy in soul and in body: the Pope blesses you all.

As a sign that God had really come down among men, He said: "The poor receive the gospel"; the poor hear the good news of salva-tion! And He also said: "Come to me, all you who are crushed under the weight of your burden, and I will give you new strength." Coming to you, I wish to remind all disciples of Christ of this great message of the Gospel, on which the love that we have for one another is based.

It must be remembered that God is also the God of mercy, as the Church is a merciful mother. In spite of the sinful, weak and hesitant character of her sons, she invites them to hope, she proposes to them a Christian ideal, holiness, not as a burden, but as a light that draws and elevates hearts. Even if evangelization experiences, here or there, progressive and laborious stages—the task of becoming a Christian never ends! The Church knows that the sons of this country are capable of a true Christian life. They have already proved it abundantly. And she counts on them a great deal.

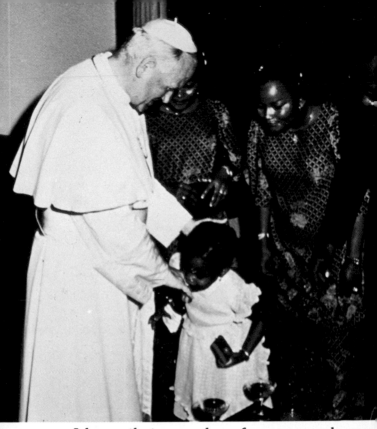

I know that a number of young people are available to cooperate in the religious instruction of school children, and to transmit to them their own reasons for hope. I know too that everywhere, in parishes as in distant stations, people are not afraid of difficulties, and are working courageously to proclaim the Good News. That is, it seems to me, a proof, as it were, of maturity. When I see all these courageous Christians here in Africa, I cannot help thinking that, nowadays, Christ has many friends in Africa, and that the Church in Africa has the maturity to face up to all vexations and all trials.

I wish to offer a particular greeting to you young people: be yourselves; under the fatherhood of God be upright citizens of your country. Be young people, and reach out to each other in generosity and fraternal service. Be young people, and do not let your hearts know selfishness or greed. I know that you carry in your hearts your dreams for the future, and in your hands the power to make those dreams come true. May peace and joy be always in your hearts!

Farewell, Africa! I take with me all that you have so generously given me and all that you have revealed to me in the course of this journey. May God bless you in each of your children, and may He let you enjoy peace and prosperity!

If I am obliged to go away, you know very well that our Lord does not leave you, that He remains with you always. In His name, I bless you again with all my heart.

TO TRANSFORM THE WORLD ACCORDING TO THE GOSPEL

On Wednesday morning, May 7, John Paul II concelebrated Mass in Uhuru Park, Nairobi, with Cardinals Otunga and Rugambwa, and with numerous bishops, in the presence of an immense crowd. After the Gospel, the Holy Father delivered the following homily.

Venerable brothers in the episcopate,
Dear brothers and sisters in Christ,

1. We gather here today to give praise and glory to our heavenly Father. We come together in this place, men and women of many different backgrounds, and yet all united in Him "who holds all things in unity" (Col. 1:17), all united at the table of God's word and at the altar of sacrifice.

My heart is filled with gratitude to God for this day and for this opportunity to celebrate the Eucharist with you, to sing praise to the Lord for having reconciled everything to Himself, "making peace by his death on the cross" (Col. 1:20).

On the day Jesus was crucified, He told Pilate: "I was born for this, I came into the world for this: to bear witness to the truth" (Jn. 18:35). Jesus came not to do His own will but the will of His heavenly Father. By His words, by His deeds, by His very existence He bore witness to the truth. In Jesus the tyranny of deceit and falsehood, the tyranny of lies and error, the tyranny of sin was defeated. For Christ is the living Word of divine truth who promised: "If you make my word your home you will indeed be my disciples, you will learn the truth and the truth will make you free" (Jn. 8:31f.).

The Church has received this same mission from Christ: to cultivate a deep love and veneration for the truth and to combine with faith the insights of learning and human wisdom—in all things to bear witness to the truth. In every age and in every land the Church proceeds in this mission, confident that if God is the supreme Source of all truth, there can be no opposition between natural wisdom and the truths of faith.

2. All of the faithful, dear brothers and sisters, have a role to play in the Church's mission on behalf of truth. That is why I stated in my encyclical that the "Church's responsibility for divine truth must be increasingly shared in various ways by all, including the specialists in various disciplines, those who represent the natural sciences and letters, doctors, jurists, artists and technicians, teachers at various levels and with different specializations. As members of the People of God, they all have their own part to play in Christ's prophetic mission and service of divine truth" (cf. *Redemptor hominis,* no. 19). Within the communion of the faithful, and especially within the local Christian community, careful attention should be given to this responsibility to bear witness to the truth. In his message to Africa my predecessor Paul VI addressed a special word to the intellectuals of this continent, precisely because he was convinced of the importance of their mission at the service of truth. And his words still ring out today: "Africa needs you,

your study, your research, your art and your teaching.... You are the prism through which the new ideas and cultural changes can be interpreted and explained to all. Be sincere, faithful to truth, and loyal" (no. 32).

HUNGER FOR GOD'S WORD

3. We must begin our witness to truth by cultivating a hunger for the word of God, a desire to receive and take to heart the life-giving message of the Gospel in all its fullness. When you listen attentively to the voice of the Savior and then put it into practice, you are indeed sharing in the Church's mission at the service of truth. You are bearing witness to the world that you firmly believe the promise God made through Isaiah: "As the rain and the snow come down from the heavens and do not return without watering the earth, making it yield and giving growth to provide seed for the sower and bread for the eating, so the word that goes from my mouth does not return to me empty, without carrying out my will and succeeding in what it was sent to do" (Is. 55:10f.). You can be messengers of the truth only if you are first of all true listeners to God's word.

IN ORDER TO TRANSFORM

4. When Pilate asked Jesus whether He was a king, His response was clear and unambiguous: "Mine is not a kingdom of this world" (Jn. 18:35). Christ came to bring life and salvation to every human being; His mission was not in the social, economic or political order. Likewise Christ did not give the Church a mission which is social, economic or political, but rather a religious one (cf. *Gaudium et*

spes, no. 42). Yet it would be a mistake to think that the individual Christian should not be involved in these areas of life in society. On this point, the Fathers of the Second Vatican Council were very clear: "One of the gravest errors of our time is the dichotomy between the faith which many profess and the practice of their daily lives.... The Christian who neglects his temporal duties neglects his duties towards his neighbor, neglects God Himself, and endangers his eternal salvation" (*Gaudium et spes,* no. 43).

Christians, therefore, and especially you who are laity are called by God to be involved in the world in order to transform it according to the Gospel. In carrying out this task, your own personal commitment to truth and honesty plays an important role, because a sense of responsibility for the truth is one of the fundamental points of encounter between the Church and society, between the Church and each man and woman (cf. *Redemptor hominis,* no. 19). The Christian faith does not provide you with ready-made solutions to the complex problems affecting contemporary society. But it does give you deep insights into the nature of man and his needs, calling you to speak the truth in love, to take up your responsibilities as good citizens and to work with your neighbors to build a society where true human values are nourished and deepened by a shared Christian vision of life.

PROMOTING TRUE CULTURE

5. One of these areas which holds a very important place in society and in the total vocation of every human person is culture. "It is a fact bearing on the very person of man that he can come to an authentic

and full humanity only through culture, that is, through the cultivation of natural goods and values. Wherever human life therefore is involved, nature and culture are very intimately connected" (*Gaudium et spes*, no. 53). A Christian will gladly collaborate in the promotion of true culture, for he knows that the Good News of Christ reinforces in man the spiritual values which are at the heart of the culture of every people and of every period of history. The Church, which feels at home in every culture, without exclusively making her own any culture, encourages her sons and daughters who are active in schools, universities and other institutions of learning to give their best to this activity. By harmonizing those values which are the unique heritage of each people or group with the content of the Gospel, the Christian will help his or her own people to achieve true freedom and the capacity to face the challenges of the times. Every Christian, united with Christ in the mystery of Baptism, will endeavor to conform to the Father's plan for His Son: "to unite all things in him, things in heaven and things on earth" (Eph. 1:10).

FOSTER HUMAN VALUES

6. Another important challenge for the Christian is that of the political life. In the state, citizens have a right and duty to share in the political life. For a nation can ensure the common good of all, and the dreams and aspirations of its different members, only to the extent that all citizens in full liberty and with complete responsibility make their contributions willingly and selflessly for the good of all.

The duties of the good Christian citizen involve more than shunning corruption, more than not ex-

ploiting others; these duties include positively contributing to the establishment of just laws and structures that foster human values. If the Christian finds
injustice or anything that militates against love, peace
and unity in society, he or she must ask: "Where have
I fallen short? What have I done wrong? What did I
fail to do that the truth of my vocation called me to
do? Did I sin by omission?"

CHRISTIAN FAMILY LIFE

7. Here today in Kenya, as I have done many
times before, I wish to address a particular message to
married couples and to families. The family is the fundamental human community; it is the first and vital
cell of any society. Thus the strength and vitality of
any country will only be as great as the strength and
vitality of the family within that country. No group
has a greater impact on a country than the family. No
group has a more influential role in the future of the
world.

For this reason, Christian couples have an irreplaceable mission in today's world. The generous
love and fidelity of husband and wife offer stability
and hope to a world torn by hatred and division. By
their lifelong perseverance in life-giving love they
show the unbreakable and sacred character of the
sacramental marriage bond. At the same time it is the
Christian family that most simply and profoundly
promotes the dignity and worth of human life from
the moment of conception.

The Christian family is also the domestic sanctuary of the Church. In a Christian home various
aspects of the whole Church are found, such as

All the families that make up the Church and all the individuals that make up the families, all of us together are called to walk with Christ, bearing witness to His truth in the circumstances of our daily lives. In doing this we can permeate society with the leaven of the Gospel, which alone can transform it into Christ's kingdom.

mutual love, attentiveness to God's word and prayer together. The home is a place where the Gospel is received and lived, and the place from which the Gospel radiates. Thus the family offers daily witness, even without words, to the truth and grace· of the word of God. For this reason, I stated in my encyclical, "Married people...must endeavor with all their strength to persevere in their matrimonial union, building up the family community through the witness of love and educating new generations of men and women capable in their turn of dedicating the whole of their lives to their vocation, that is to say, to the 'kingly service' of which Jesus Christ has offered us the example and the most beautiful model" (Redemptor hominis, no. 21).

BEARING WITNESS

8. Beloved brothers and sisters: all the families that make up the Church and all the individuals that make up the families, all of us together are called to walk with Christ, bearing witness to His truth in the circumstances of our daily lives. In doing this we can permeate society with the leaven of the Gospel, which alone can transform it into Christ's kingdom—a kingdom of truth and life, a kingdom of holiness and grace, a kingdom of justice, love and peace! Amen.

THE GOSPEL MESSAGE
BEARS FRUIT IN PRAYER

The Holy Father's last engagement on Wednesday morning, May 7, was a visit to the Carmel of Nairobi, which is situated close by the Nunciature. The Carmel was founded in 1939 from the Irish Carmel of Hampton in Dublin, and at present the community includes members from Ireland, Scotland, India, United States, Germany and Austria. On the occasion of the Pope's visit the Carmel was host to forty other cloistered religious of various Orders. The Holy Father addressed them as follows.

Dear sisters in our Lord Jesus Christ,

1. Being your neighbor for two days, I could not fail to come and visit your Carmel. It gives me great joy to know that, near the house of the Pope's representative, there is a house of prayer where God's praises are constantly sung and where the sacrifice of your cloistered life is offered in joyful generosity to the Father. The fact that other contemplative communities in Kenya have gathered here with you gives me added joy. My dear sisters, I bring you the greetings and love of the whole Church, and I thank you for your contribution to evangelization and for the inspiration of your lives. Yes, it is a great tribute to the grace of God and to the power of the death and resurrection of the Lord that many years ago the contemplative religious life took root in African soil, bringing forth abundant fruits of justice and holiness of life. You are indeed the recipients of a particular gift from God: the contemplative vocation in the Church. The introduction of the contemplative life in a local Church is an important indication of the dynamic implantation of the Gospel in the heart of a

people. This is a sign which, together with missionary activity, shows the maturity of the local Church. To live the holiness of Christ and to share the ardent desire of His heart—"I must preach the Good News of the kingdom of God to the other cities also; for I was sent for this purpose" (Lk. 4:43)—these are hallmarks of Christ's Church.

2. Here in the heart of Kenya you are called to fulfill your exalted mission in the Body of Christ: to perpetuate Christ's life of prayer and loving immolation. The Church has learned from her Founder—and centuries of experience have confirmed her profound conviction—that union with God is vitally necessary for fruitful activity. Jesus has told us: "I am the vine, you are the branches...apart from me you can do nothing" (Jn. 15:5). The Church is deeply aware, and without hesitation she forcefully proclaims, that there is an intimate connection between prayer and the spreading of the Kingdom of God, between prayer and the conversion of hearts, between prayer and the fruitful reception of the saving and uplifting Gospel message. This alone is enough to assure you and all contemplative religious throughout the world just how necessary your role is in the Church, just how important your service is to your people, just how great your contribution is to the evangelization of Kenya and all Africa.

3. In your lives of prayer, moreover, Christ's praise of His eternal Father goes on. The totality of His love for His Father and of His obedience to the Father's will is reflected in your own radical consecration of love. His selfless immolation for His Body, the Church, finds expression in the offering of your lives in union with His sacrifice. The renuncia-

tion involved in your vocation shows the primacy of Christ's love in your lives. In you the Church gives witness to her fundamental function, which is, as I said in my encyclical: "to point the awareness and experience of the whole of humanity towards the mystery of God..." (*Redemptor hominis,* no. 10).

4. Your lives and your activities are very much a part of the whole Church; they are in the Church and for the Church. You live in the very heart of the Church as did St. Thérèse of the Child Jesus and so many other contemplative nuns throughout the Church's past. And as you pursue your vocation in fidelity to the Christ who called you, you remain spiritually very close to your families and the communities from which you come. As you live out your lives totally for Jesus Christ, your Spouse, and for all who have been called to life in Him—the entire Christian family—you can rightly feel near to all your brothers and sisters as they strive for salvation and the fullness of human dignity. In your lives of material detachment and in the earnest work that you perform each day, you show your solidarity with the whole working community to whose service you are called. And through your prayers and the fruitfulness of your spiritual activities, you are in a position to contribute effectively to the great cause of justice and peace and to the human advancement of countless men and women. Through your cloistered lives children are brought to Christ, the sick are comforted, the needy assisted, human hearts reconciled and the poor have the Gospel preached to them.

In certain places in Africa, a monastery of contemplative religious has been established in the vicinity of the major seminary. Is it not especially meaningful that those who saw the necessity of promoting vocations to the priesthood, so as to enable the young churches to become fully implanted in the native soil, also professed their conviction that only the grace of God, humbly sought in constant prayer, could sustain the fervor of the priesthood? I ask you therefore, as a special request on this occasion, to make it one of the primary intentions of your prayers, to beseech the Lord of the harvest to send out laborers into His harvest (cf. Mt. 9:38), and to bless His Church in Africa with many good, generous, and committed priests, whose example of a holy and truly pastoral life constitutes the best guarantee for the life of the Church and the propagation of the Faith.

5. Yours is then a truly important life of faith in Jesus Christ. In the words of St. Peter: "Without having seen him, you love him; though you do not now see him, you believe in him and rejoice with unutterable and exalted joy" (1 Pt. 1:8). And precisely because of this, your lives become lives of great service to the Church. With Mary you are called to meditate on the word of God, and to cooperate in bringing forth to spiritual life those who believe in Christ. For you, therefore, the future is clear. You are on the right path—the path of total, joyful consecration to Jesus Christ and of loving service to all your brothers and sisters in Africa and throughout the Church.

Dear sisters: in all your efforts to walk with Mary and to ascend the mountain that is Christ by loving more deeply and serving more generously, remember that "your life is hid with Christ in God" (Col. 3:3), for the glory of the Most Holy Trinity: the Father, and the Son, and the Holy Spirit.

Amen.

FUNDAMENTAL ATTITUDE FOR REAL PROGRESS

In the early afternoon of May 7, John Paul II had a private meeting with the President of the Republic of Kenya, Daniel Arap Moi, during which he delivered the following address.

Mr. President,

1. I wish to express my gratitude to you for your invitation to the State House. I am very pleased to have a meeting with Your Excellency and to be able to greet so many distinguished personages of your nation. The few hours I have already spent in Kenya have enabled me to experience for myself traditional African hospitality, which is a deeply human and warm reality.

In addressing you today, and through you the whole nation of Kenya, I consider it fitting to pay tribute in the first place to the memory of the Founding Father of this Republic, the late President Mzee Jomo Kenyatta, who completed his life of service to his people less than two years ago. In the eulogy which you delivered during the state funeral of the one you called "my father, my teacher and my leader," you summed up the meaning of his contribution in the following words: "In life, Mzee Kenyatta championed justice and equality. He advocated respect for human dignity and the preservation of our culture. His concern for the welfare of all Kenyans was deep and binding. We are all indebted to him...." During the early years of this nation, he achieved unity, created a spirit of brotherhood, and instilled the determination to go on building the nation through the common efforts of all. He left to Kenya a beautiful heritage and a challenging program.

2. Respect for human dignity, for the dignity of every man, woman and child, for the dignity that all human beings possess, not because it has been conferred on them by their fellow men but because they have received it from God: this is the fundamental attitude to be adopted if real progress is to be made. It is precisely in this conviction and in this commitment to the dignity of every human being that the Church and the state find themselves on the same path.

I know, Mr. President, that on many occasions you have publicly expressed your appreciation of the contribution which the Catholic Church in your country makes to the advancement of the peoples. This, together with the existence of good relations between your nation and the Holy See, together also with the collaboration which exists in the field of education, health care and other areas of human development, is reason for much satisfaction. It also augurs well for the future.

3. On this occasion, I wish to repeat that the Church is deeply concerned for all the needs of the people. Precisely because she values so highly the dignity of every human being, the Church will always continue to exercise her mission, in accordance with her own nature, for the real good of man and society, and for the benefit of the whole human person.

In this spirit, the Church contributes to development, unity, brotherhood and peace among people and among nations. For this reason, the Church will raise her voice and call upon her sons and daughters every time that the conditions of life of individuals and communities are not truly human, every time they are not in accord with human dignity. This too is a reason why I have undertaken my first journey through the African continent—to proclaim the dignity and basic equality of all human beings and their right to the full development of their personality in every sphere, material as well as spiritual.

Mr. President, I should like this brief meeting with you and with all your distinguished guests to be for each and every one, for all the people of Kenya, a fraternal encouragement to advance along the road of truly human progress. May God, the Creator of man and nature, accompany you in your endeavors to lead Kenya forward, to build a prosperous Africa, and to construct a world community in unity, justice and peace.

PROMOTION OF PEACE, SOCIAL JUSTICE, AND MORAL VALUES AMONG THE NATIONS

After his visit to the President of Kenya, John Paul II returned to the Nunciature, and there, on Wednesday evening, May 7, he had meetings with the representatives of various Christian and non-Christian religons. First of all, he met the Muslim leaders and addressed them as follows.

Dear friends,

1. During my visit to Kenya I am very pleased to be able to greet a group of Muslim leaders. Your coming here today is deeply appreciated as an expression of your fraternal courtesy and respect. Be assured that I reciprocate these sentiments in your regard and towards all the Muslim people of this land.

2. On other occasions I have spoken of the religious patrimony of Islam and of its spiritual values. The Catholic Church realizes that the element of worship given to the one, living, subsistent, merciful and almighty Creator of heaven and earth is common to Islam and herself, and that it is a great link uniting all Christians and Muslims. With great satisfaction she also notes, among other elements of Islam which are held in common, the honor attrib-

Prayer, almsgiving and fasting are highly valued in both of our respective traditions and are beyond doubt a splendid witness to a world that runs the risk of being absorbed by materialism. Our relationship of reciprocal esteem and the mutual desire for authentic service to humanity urge us on to joint commitments in promoting peace, social justice, moral values and all the true freedoms of man.

uted to Jesus Christ and His Virgin Mother. As the Catholic Church makes every effort to sustain religious dialogue with Islam on the basis of existing bonds, which she endeavors ever more to reflect on, she likewise extends the invitation that her own heritage be fully known, especially to those who are spiritually attached to Abraham, and who profess monotheism.

3. On my part I wish, therefore, to do everything possible to help develop the spiritual bonds between Christians and Muslims. Prayer, almsgiving and fasting are highly valued in both of our respective traditions and are beyond doubt a splendid witness to a world that runs the risk of being absorbed by materialism. Our relationship of reciprocal esteem and the mutual desire for authentic service to humanity urge us on to joint commitments in promoting peace, social justice, moral values and all the true freedoms of man.

4. It is in this perspective that our meeting today offers us much hope. May it prove beneficial to humanity and give glory to God, who made us in His image and likeness, and who has revealed Himself to us.

With renewed sentiments of brotherhood I would ask you to carry my greetings to all the communities from which you come. Thank you again.

DIALOGUE ON THE MYSTERY OF MAN

After his meeting with the Muslims on May 7, the Holy Father then met the leaders of the Hindu community and spoke to them as follows.

Dear friends,

The presence here today of members of the Hindu community gives me great pleasure. In visiting the people of Kenya, I am happy to become acquainted with all those who live in this land and have a part in the life of this nation.

Your own roots are found in the venerable history of Asia, for which I have much respect and esteem. In greeting you I willingly recall the fact that the Second Vatican Council, in its Declaration *Nostrae aetate* manifested the fraternal attitude of the whole Catholic Church to non-Christian religions. In this she showed her task of fostering unity and love among individuals and nations and her commitment to advance fellowship among all human beings. Special reference in the document was made to Hinduism and to the religious values embraced by its followers.

And today the Catholic Church is willingly associated with all her brethren in a dialogue on the mystery of man and the mystery of God. The purpose of life, the nature of good, the path to happiness, the meaning of death and the end of our human journey—all these truths form the object of our common service of man in his many needs, and to the promotion of his full human dignity. And under the sign of this human dignity and brotherhood I greet you today with sincerity and fraternal love.

DIVISION
OF CHRISTIANS
A SCANDAL FOR
THE WORLD

On May 7, after his meeting with the Hindus, His Holiness then met the heads of the non-Catholic Christian churches in Kenya and addressed them as follows.

Dear brothers and sisters from the Christian Churches and Communities of Kenya,

"Grace to you and peace from God our Father and the Lord Jesus Christ" (Rom. 1:7).

1. I have come to Kenya to be with the bishops and people of the Catholic Church, since my task as bishop of Rome is a fraternal service of unity to support them in their fidelity to the Gospel and in their life in the one Catholic Communion. Humbly I see it as part of this ministry that I should also come to greet you, "holy brethren, who share in a heavenly call" (Heb. 3:1), for, despite those factors that still divide us, we are nevertheless linked by a real fellowship that remains true even though it is still imperfect (cf. *Unitatis redintegratio,* no. 3).

2. Because of this one Baptism, in which we profess one basic faith that Jesus is Lord and that God raised Him from the dead (cf. Rom. 10:9), we stand

together before the world of today with a common responsibility which stems from obedience to Christ. This common responsibility is so real and so important that it must impel us to do all we can, as a matter of urgency, to resolve the divisions that still exist between us, so that we may fulfill the will of Christ for the perfect unity of His followers.

Without full organic unity, Christians are unable to give a satisfactory witness to Christ, and their division remains a scandal to the world, and especially to the young Churches in mission lands. Your presence here testifies to a deep insight: that especially in the young Churches of Africa, in a continent that hungers and thirsts for God—a longing that can be fulfilled only in Christ—the common apostolic faith in Christ the Savior must be held and manifested, for in Christ there can be no division. Your presence, together with the sincere ecumenical efforts which are developing, show our common desire for full unity. For truly the credibility of the Gospel message and of Christ Himself is linked to Christian unity.

3. This is why, at the international level, many of your churches are now engaged in a theological dialogue with the Catholic Church—a dialogue that is already offering new hope for much greater understanding among us. This is also why, here in Kenya, the Christian people are striving to reach one mind in the faith of Christ. For whether they live in Africa or in Europe, in Asia or in America, Christians are the heirs of sad divisions. These divisions have to be first faced in a dialogue of mutual understanding and esteem, "speaking the truth in love" (Eph. 4:15), and then dealt with in accordance with the promptings of the Holy Spirit.

This task is, I repeat, an urgent one. Jesus calls us to bear witness to Him and to His saving work. We can do this adequately only when we are completely united in faith and when we speak His word with one voice, a voice that rings with that warm vitality which characterizes the whole Christian community when it lives together in full communion.

4. Our divisions impair that vitality and prevent our neighbors from hearing the Gospel as they should. And yet, even now, thanks to what we already have in common, it is possible for us, despite those divisions, to give a sincere even if limited witness together before a world that so sorely needs to hear that message of love and hope which is the Good News of the salvation won for all mankind by Jesus Christ, who "was crucified in weakness but lives by the power of God" (2 Cor. 13:4). It is possible for us to collaborate frequently in the cause of the Gospel. Although we cannot yet do everything together—especially the fullness of Eucharistic worship—we can still accomplish much together.

Wherever possible, then, let us find ways of engaging in acts of common witness, be it in joint Bible work, in promoting human rights and meeting human needs, in theological dialogue, in praying together when the opportunity allows—as it does so beautifully today—or in speaking to others about Jesus Christ and His salvation. As we do these things we must continue to ask the Holy Spirit for light and strength to conform perfectly to God's holy will for His Church.

5. The task that faces Christians as we near the end of the twentieth century is indeed a mighty challenge, and it is good to see how much is already

being done by divine grace to respond to it. May this response grow and develop in every part of the world. It is in this hope that I earnestly pray to God our Father that the churches and communities you represent, and the All African Council of Churches and the Christian Council of Kenya, of which so many of you are members, may be ever more faithful servants of Christ's will that all of us who believe in Him may be one, even as He and His Father are one. May you "stand firm in one spirit, with one mind striving side by side for the faith of the Gospel" (Phil. 1:27) for the glory of the most Holy Trinity, the Father, and the Son, and the Holy Spirit. Amen.

TWO DYNAMIC ASPECTS OF THE LIFE OF CHRIST

On Wednesday evening, May 7, the Holy Father met the visiting bishops from the countries bordering on Kenya. Among them was Cardinal Laurean Rugambwa, Archbishop of Dar-es-Salaam. To them His Holiness delivered the following address.

My dear brothers in the episcopate,

1. It is a great pleasure for me to greet you here today. You have come as visitors to Kenya to show your solidarity with your brother bishops and with their people. Since this is an extraordinary ecclesial celebration for them, you have wished to be close to them in the joy of the Faith. In coming, you have brought with you not only the fellowship of your own local churches, but a special manifestation of Catholic unity. And because you are members of the universal College of Bishops united with the successor of Peter, you bear collective pastoral responsibility for the good of the whole Church and for her pastoral activities throughout the world. Hence, with an awareness of the deep reality of the episcopate you have gathered in prayerful and fraternal solidarity.

2. Our being together today evokes quite naturally a consideration of our common ministry, our shared responsibility and our common likeness to Jesus Christ, the Incarnate Word and the High Priest of the New Testament.

In Jesus Christ, the Son of God, we find a fundamental insight into our deepest Christian identity. In Jesus Christ, the Good Shepherd, we have a full perception—in simplicity and profundity—of all pastoral ministry in the Church of God. In Jesus Christ, the Suffering Servant, we discern the complete meaning of a sacrificial life. In Jesus Christ, the Risen Lord, we comprehend the final goal of the Paschal Mystery—to which all our preaching and catechesis are directed.

3. All I wish to do in these moments with you is to direct my thoughts and yours to Jesus Christ—to Him who is *Unigenitus Dei Filius*, but who has become *Primogenitus in multis fratribus* (Rom. 8:29). This Son of God, this Son of Mary, this Priest and Victim of Redemption explains us to ourselves and declares the meaning of our ministry today and always: "Jesus Christ is the same yesterday and today and for ever" (Heb. 13:8).

As He called His Apostles, so He has also called us: to be His companions, to remain in His love, and to proclaim His Gospel. And in our full pastoral role as successors of the Apostles we are called to communicate Christ to our people. Sharing in His Sonship by divine adoption, we are instruments of grace for others, as we lead our people to the fullness of His life revealed in the mystery of the Church, the Body of Christ.

4. Our identity and our mission, as well as the term of our mission, are all linked to Christ in His Sonship; we are conformed to Him. Because of this likeness to Christ, we have great joy and comfort in living two dynamic aspects of Christ's life. With Christ we are conscious of loving the Father; His

words pervade our consciousness and our daily activity as bishops: "I love the Father" (Jn. 14:30). At the same time each of us in Christ can say: "The Father loves me," precisely because Jesus has said: "The Father loves the Son" (Jn. 3:35). This awareness of being in Christ, of loving His Father and being loved by Him is a source of pastoral strength. It confirms the meaning of our lives. It is a reason for thanksgiving to the Father and for endless praise of Jesus Christ.

Dear brother bishops: in the months and years ahead, may it bring us gladness to recall that in Kenya we manifested our episcopal unity together by praising Jesus Christ, the Eternal Son of God. To Him be glory for ever, with the Father, in the unity of the Holy Spirit. Amen.

EPISCOPAL MINISTRY AT THE SERVICE OF LIFE

The Holy Father's final engagement on Wednesday evening, May 7, was a meeting with the Kenyan bishops in the Nunciature at Nairobi. John Paul II spoke to them as follows.

Venerable and dear brothers in our Lord Jesus Christ,

1. Today during this Easter season it is a cause of deep joy and a source of pastoral strength for us to assemble in Nairobi, to gather together in the name of Jesus who said: "I am the resurrection and the life" (Jn. 11:25).

We are extremely conscious that our ministry in Africa and our service to the universal Church is placed under the sign of the Risen Christ. For, together with all our brother bishops throughout the world, we are successors of the body of Apostles that was chosen to witness to the resurrection. The knowledge that "with great power the apostles gave their testimony to the resurrection of the Lord Jesus" (Acts 4:33) truly strengthens us and uplifts us, because we know that we have received the inheritance of the Apostolic College. For us bishops this is an hour of trust in the Risen Lord, an hour of Easter joy an hour of great hope for the future of Africa.

AMECEA'S INSTITUTE

2. On this occasion my thoughts go to all the bishops of Africa, and I note with deep satisfaction

that the members of the Episcopal Conference of Kenya are resolutely engaged in many programs of collaboration and joint action with their fellow bishops from the AMECEA countries of Tanzania, Uganda, Zambia, Malawi, the Sudan and Ethiopia. In the abundant strength that comes from charity and mutual support, your ministry is sustained and enriched. Be assured of my admiration and esteem for the unity that you express in diversity and in fraternal collaboration, and for your concerted efforts on behalf of the evangelization of those countries that have so much in common.

An initiative worthy of particular mention is AMECEA's Pastoral Institute at Eldoret. This institute offers special opportunities to reflect on the Church's mission to guard and teach ever more effectively the word of God. The Holy Spirit Himself is directing the Church in Africa to scrutinize "the signs of the times" in the light of the sacred deposit of God's word as it is proclaimed by the magisterium. It is only on this sound basis that true answers can be found to the real problems that touch people's lives. It is in judging according to this sacred norm that the bishops will exercise their personal responsibility to evaluate what pastoral activities and solutions are valid for Africa today.

MINISTRY OF SERVICE

3. Venerable brothers, the episcopal ministry is a ministry at the service of life, bringing the power of the resurrection to your people, so that they may "walk in newness of life" (Rom. 6:4), so that they may be ever more aware of the Christian life to which

they are called by virtue of their Baptism, and so that in their daily lives—in the setting of Africa—they may have fellowship with the Father and His Son Jesus Christ in the unity of the Holy Spirit. And because this fellowship is fully achieved only in heaven, your ministry likewise involves a clear proclamation of eternal life.

PASTORS OF THE FLOCK

4. As Successor of Peter in the See of Rome and as your brother in the College of Bishops, I have come to Africa to encourage you in your efforts as pastors of the flock; in the efforts of each of you to offer to Christ a local church in which unity reigns between the bishop and the priests, the religious and the laity; in your efforts to enlighten communities with the Gospel and make them vibrant with the life of Christ; in your efforts to bring the dynamic power of the resurrection into human life and by it to transform and elevate all levels of society.

I have come to confirm you in your total acceptance of God's holy word as it is authentically proclaimed by the Catholic Church at all times and in all places. I wish to support you in the conviction, so splendidly expressed by the bishops of Kenya in their Pastoral Letter of April 27, 1979, that fidelity to the teachings of Christ and the magisterium of His Church is truly in the interests of the people. By following your clear insights of faith you showed yourselves true pastors of the flock, exercising real spiritual leadership when you declared: "We, your bishops, would do a disservice to the people if we did not expect of them the goodness and the fidelity that they are capable of by the grace of God" (Pastoral Letter, p. 10). Your greatest contribution to your people and to all Africa is indeed the gift of God's word, the acceptance of which is the basis for all community and the condition for all progress.

RESPECT FAMILY VALUES

5. As the *servus servorum Dei* I have come to uphold with you the priorities of your ministry. In the first place I offer my support for your pastoral efforts on behalf of the family—the African family. The great African tradition is faithful to so many family values, and to life itself, which takes its origin in the family. A profound respect for the family and for the good of children is a distinctive gift of Africa to the world. It is in the family that each generation learns to absorb these values and to transmit them. And the whole Church appreciates everything you do to preserve this heritage of your people, to purify it and uplift it in the sacramental fullness of Christ's new and original teaching. Hence we see the great value of presenting the Christian family in its relationship to the most Holy Trinity, and of maintaining the Christian ideal in its evangelical purity. It is the divine law proclaimed by Christ that gives rise to the Christian ideal of monogamous marriage, which in turn is the basis for the Christian family. Only a week before he died, my predecessor, John Paul I, spoke to a group of bishops in these words, which I consider very relevant here today in Africa: "Let us never grow tired of proclaiming the family as a community of love: conjugal love unites the couple and is procreative of new life; it mirrors the divine love, is communicated, and in the

words of *Gaudium et spes,* is actually a sharing in the covenant of love of Christ and His Church" (*AAS* 70 [1978], p. 766).

Be assured of my solidarity with you in this great task involving the diligent preparation of the young for marriage, the repeated proclamation of the unity and indissolubility of marriage, and the renewed invitation to the faithful to accept and foster with faith and love the Catholic celebration of the sacrament of marriage. Success in a pastoral program of this nature requires patience and perseverance and a strong conviction that Christ has come to "make all things new" (Rev. 21:5).

HUMANAE VITAE ENCYCLICAL

Know also that in all your efforts to build up strong united families, in which human love reflects divine love and in which the education of children is embraced with a true sense of mission, you have the support of the universal Church. With the love and sensitivity of pastors, you have well illustrated the great principle that any pastoral approach that does not rest on the doctrinal foundation of the word of God is illusory. Hence with true pastoral charity you have faced various problems affecting human life and repeated the Church's teaching at the true service of man. You have clearly insisted, for example, on the most fundamental human right: the right to life from the moment of conception; you have effectively reiterated the Church's position on abortion, sterilization and contraception. Your faithful upholding of the Church's teaching contained in the encyclical *Humanae vitae* has been the expression of your pastoral concern and your profound attachment to the integral values of the human person.

Every effort to make society sensitive to the importance of the family is a great service to humanity. When the full dignity of parents and children is realized and is expressed in prayer, a new power for good is unleashed throughout the Church and the world. John Paul I expressed this eloquently when he said: "The holiness of the Christian family is indeed a most apt means for producing the serene renewal of the Church which the Council so eagerly desired. Through family prayer, the *ecclesia domestica* becomes an effective reality and leads to the transformation of the world" (*Ibid.*, p. 767). Upon you, brethren, rest the hope and trust of the universal Church for the defense and promotion of the African family, both parents and children. The Holy Spirit of truth, who has implanted so many values in the hearts of the African people, will never cease to assist you as pastors in bringing the teaching of Jesus ever more effectively into the lives of your brothers and sisters. We need never be afraid to preach the fullness of His message in all its evangelical purity, for, as I stated on another occasion: "Let us never fear that the challenge is too great for our people: they were redeemed by the precious blood of Christ; they are His people. Through the Holy Spirit, Jesus Christ vindicates to Himself the final responsibility for the acceptance of His word and for the growth of His Church. It is He, Jesus Christ, who will continue to give the grace to His people to meet the requirements of His word, despite all difficulties, despite all weaknesses. And it is up to us to continue to proclaim the message of salvation in its entirety and purity, with patience, compassion and the conviction that what is impossible with man is possible with God" (*AAS* 71, [1979], pp. 1424f.).

CATECHESIS—A PRIORITY

6. Another great priority of your ministry is catechesis: developing the initial faith of your people and bringing them to the fullness of Christian life. I am close to you, in praise and encouragement, in every undertaking of yours to communicate Christ, to make His Gospel incarnate in the lives and culture of your people. In union with the universal Church, an in openness to the patrimony of her long history, you are striving to lead your people in the reality of their daily lives to look to Christ for light and strength. The aim of your local churches is to have the faithful living through, with and in Christ. Your efforts, in which you rightfully endeavor to associate the whole community—and in a special way the catechists—must have constant reference to Christ, to His divine Person, His Spirit, and His Gospel.

The "acculturation" or "inculturation" which you rightly promote will truly be a reflection of the Incarnation of the Word, when a culture, transformed and regenerated by the Gospel, brings forth from its own living tradition original expressions of Christian life, celebration and thought (cf. *Catechesi tradendae*, no. 53). By respecting, preserving and fostering the particular values and riches of your people's cultural heritage, you will be in a position to lead them to a better understanding of the mystery of Christ, which is to be lived in the noble, concrete and daily experiences of African life. There is no question of adulterating the word of God, or of emptying the cross of its power (cf. 1 Cor. 1:17), but rather of bringing Christ into the very center of African life and of lifting up all African life to Christ. Thus, not only is Christianity relevant to Africa, but Christ, in the members of His Body, is Himself African.

PROPER FORMATION

7. Again, with good reason, you attribute great pastoral importance to the proper formation of priests and religious, as well as to fostering these vocations in the Church. This attitude is an expression of your deep understanding of the needs of the Body of Christ.

Since the beginning of my pontificate I have striven to point out the importance of religious consecration in the Church and the value of religious life as it affects the whole community of the faithful. Religious have the task of showing forth the holiness of the whole Body of Christ and of bearing witness to a new and eternal life acquired by the redemption of Christ (cf. *Lumen gentium*, no. 44). At the same time they are called to many different apostolates in the Church. Their service in the Gospel is very necessary for the life of the Church. Missionary religious in Kenya have labored with great fidelity in the cause of the Gospel; only the Lord Jesus can adequately thank them and reward them for what has been accomplished for the implantation of the Church. Their mission now goes on side by side with their Kenyan fellow religious, who have heard the call of Christ and are working generously for the cause of the Gospel. The future of evangelization in this land will continue to owe much to the men and women religious, both autochthonous and from abroad.

I have likewise sought to draw attention to the essential nature, role and function of the priesthood in its unchanging relationship to the Eucharist, which is the summit of all evangelization (cf. *Presbyterorum ordinis,* no. 5).

In particular I wish to confirm the vital importance for the Christian people of having their priests properly trained in the word of God, in the knowledge and love of Jesus Christ and His cross. In the divine plan, the transmission of the life-giving Gospel of Christ is linked with the preparation of the priests of this generation. To provide this proper seminary training is one of our greatest responsibilities as bishops of the Church of God; it can be one of our most effective contributions to the evangelization of the world.

UNITY AND COOPERATION

8. An important element that affects every community in the Church is the unity and cooperation between bishops and priests. By reason of his ordination, the priest is "a co-worker with the order of bishop," and to live out the truth of this vocation he is called to collaborate with the bishop and to pray for him. To explain the unity of the priests with the bishop, St. Ignatius of Antioch compared it to the relationship between the strings and the lute (Letter to the Ephesians, IV).

On the part of the bishop this relationship requires that he should be close to his priests as a brother and father and friend. As such he must love them and encourage them, not only in their pastoral activities, but in their lives of personal consecration. The bishop is called to strengthen his priests in faith and to urge them to look constantly to Christ, the Good Shepherd, in order that they may realize ever more their priestly identity and dignity.

The Church renews her debt of gratitude to all the missionary and *Fidei Donum* priests who are laboring in the cause of Christ's Gospel. Their generosity is an expression of the power of Christ's grace, and their ministry is a great proof of Catholic unity.

9. In the building up of the Church, I am aware of your sustained work to build small Christian communities in which the word of God is the guideline of action and in which the Eucharist is the true center of life. The whole community of the faithful benefits from these initiatives that make it possible for people to recognize the Church in her concrete expression and human dimension as a visible sacrament of God's universal love and saving grace. It is certainly the will of Jesus Christ that the love of Christians should be manifested in such a way that individual communities exemplify the universal norm: "By this will all men know that you are my disciples, if you have love for one another" (Jn. 13:35). In your pastoral zeal you know the wise criteria laid down by Paul VI and which remain a sure guide for the effectiveness of these communities (cf. *Evangelii nuntiandi*, no. 58). At this time I would just stress the great power which those communities have to fulfill an active ecclesial role in the evangelization of Africa. May they go forward with you, their pastors, and with the priests, to communicate "the unsearchable riches of Christ" (Eph. 3:8).

10. Before concluding my words to you today, my dear brethren in Christ Jesus, I wish to emphasize once more the great need for holiness in our lives. To

exercise fruitfully our role as pastors of God's people, we must know Christ and love Him. In a word, we are called to friendship with the Lord, just as the Apostles were. Like Jesus we are the object of the Father's love and the Holy Spirit is alive in our hearts. The effectiveness of everything we do depends on our union with Jesus, on our holiness of life. There is no other way to be a worthy bishop, a good Shepherd of the flock. There is no pastoral leadership without prayer, for only in prayer is union with Jesus maintained. Only by being like Jesus, Son of Mary, who is the Mother of us all, can we fulfill our mission to the Church.

May Mary, Queen of Apostles, sustain you in holiness and love, in prayer and pastoral charity, and help you to bring Jesus to all your people, to all Kenya, to all Africa.

Praised be Jesus Christ, "the chief Shepherd" (1 Pt. 5:4) of God's people, "the Bishop and Shepherd of our souls" (1 Pt. 2:25).

A NATION THAT HONORS GOD WILL RECEIVE HIS BLESSINGS

Early on Thursday morning, May 8, John Paul II travelled by helicopter to Nairobi Airport. There, to greet him on his departure, were President Daniel Arap Moi of Kenya, together with numerous members of the government, the bishops of Kenya and the Diplomatic Corps. The Holy Father reviewed the Guard of Honor, and after a farewell address by the President of Kenya, His Holiness spoke as follows.

Dear friends,

1. After two unforgettable days, I wish to express my profound gratitude for the truly African hospitality which I have received here. The kindness, the openness and the joy of the people of Kenya have impressed me deeply. Now I know what it means to be swept up by the enthusiastic reception of an African community. More than ever, I now feel that I belong to you.

My mission now takes me to other African countries. Thank you for the strength and the joy you have given me. Thank you for having made me so much a part of your hopes and achievements, for having shared with me your determination to go on building a nation, united in its pursuit of just progress for all, faithful to its culture and traditions, strong in its belief that joint efforts will succeed.

Thank you for the strength and the joy you have given me. Thank you for having made me so much a part of your hopes and achievements, for having shared with me your determination to go on building a nation, united in its pursuit of just progress for all, faithful to its culture and traditions, strong in its belief that joint efforts will succeed.

I keep in my heart and I shall cherish forever all the moments of this wonderful visit, all the people I have met; I shall remember your music and your songs. In the prayers we shared, I have felt deep communion with you, a communion that neither distance nor time can diminish.

2. My gratitude goes to His Excellency, the President of Kenya, to all the authorities of the nation and of the city of Nairobi, to those responsible for public order during these days. I feel indebted to all the people who have contributed their time, their work and their services to create the conditions that have made this visit such a rewarding experience. A very special word of thanks to the management and staff of the *Voice of Kenya* and the local press, as well as to the foreign media, which made it possible for me to enter, with my friendship and message, the homes and villages of many who could not be here. How much I would have liked to travel across your land and to meet each one of you, to greet and bless you, and to learn firsthand about your lives and struggles. I hope that the words and the pictures which the media have brought to you were able to convey my esteem, my encouragement and my deep love for every human being in this beautiful land.

3. How can I adequately express my gratitude to my brother bishops for the moments of grace which we shared in our meetings and liturgical celebration? Moments of grace, yes, moments of divine grace; for I have seen that you have accepted the message of Christ. Your churches in the cities and villages, your schools and hospitals, the ministry of your priests, the dedication of your men and women religious, the sacramental life of your faithful, the many activities by

which the laity assume their share of the mission of evangelization—all of this bears witness to the grace of God which is at work in your midst. At this moment of departure, I wish, therefore, to thank God with you for the dynamic Church in Kenya.

4. One last thought I wish to leave with you. A nation that holds God in honor cannot fail to receive the blessings of God. Even when you meet problems, even when new difficulties arise, your trust in God will be the guarantee that you will overcome all obstacles, and that you will build a nation where unity and love reign, where brotherhood and peace flourish, where everyone works together for the future in the spirit of *Harambee*. The Creator has given every human being a dignity that is unsurpassed and that is equal for all. Your common efforts in the further development of your nation will succeed when they are inspired by respect for the fundamental God-given dignity and rights of every man, woman and child, and by the desire to create the necessary conditions so that families and all people may enjoy the dignity that is theirs as children of God.

Assuring you once again of my fraternal affection and esteem, I now take leave of Kenya.

To all of you, to all the people of Kenya, I wish to say once more: thank you all! *Asanteni sana!*

Till we meet again! *Kwa herini, kwa herini ya kuonana!*

May God bless you! *Mungu awabariki!*

May God bless all Kenya!

A VISIT OF
FRIENDSHIP AND PEACE

On his arrival at Kotoka Airport (Accra) at 10:30 a.m. on May 8, John Paul II was welcomed with a 21-gun salute. Present at the airport to receive him were the President of Ghana, Hilla Limann, and many members of the government, the Bishop of Accra, Most Reverend Dominic Kodwo Andoh, together with all the bishops of the country, and of some neighboring countries, the Pro-Nuncio, Most Reverend Giuseppe Ferraioli, other civil authorities, and the members of the Diplomatic Corps. In reply to the President's speech of welcome, the Holy Father delivered the following address.

Mr. President,

1. Your very kind welcome on my arrival in Ghana gives me much pleasure, and I am grateful for the expression of esteem which you have directed to my person in your own name and on behalf of all the people of this country. On my part I assure you and all your fellow citizens of my respect and friendship.

It is indeed a great joy to be in Ghana. Yours is a country blessed in so many ways. The rich variety of nature—low coastlands and high plains, forests and savannahs—marks the home of a people rich in linguistic and cultural expressions. At the same time they are united in a common resolve to be a nation where every man, woman and child, where every family and group feel respected in their dignity and in their desire to develop their potential to the full. My affectionate greeting goes to all the people of Ghana, wherever they may be. I greet them in the cities and the villages. I greet the authorities and the elders, the fathers and the mothers, and in a special way the young people and the children. To all I say: I have come as your friend. I have come to be with the poor, to comfort the sick, to speak a word of encouragement and hope to those who are lonely, abandoned or in pain.

2. At the moment of my arrival, I wish also to express my special joy at the opportunity to meet the beloved sons and daughters of the Catholic Church in Ghana. My warm greeting and blessing goes in the first place to my brothers in the Episcopate, the zealous and faithful pastors of the People of God. To all the clergy, Ghanaian and from abroad, to the men and women religious, and to all the laity, I say: may the joy and peace of our Lord Jesus Christ be with you on this day and always. I have come to you as Bishop of Rome and Successor of Peter, as a father and brother to rejoice with you in our common faith, hope and charity, and to celebrate with you the communion that unites us.

3. I gladly avail myself of this opportunity to express to you, Mr. President, and to all the civil authorities, my deep appreciation for the esteem and understanding which you manifest towards the Catholic Church, and which you translate into an effective collaboration in the field of education, health care and the many sectors of human advancement. The Church will always be grateful for the freedom to carry out her mission, which is religious in nature. And because she is the servant of mankind, the

Church will always be ready to cooperate in promoting justice, peace and human dignity through the active participation of her members in common efforts, and through her continuous proclamation that all human beings are created in the image and likeness of God and therefore endowed with equal dignity and rights.

At the beginning of my visit of friendship and of peace in Ghana, I invoke upon this land and its people abundant blessings from Almighty God.

EVANGELIZATION
IS THE DUTY
OF EACH OF YOU

After the official welcome at Accra Airport, on May 8, the Holy Father drove in an open car to Accra Cathedral which was packed with priests, men and women religious, seminarians, and numerous groups of the laity. He spoke to them as follows.

Venerable and dear brothers in the Episcopate,
Beloved brothers and sisters in Christ,

1. After His Ascension into heaven, our Lord Jesus Christ sent the Holy Spirit upon His Apostles and into His Church. The Holy Spirit was Jesus' first gift to those who believe. Jesus Himself had foretold the coming of the Spirit of Truth when He said: "...he will bear witness to me and you also are witnesses" (Jn. 15:26-27).

And today in Accra, in this Cathedral dedicated to the Holy Spirit, we have assembled to celebrate this mystery, this great reality of the Holy Spirit's presence in the Church—the presence of the Holy Spirit who continues to bear witness to Jesus and who stirs up new witnesses among the faithful in every generation. We rejoice to know that the Holy Spirit is with us still, that He unites the Church in her communion and in her ministry (cf. *Lumen gentium*, no. 4). We rejoice that through the power of the Holy Spirit the great life-giving message of the death and resurrection of Jesus has been passed on down the centuries, and that it has been brought to Ghana.

2. After the efforts at evangelization that had been made in previous centuries, two generous priests, Father Moreau and Father Murat, succeeded a hundred years ago in establishing the Catholic Church in this land. We praise the grace of God that brought them to the people of Ghana on that Pentecost Tuesday in 1880. And we bless the memory of all the missionaries who came subsequently, in order to bear witness to Christ through the power of His Holy Spirit. The seed of God's word, planted on Ghanaian soil, has taken root; it has grown into a large tree and has brought forth fruits of holiness for the glory of the Most Holy Trinity.

In spite of difficulties and the vicissitudes of history, the Gospel has been freely offered and freely accepted. The kingdom of God has been preached, and over and over again evangelization has reached its dynamic summit in the "clear proclamation that in Jesus Christ, the Son of God made man, who died and rose from the dead, salvation is offered to all men as a gift of God's grace and mercy" (Evangelii nuntiandi, no. 27).

The genuine charity of Christ was the motivation for one missionary congregation after another in sending its members to serve Ghana and her people, and the same genuine charity of Christ was the authentic means that bore such effective witness to the Gospel. Priests, sisters and brothers came on a mission of salvation and service. Each fulfilled his or her role. All of them together, through the power of the Holy Spirit, built up the Church by word and deed, by

prayer and sacrifice. At a later date lay mission
helpers came too, bearing witness to the universal
missionary nature of the Church. And all of these
laborers for the Gospel have served valiantly—and
with God's help they will continue to work generously, side-by-side with their Ghanaian brothers and
sisters, in the harvest of the Church.

3. But the same Holy Spirit who sustained dedicated missionaries also raised up new followers for
Christ, vivifying the local Church and calling its
members in turn to share the great task of evangelization. In the strength of the Paschal Mystery, people
accepted the word of God; they believed and were
baptized; they were nurtured on the Eucharist and
came to maturity in Christian living. Entire Christian
communities accepted the challenge to "walk in
newness of life" (Rom. 6:4) and to embrace the
challenge of the Beatitudes in their fullness. The missionary contact that had begun with human affability
and kindness led finally to the full flowering of
parishes, which became "the prime mover and the
pre-eminent place for catechesis" and "a major point
of reference for the Christian people" (Catechesi
tradendae, no. 67).

From the midst of these parishes and other Christian communities there came forth those generous
young people who would heed God's call to the
priesthood and religious life and thus, together with
the laity, fulfill their distinctive role in the one
Church of God, as "a chosen race, a royal priesthood,
a holy nation, God's own people" (1 Pt. 1:9).

In due time, Ghanaian bishops were appointed to
the pastoral leadership of the People of God. With
gratitude for what had already been achieved in the

work of evangelization, they entered into the continuity of apostolic succession. The fact that all the bishops of this country are now native Ghanaians is an eloquent testimony to the success of the work of the missionaries and to the solid implantation of the Church in this land. For this we give special thanks to God on the occasion of the celebration of this centenary.

4. The one Body of Christ was likewise to perceive its common task, its essential mission, its deepest identity, which was later so accurately expressed by Paul VI in this way: "Evangelizing is, in fact, the grace and vocation proper to the Church" (*Evangelii nuntiandi,* no. 14). Above all, the spread of the Gospel was to be linked with the witness of love, in accordance with Christ's words: "This is my commandment: that you love one another as I have loved you" (Jn. 15:12). In the observance of this commandment all Christian societies find their secure basis. And the love to which all Christians are called is itself the ladder by which every generation ascends to God and to eternal life.

5. You, my brother priests, at the service of your brothers and sisters of the laity—all of whom are called to holiness of life, all of whom are witnesses for the kingdom of God—you have the particular mission of proclaiming the Gospel in its fullest enactment, which is the celebration of the Eucharist, wherein the work of redemption is renewed. In a special way you participate in the mission of Jesus for the benefit of the whole Body of Christ; you share deeply in the burning desire of His soul: "I must proclaim the Good News of the Kingdom...for I was sent for this purpose" (Lk. 4:43). It is because of this that you have offered your

lives in celibacy and pastoral charity, to stay close to your people, to lead them in the path of salvation, building up the Church in faith and love, and in the unity and peace of Christ.

And you, men and women religious of Ghana, you are called to the service of your brothers and sisters through a multiplicity of activities motivated by love. But your greatest contribution is not what you do, but what you are. By your consecration to the Lord Jesus Himself you show that the Gospel is the full expression of all human values and that the love of Jesus Christ has first place in the pilgrim Church. Yes, your consecration is a normal expression of the full and healthy life of the Church. The maturity of ecclesial life in Ghana requires the oblation of your lives —made with generosity and lived out in persevering charity and joy. In your self-sacrifice for the sake of the kingdom of God you become ever more intimately united with all your people, sharing the hopes of their everyday lives and helping them to fulfill their deepest aspirations for eternal life.

And to you, the seminarians, I say this: Remember that you are called to be close to Christ. You are meant to be His friends, His companions, His collaborators in the mystery of salvation. To accomplish this you must pray, for only in prayer will you come to know Jesus, to love Jesus and to understand fully the needs of His people. There are many aspects to your seminary training. The good of God's people requires that you should be intellectually prepared in ecclesiastical and secular sciences, that you should understand deeply your own culture, so that you will be able to bring the word of God to it effectively. But all your studies and activities must be preceded and followed by prayer. Only through prayer will you be sustained in the love of Christ, only through prayer will your lives be relevant. When the Pope goes back to Rome, remember that he told you this: "Let us not lose sight of Jesus, who leads us in our faith and brings it to perfection" (Heb. 12:2).

Viewing the Church in Ghana, I cannot but say a special word about the family. Since it is the community in which every person is born, the family is, therefore, the foundation on which all wider communities are built. Let every family truly be a "domestic Church," a community where the Lord Jesus has the central place, where children learn to know and love God, where prayer is the binding force. In this community of love and life, the future of society is decided, and the peace of the world is built.

6. And together with your bishops and with the Church throughout the world, you, the faithful of Ghana, all the clergy, religious, seminarians and laity, are called to holiness of life, to bear witness to Christ, and to spread the Good News of salvation. To all of you belongs a share in the evangelization of the world. It is the work of the Holy Spirit; it is He who gives witness to Jesus in this our age and confirms all His members as witnesses to the Lord Jesus and to His Gospel of love. All of you in this centenary year of grace are summoned to hear Christ's words: "Let your light so shine before men that they may see your good works and give glory to your Father who is in heaven" (Mt. 5:16).

Beloved brothers and sisters, this is why I have come to Ghana: to bear witness to Christ, who was crucified and who rose from the dead, and to tell you all that we share a common mission in bringing Jesus to the world.

In our task of bearing witness to her Son, Mary the Mother of Jesus will assist us. She is the Mother of the entire Body just as she is the Mother of the Head. She is the help of Christians; she is the cause of our joy.

And to her Son, Jesus Christ, and to His eternal Father be all praise and glory in the unity of the Holy Spirit, for ever and ever. Amen.

I do not forget either the Christians of Togo and the Christians of Benin who have made a point of coming here, with their pastors, to see the Pope, to listen to his word, to pray with him and give him the testimony of their attachment. I am sorry I was not able to visit your countries and your Churches this time. I ask God to bless you, and to bless your families, especially those who are sorely tried. And be sure to tell your fellow countrymen that the Pope thinks also of your Churches and that he prays for them, supporting the ministry of your bishops who are my brothers. To each of you, my affection and my encouragement.

AFRICA HAS SOMETHING SPECIAL TO OFFER TO THE WORLD

In the early afternoon of May 8, John Paul II left the nunciature, accompanied by the Pro-Nuncio, Most Reverend Ferraioli, to visit the President of Ghana, Mr. Hilla Limann. After an address by the latter, in the course of which he again thanked the Pope for his visit to Ghana, the Holy Father replied as follows.

Mr. President,

1. I express my sincere thanks for the words which you have addressed to me on this occasion of our meeting here in the capital city of Accra. I feel deeply honored by the sentiments of esteem which you have manifested towards my person. I accept them gratefully, for I know that they are meant to honor not my person but the Head of the Catholic Church coming to the beloved nation of Ghana as a pilgrim of peace. I wish to renew once more my appreciation for the invitation which you so kindly extended to me—as did also my brother bishops—to visit your country and your people.

As I had the occasion to say when I officially announced my visit to Africa, the purpose of this journey is to perform my universal ministry and to honor personally the Church in Africa. With regard to Ghana,

I also noted that this is the year in which the Catholic Church celebrates the centenary of her implantation in this part of the great African continent. It was, therefore, important for me to express in a special way the joy of the whole Church on this happy occasion. I also hope that my visit will contribute to the promotion of authentic human progress in Ghana and in all Africa, at the service of universal brotherhood and peace. Since my arrival this morning, I have already received many kindnesses from the people of the capital city; I wish to take this opportunity to express, through your person, my joyful gratitude to everyone.

2. By my presence here today, Mr. President, I desire to honor the whole Ghanaian nation, with the wealth of its history, people, culture and achievements—in a word, with its own authentically African and Ghanaian heritage and genius, and in its own rightful place among the nations of this continent and of the world. The history of my own native country, a history made up of moments of great achievement and joy but also of periods of suffering and sadness, has made me acutely aware of how necessary it is to respect the specific values of each people and of each nation. its traditions, its aspirations and its rights among all the member nations of the world community, Africa and each of the nations that form part of it—has so much to offer to the common endeavors of all peace-loving peoples.

Too often relations between states and governments, especially when viewed in the context of political and economic development, are seen in terms of mere self-interest, of strengthening already dominant positions, and of pressure applied through aid, with the result that older and economically more advanced nations fail to see that the young countries have much more to offer than simply a share of their natural resources or being a market for the products of the industrialized nations.

3. So many of the values that are embodied in the culture of the African nations not only contribute to the building of each nation, but can add to the enrichment of other nations and peoples as well. For Africa has something distinctive to offer to the world. One of the original aspects of this continent is its diversity, but a diversity that is bound together by the undeniable unity of its culture: a vision of the world where the sacred is central, a deep awareness of the link between Creator and nature, a great respect for all life, a sense of family and of community that blossoms into an open and joyful hospitality, reverence for dialogue as a means of settling differences and sharing insights; spontaneity and the joy of living expressed in poetic language, song and dance. All these aspects manifest a culture with an all encompassing spiritual dimension. This is what makes the African culture unique. This is what binds the many people of Africa together without hampering in the least that immense richness of local expressions or the heritage of single groups and regions.

By my own origin, education and history, I have learned to value highly the power that culture has for every people. During my visit to my native Poland, I stated this conviction as follows: "Culture is an expression of man, a confirmation of humanity. Man creates culture and through culture creates himself. He creates himself with the inward effort of the spirit, of thought, will and heart. At the same time he creates culture in communion with others. Culture is an expression of communication, of shared thought and collaboration by human beings. It is born of service of the common good and becomes an essential good of human communities" (Gniezno, June 3, 1979). I therefore say to Ghana and all Africa: Preserve your culture. Let it become enriched through exchange with other cultures, but do not let your own culture die. Keep it alive, and offer it as your contribution to the world community.

Each nation brings to the family of nations its own cultural contribution, and through the legitimate expression of values and traditions there is possible a harmony among peoples that transcends partisan differences, prejudices and rivalries. Such a harmony, built on respect for and openness towards the values of others, in particular their moral and spiritual values, facilitates the possibility of concerted action on problems that extend beyond the borders of individual nations. Africa is called to bring fresh ideals and insights to a world that shows signs of fatigue and selfishness. I am convinced that you Africans can do this.

4. In stressing respect for moral and spiritual values in the sphere of international collaboration, I have touched on what I consider to be basic in all relationships in society. All structures that are created as expressions of needs and aspirations relate to the human person, for they are meant to serve each human person and the whole human community. This holds true especially of political structures and activities. In my address to the General Assembly of the United Nations last October, I said that all political activity "...comes from man, is exercised by man and is for man. And if political activity is cut off from this

fundamental relationship and finality, if it becomes in a way its own end, it loses much of its reason to exist. Even more, it can also give rise to a specific alienation. It can become extraneous to man; it can come to contradict humanity itself. In reality, what justifies the existence of any political activity is service to man, concerned and responsible attention to the essential problems and duties of his earthly existence in its social dimension and significance, on which also the good of each person depends" (no. 6).

If I have stressed this point once more, Mr. President, I have done so out of deep conviction, and because such is the teaching of the Church which God has called me to lead, namely, that no effort to achieve human advancement can succeed if the lofty dignity of every human being is not respected, defended and promoted in every situation. Such must be the motivation not only of the authorities but also of every single citizen, of all the men and women of this beautiful land who are called to work together so that everyone may be given the possibility to live a life in keeping with human dignity.

5. Yes, Mr. President, Ghana is a beautiful country, rich in cultural traditions and in the potential of its people, endowed also with natural resources, especially in the agricultural domain. It is my hope that, under the guidance of the authorities, all the citizens will loyally work together, without having to give up any of their own cultural values, but also without letting barriers arise between individuals and groups; that they will wholeheartedly and industriously work together to make the earth yield bountiful fruit. You have your cities, with ever larger concentrations of people, where problems of housing, education and

employment may arise and demand bold action to ensure that nobody is excluded from the benefits of progress. But there are also the rural areas, where most of the people still live, and where there exists a real potential for contributing to the national effort for development. Since justice demands that nobody should go hungry or lack the opportunity to achieve his or her full potential, both spiritually and materially, then society should also regard agricultural labor as ennobling, and the status and dignity of the rural population should be constantly improved.

6. I can assure you, Mr. President, that the Catholic Church stands always ready to offer her specific contribution, through the collaboration of her leaders and all her members. The Church has no political or economic designs or projects. The most efficient long-term contribution that she can make to the development of a nation is in raising the moral and ethical awareness of people with regard to the demands of justice, social love and fraternal collaboration; and in stressing the development of the whole person, to ensure that this development is not understood in the materialistic sense; in making each person aware of his or her dignity as given by God. It is also well known that, right from the beginning, the Church in Africa has encouraged and participated in concrete efforts in education, health care, literacy and many other fields. She is prepared to continue this collaboration and this commitment in accordance with her own mission and nature, while fully respecting the lawful role and authority of the state.

Mr. President, the dynamism and the virtues of its people can ensure a great future for Africa. That Ghana may fulfill her role of destiny in this continent is my fervent wish and prayer today.

CHRIST'S PRAYER FOR UNITY, OUR REASON FOR HOPE

On Thursday evening, May 8, before the Mass in Independence Square, the Holy Father met the heads of the other Christian communities in Ghana, and spoke to them as follows.

Dear friends in our Lord Jesus Christ,

1. I am deeply honored by your presence here today. It is a pleasure for me to meet distinguished representatives of my Christian brethren of Ghana. I wish to greet you all in the charity of Jesus Christ. It means so much to me to have this opportunity to tell you of my intention, and the intention of the whole Catholic Church, to pray and to work sincerely and perseveringly for the restoration of unity in faith and love among all Christians.

The commitment of the Second Vatican Council, of my predecessors and of my own pontificate is based on the desire which Christ expressed at the Last Supper in His prayer to His Father for His disciples: "...that they may all be one" (Jn. 17:21).

2. All of us realize the great value that prayer has in accomplishing what is humanly difficult or even

impossible. Jesus Himself has told us: "What is impossible with men is possible with God" (Lk. 18:24). We know how important it is to turn humbly to God, day after day, asking Him for the gift of constant conversion of life, which is so closely linked to the question of Christian unity. An occasion such as this inspires in our hearts an ever greater desire for this unity and for the means that dispose us to receive it as God's free gift. Hence this meeting inspires us to pray together, to lift up our hearts in unison to "the Father of mercies and God of all comfort" (2 Cor. 1:3).

3. At the same time as we pursue our efforts towards the goal of perfect unity, we give thanks for the great bonds that already unite us in faith in the divinity of Christ. We praise God for our common faith in Baptism as an incorporation into the death and resurrection of the Lord. We praise Him for the common love and esteem that we have for the holy Scriptures, which speak to us of Christ and His Church. And by the grace of God we are already in a position to confess together that "Jesus Christ is the Son of God" (1 Jn. 4:15) and that "there is one Mediator between God and men, the man Christ Jesus" (1 Tm. 2:5).

4. Because we believe in Christ and in "the unsearchable riches of Christ" (Eph. 3:8), we feel led by the Spirit to do everything possible to remove the divisions in faith that impair our perfect common witness to the Lord and His kingdom, so that we may better serve our neighbor and more effectively bring the Good News of salvation to the world that continues to see in us a divided Christ. And yet we know that Christ has prayed for unity, and that the Father

listens to His prayer. Christ's prayer is the reason for our hope and we know that "hope does not disappoint us" (Rom. 5:5).

It gives me great pleasure to be informed of the worthy ecumenical activities taking place in Africa. I pray that the relationship between individual Christians and the relationship between Churches and ecclesial communities will make ever greater progress in truth and love for the glory of the most Holy Trinity.

IN FRIENDSHIP
LET US PROMOTE
THE DIGNITY OF MAN

After meeting the heads of the non-Catholic Christian Churches, the Holy Father then met the leaders of the Muslim community and delivered to them the following address.

Dear friends,

At this time I wish to express my respect for the Muslim representatives present here. Through you I send my cordial greetings to the entire Muslim community throughout Ghana.

During my recent visit to Turkey, I had the occasion to speak special words of friendship for my Islamic brothers and sisters. My words were the expression of a contact that was fostered by the Second Vatican Council, and that found an important reference in the memorable message to Africa of Paul VI in 1967. On that occasion he stated: "We also wish to express our esteem for all the followers of Islam living in Africa, who have principles in common with Christianity, which gives us glad hope for an effective dialogue. Meanwhile, we express our wish that as Muslims and Christians live as neighbors, mutual respect will be constantly present in social life also, and common action to promote the acceptance and the defense of man's fundamental rights" (no. 5). Yes, mutual respect based on mutual understanding and directed to the joint service of humanity is a great contribution to the world.

Hence today I renew my own sentiments of esteem and those of the whole Catholic Church for the Muslims of Ghana and of all Africa, praying that the almighty and merciful God will grant peace and brotherhood to all the members of the human family. And may the harmony of creation and the great cause of human dignity be advanced through our fraternal solidarity and friendship.

THE FAITH
IS AFRICA'S MOST
PRECIOUS TREASURE

On the evening of May 8, the Holy Father celebrated Mass in Independence Square which was attended by President Limann and his wife. During the Mass, His Holiness administered the sacraments of Baptism and Confirmation to ten adults, and those were among the 150 to whom the Pope later distributed Communion. The following is the text of his homily.

Dear brothers and sisters in Christ,

1. A little less than ten years ago, the first Pan African and Malagasy Meeting of the Laity was held here in Accra. As Archbishop of Krakow and also consultor to the Council for the Laity, I had the opportunity at that time, although I was not present, to follow with particular attention, interest and admiration the highlights of that historic event. The lay men and women who had come from thirty-six African countries were, in effect, saying in unison: "Present!" They were telling the world: "We are present in the communion of the faithful; we are present in the mission of the Church of Christ in Africa!"

2. Ten years later, God has granted me the opportunity to come to Accra, to be with you today, to celebrate the Eucharist together with you, to speak to you, and through you to address a message to all the

Catholic laity of Africa. Today it is the Successor of Peter, it is Pope John Paul II who says: "Present!" Yes, I am present with the laity of Africa; I come as your father and as Pastor of the universal Church. I am present as your brother in the Faith! As a brother in Christ I wish to tell you how close l am to you in the infinite charity of the crucified and risen Lord. How much I love you, how much I love the laity of Africa!

As your Pastor, I wish to confirm you in your efforts to remain faithful to the Gospel, and in your mission to carry to others the Good News of our salvation. I wish to exhort you, the laity, to renew through the Eucharist the strength of your Christian commitment, to revive the joy of being members of the Body of Christ, to dedicate yourselves once again as Christians in Africa to promote the true and integral development of this great continent. Together with you I wish to give thanks to the heavenly Father, remembering "how you have shown your faith in action, worked for love and persevered through hope, in your Lord Jesus Christ" (1 Thes. 1:3).

3. Brothers and sisters in Christ, I desired to direct my words, my greeting and my blessing to the Catholic laity in every country of Africa. I want to reach beyond the boundaries of language, geography and ethnic origin, and, without distinction, to entrust each one to Christ the Lord. Thus I ask everyone of you who hears my message of fraternal solidarity and pastoral instruction to pass it on. I ask you to make my message travel from village to village, from home to home. Tell your brothers and sisters in the Faith that the Pope loves you all and embraces you in the peace of Christ.

4. This vast continent of Africa has been endowed by the Creator with many natural resources. In our own day we have witnessed how the development and use of these numerous resources have greatly served to advance the material and social progress of your individual countries. As we thank God for the benefits of this progress, we must not forget, we dare not forget, that the greatest resource and the greatest treasure entrusted to you or to anyone is the gift of Faith, the tremendous privilege of knowing Christ Jesus as Lord.

You who are lay persons in the Church, and who possess faith, the greatest of all resources—you have a unique opportunity and crucial responsibility. Through your lives in the midst of your daily activities in the world, you show the power that faith has to transform the world and to renew the family of man. Even though it is hidden and unnoticed like the leaven or the salt of the earth spoken of in the Gospel, your role as laity is indispensable for the Church in the fulfillment of her mission from Christ. This was clearly taught by the Fathers of the Second Vatican Council when they stated: "The Church is not truly established and does not fully live, nor is she a perfect sign of Christ among people, unless there exists a laity worthy of the name, working alongside the hierarchy. For the Gospel cannot be deeply imprinted on the mentality, life and work of any people without the active presence of lay people" (*Ad gentes,* no. 21).

5. The role of lay people in the mission of the Church extends in two directions: in union with your pastors and assisted by their guidance you build up the communion of the faithful; secondly, as responsible citizens you permeate with the leaven of the Gos-

pel the society in which you live, in its economic, social, political, cultural and intellectual dimensions. When you faithfully carry out these two roles as citizens of both the earthly city and the heavenly kingdom, then are the words of Christ fulfilled: "You are the salt of the earth.... You are the light of the world" (Mt. 5:13-14).

6. Today our brothers and sisters receive new life through water and the Holy Spirit (cf. Jn. 3:3ff.). By Baptism they are incorporated into the Church and reborn as children of God. They receive the greatest dignity possible for any person. As St. Peter said, they become "a chosen race, a royal priesthood, a consecrated nation, a people set apart to sing the praises of God" (1 Pt. 2:9). In the sacrament of Confirmation they are more intimately joined to the Church and endowed by the Holy Spirit with special strength (cf. *Lumen gentium*, no. 11). By means of these two great sacraments Christ summons His people, Christ summons each one of the laity to assume a share in the responsibility for building up the communion of the faithful.

As members of the laity, you are called to take an active part in the sacramental and liturgical life of the Church, especially in the Eucharistic Sacrifice. At the same time you are called to spread the Gospel actively through the practice of charity and through involvement in catechetical and missionary efforts, according to the gifts which each one of you has received (cf. 1 Cor. 12:4 ff.). In every Christian community, whether it be the "domestic Church" constituted by the family, or the parish collaborating with the priest, or the diocese united around the bishop, the laity strive, like the followers of Christ in the first century, to remain faithful to the teaching of the Apostles, faithful to fraternal service, faithful to prayer and to the celebration of the Eucharist (cf. Acts 2:42).

7. Your Christian vocation does not take you away from any of your other brothers and sisters. It does not inhibit your involvement in civic affairs nor exempt you from your responsibilities as a citizen. It does not divide you from society nor relieve you of the daily trials of life. Rather your continued engagement in secular activities and professions is truly a part of your vocation. For you are called to make the Church present and fruitful in the ordinary circumstances of life—in married and family life, in the daily conditions of earning a living, in political and civic responsibilities and in cultural, scientific and educational pursuits. No human activity is foreign to the Gospel. God wishes all of creation to be ordered to His kingdom, and it is especially to the laity that the Lord has entrusted this task.

8. The laity of the Church in Africa have a crucial role to play in meeting the urgent problems and challenges which face this vast continent. As Christian laity, the Church expects you to help shape the future of your individual countries, to contribute to their development in some particular sphere. The Church asks you to bring the influence of the Gospel and the presence of Christ into every human activity, and to seek to build a society where the dignity of each person is respected and where equality, justice and freedom are protected and promoted.

9. Today, I also wish to emphasize the need for the continuing instruction and catechesis of the laity. For only a serious spiritual and doctrinal formation in your Christian identity, together with an adequate

civic and human preparation in secular activities, can make possible that contribution of the laity to the future of Africa which is so greatly desired. In this regard we are reminded of the exhortation of St. Paul: "...we urge you and appeal to you in the Lord Jesus to make more and more progress in the kind of life you are meant to live: the life that God wants..." (1 Thes. 4:1). In order to accomplish this goal, greater knowledge is needed of the mystery of Christ. It is necessary for the laity to enter into this mystery of Christ and to be trained especially in the word of God, which leads to salvation. The Holy Spirit is calling upon the Church to pursue this path with loving tenacity and perseverance. Hence I wish to encourage the worthy initiatives on all levels which have already been undertaken in this field. May these efforts continue and increasingly equip the laity for their mission, so that with holiness of life they may meet the many needs that lie ahead, so that the whole Church in Africa will ever more effectively communicate Christ.

10. My brothers and sisters, we were reminded today by the second reading that Jesus Christ "is the living stone..." (1 Pt. 2:4). Jesus Christ is the One on whom the future of the world is built, on whom the future of every man and woman depends. At all times we must look to Him. At all times we must build on Him. Thus I repeat to you what I said to the world on Easter Sunday of this year: "Do not reject Him, you who, in whatever way and in whatever sphere, are building the world of today and of tomorrow: the world of culture and civilization, the world of economics and of politics, the world of science and information. You who are building the world of peace, ...do not refuse Christ: He is the cornerstone!"

11. With the words of the apostle Peter, I invite you to "set yourselves close to him so that you too... may be living stones making a spiritual house" (1 Pt. 2:4f.), building up the Church in Africa, advancing the kingdom of God on earth.

It is in this spirit that we pray to our heavenly Father: "Thy Kingdom come, thy will be done on earth as it is in heaven." Amen.

Dear brothers and sisters of Togo and Benin,

Thank you for having come in such large numbers, for having walked for such a long time to meet the Vicar of Christ. I call upon you, too, to remain firm in the Faith, and very united among yourselves. The Lord is faithful; He will not abandon you if you give Him your trust. He will make you strong so that you may bear witness to your Faith, not only in church, but in the acts of your everyday life, where it is continually necessary to choose to live according to truth, according to purity, according to the charity of the Gospel. Continue to acquire knowledge about the truths of the Faith. Approach with joy the sacraments of Penance and the Eucharist, remembering that it is the Lord who forgives you, who nourishes you, who gives you His grace. It is the visible sign of His invisible presence. As the risen Christ said: "Peace be with you." "Do not be afraid." May the Lord bless you.

A PRAYER TO MARY, MOTHER OF THE CHURCH

At the conclusion of the Mass in Independence Square on May 8, the Holy Father recited the following prayer in which he entrusted to Mary the Church in Ghana and in Africa.

On this day of joy as we gather in your presence, O Mary, Mother of Jesus and Mother of His Church, we are mindful of the role you played in the evangelization of this land. We are mindful of how—in the beginning—the missionaries came with the power of Christ's Gospel and committed the success of their work to you.

As Mother of Divine Grace you were with the missionaries in all their efforts, and you were with Mother Church, of whom you are the type, the model and the supreme expression, in bringing Christ into Africa.

And as the Mother of the Church you presided over all the activities of evangelization and over the implantation of the Gospel in the hearts of the faithful. You sustained the missionaries in hope and you gave joy to every new community that was born of the Church's evangelizing activity.

You were there, with your intercession and your prayers, as the first grace of Baptism developed, and as those who had new life in Christ your Son came to a full appreciation of their sacramental life and Christian calling.

And you are here today as the Christian family gathers to celebrate the Gospel, to recall the mighty works of God, and to commit itself to the continued evangelization of this land and continent "so that the word of the Lord may speed on and triumph" (2 Thes. 3:11).

We ask you, Mary, to help us to fulfill this mission which your Son has given to His Church and which, in this generation, falls to us. Mindful of your role as Help of Christians, we entrust ourselves to you in the work of carrying the Gospel ever deeper into the hearts and lives of all the people. We entrust to you our missionary mandate and commit our cause totally to your prayers.

And, as Pastor of the universal Church, Vicar of your Son, I, John Paul II, through you, O Mary, entrust the whole Church in Ghana and in all Africa to Christ our Lord. Through you I present to Christ, the Savior, the destiny of Africa, praying that His love and justice will touch the hearts of every man, woman and child of this continent.

Mary, I entrust all this to Christ through you, and I entrust all this to you for Christ, your Son. I do it at a moment when I am closely united with my brother bishops in celebrating the Gospel as "the power of salvation to all who believe" (Rom. 1:16). I do it now, at this special moment when my brothers are so close to me in the exercise of our common responsibility for the Church in Africa. Accept, O Mary, this offering from all of us, and from all God's people, and present it to your Son. Present Him a Church "holy and without blemish" (Eph. 5:27).

Be mindful, O Mother, of all who make up the Church in Africa. Assist the bishops and their priests to be ever faithful to the word of God. Help sanctify the religious and the seminarians. Intercede so that the love of your Son will penetrate into all families, so that it will console all those in pain and suffering, all those in need and want. Look kindly upon the catechists and all who fulfill a special role of evangelization and Catholic education for the glory of your Son. Accept this, our loving consecration, and confirm us in the Gospel of your Son.

As we express our deepest gratitude to you for a century of your maternal care, we are strong in the conviction that the Holy Spirit is still overshadowing you, so that in Africa you may bring forth Christ in every generation.

To Jesus Christ your Son, with the Father, in the unity of the Holy Spirit be praise and thanksgiving for ever and ever. Amen.

CATECHESIS CONTINUES ACTIVITY OF JESUS, THE TEACHER

Early on Friday morning, May 9, the Holy Father left Bamboko Airport by plane for Kumasi. Shortly after noon he celebrated Mass in the stadium for catechists. After the Gospel, he preached the following homily.

Dear brothers and sisters,

1. Today is a day of great joy, and I have looked forward to this day for a long time. I have wanted to come and tell the catechists how much I love them, how much the Church needs them. Today is also a day of deep meaning because Jesus Christ, the Son of God, the Lord of history, the Savior of the world, is present in our midst. Through His holy Gospel He speaks to us in the words that He once addressed to His disciples: "All authority in heaven and on earth has been given to me. Go therefore and make disciples of all nations, baptizing them in the name of the Father and of the Son and of the Holy Spirit, teaching them to observe all that I have commanded you; and lo, I am with you always..." (Mt. 28:19).

2. This command and this promise of Jesus were the inspiration for the evangelization of Ghana and all Africa, and they have shaped the lives of all who have collaborated in the cause of the Gospel. In a special way these words have been taken to heart by numerous catechists over the past century. And today I wish to manifest the Church's profound esteem for these devoted workers in the service of the Gospel. I express the gratitude of the whole Catholic Church to these catechists who are here today, to their predecessors in the Faith, and to their fellow catechists throughout the continent of Africa—gratitude for helping to make disciples for Christ, for helping people to believe that Jesus is the Son of God, for helping to instruct their brothers and sisters in His life, and thus to build up His Body, the Church. This catechizing activity has been accomplished by word and example; and the dedication of countless catechists and their deep attachment to the person of Jesus Christ remain a chapter of glory in the history of this land and this continent.

3. The Church recognizes in these catechists people called to exercise a particular ecclesial role, a special sharing in the responsibility for the advancement of the Gospel. She sees them as witnesses of faith, servants of Jesus Christ and His Church, effective collaborators in the mission of establishing, developing and fostering the life of the Christian community. In the history of evangelization many of these catechists have in fact been teachers of religion, leaders in their communities, zealous lay missionaries, and examples of faith. They have stood faithfully by the missionaries and the local clergy, supporting their ministry while fulfilling their own distinctive tasks. The cate-

chists have rendered many services connected with communicating Christ, implanting the Church and bringing the transforming and regenerative power of the Gospel ever more into the lives of their brothers and sisters. They have assisted people in many human needs and contributed to development and progress.

4. In all this they have explicitly made known the name and person of Jesus Christ, His teaching, His life, His promises and His kingdom. The communities that they have helped to build up were based on the same elements as were found in the early Church: on the Apostles' teaching and fellowship, on the Eucharist and prayer (cf. Acts 2:42). Thus the Lordship of Christ was fostered in one community after another, from one generation to the next. Through their generous work, Christ's command is continually fulfilled and His promise verified.

5. The Church is not only grateful for what has been accomplished by the catechists in the past, but she is confident for the future. Despite new conditions, new requirements and new obstacles, the relevance of this great apostolate will remain undiminished, because there will always be a need to develop an initial faith and to lead people to the fullness of Christian life. An increased realization of the dignity and importance of the role of the catechist is but one consequence of the Second Vatican Council's insistence on the fact that the whole Church shares responsibility for the Gospel. Only with the collaboration of her catechists will the Church be able to fulfill adequately the challenge that I described in my Apostolic Exhortation on Catechesis in Our Time: "As the twentieth century draws to a close, the Church is bidden by God and by events—each of them a call from Him—to renew her

trust in catechetical activity as a prime aspect of her mission. She is bidden to offer catechesis her best resources in people and energy, without sparing effort, toil or material means, in order to organize it better and to train qualified personnel. This is no mere human calculation; it is an attitude of faith" (*Catechesi tradendae*, no. 15).

6. The Sacred Congregation for the Evangelization of Peoples, numerous bishops and episcopal conferences have placed strong emphasis on the formation of catechists, and in this they are worthy of the highest praise. The destiny of the Church in Africa is undoubtedly linked with the success of this initiative. I wish, therefore, to give full encouragement to this wonderful work. The future of catechetical activity will depend on sound programs of preparation, where there is ever greater instruction for the catechists, where priority is given to the spiritual and doctrinal formation of the catechists, and where catechists are able to experience in some measure the authentic sense of Christian community that they are called upon to build.

The instruments of catechesis must also be given due attention, including effective catechetical materials that take into account the need for the incarnation of the Gospel in determined local cultures. Moreover, the whole Church must feel committed to help face the difficulties and problems inherent in sustaining catechetical programs. In a special way, the whole community of the Church must show its esteem for the important vocation of catechists, who must feel supported by their brothers and sisters.

7. Above all, to ensure the success of all catechetical activity, the aim of catechesis itself must

remain crystal clear: catechesis is a work of faith that is far beyond any technique; it is a commitment of Christ's Church. Its primary and essential object is the mystery of Christ; its definitive aim is to put people in communion with Jesus Christ (cf. *Catechesi tradendae*, no. 5). Through catechesis the activity of Jesus the Teacher goes on. He elicits from His brethren an adherence to His Person, and through His word and sacraments He leads them to His Father and to the fullness of life in the most Holy Trinity.

8. Gathered here today to celebrate the Eucharistic Sacrifice, we express our trust in the power of the Holy Spirit to continue to raise up and sustain, for the glory of God's kingdom, new generations of catechists, who will faithfully transmit the Good News of salvation and bear witness to Christ and Him crucified.

9. Today the Church offers to the catechists the sign of Christ's love, the great symbol of Redemption: the cross of the Savior. For catechists of every age the cross is the credential of authenticity and the measure of success. The message of the cross is truly "the power of God" (1 Cor. 1:18).

Dear catechists, dear brothers and sisters: in fulfilling your role, in communicating Christ, remember the words of a pioneer catechist of the fourth century, St. Cyril of Jerusalem. "The Catholic Church is proud of all Christ's actions, but her greatest boast is the cross" (*Cat.* no. 13).

With this cross, with the crucifix that you receive today as a sign of your mission in the Church, go forward confidently and joyfully. And remember too that Mary is always standing next to Jesus, close to you; she is always by the cross. She will lead you safely to the victory of the resurrection; and she will help you to communicate to others the Paschal Mystery of her Son.

Beloved catechists of Ghana and all Africa: Christ calls you to His service; the Church sends you forth. The Pope blesses you, and he commends you to the Queen of heaven. Amen.

Pope John Paul II tries his hand at a set of native drums.

THE CATECHISTS
OF AFRICA
ARE THE HERALDS
OF PEACE

At the end of the Mass at Kumasi on May 9, the Holy Father conferred the John XXIII International Peace Prize on six catechists—one from each country visited by the Pope during his African pilgrimage. Unfortunately, due to a series of coincidences, the two catechists from Zaire and the People's Republic of the Congo did not arrive at Kumasi in time for the conferring of the prize. During the ceremony of the conferring the Holy Father delivered the following address.

Peace to all of you here present!
Peace to Africa and the world!
Dear friends,

It is with great pleasure that I accept and approve the proposal of the John XXIII International Peace Prize Foundation to honor the six catechists here present, who have been chosen to receive the John XXIII International Peace Prize.

This award is linked to the figure of John XXIII. In his Encyclical *Pacem in terris* he set forth in broad outline the principles on which a peaceful order of relations must be built: "founded on truth, built up on justice, nurtured and animated by charity, and brought into effect under the auspices of freedom" (*Pacem in terris*, no. 5). In the example of his life he showed that peace must always be the first concern of all human beings, whatever their function or social condition may be. By establishing an award for peace he wished to encourage every initiative that has as its goal the fostering of fraternal relations between individuals and peoples.

The objective of the awarding of this prize, according to the intention of its founder, is to give solemn recognition to the merits of persons or institutions who have made an outstanding contribution to peace on earth. After Mother Teresa of Calcutta and the United Nations Educational, Scientific and Cultural Organization (UNESCO), the Foundation now proposes as recipients of the Prize six individuals who represent a group of thousands upon thousands of faithful servants who effectively uphold the ideal of peace. These are the catechists of Africa.

Chosen from among their people, the catechists of Africa have unceasingly worked for their people. Accepting hardship and personal sacrifice, they have given without reserve the best of themselves to their brothers and sisters. Faithful believers in the teachings of Christ, they have been instrumental in helping their fellow Africans to revere God, the Father of all, to respect the dignity of every person, to love their fellow human beings, and to foster reconciliation and pardon. Often untiring travelers, and always faithful servants of the local community, they have helped to break down divisive barriers and to assist their brothers and sisters in need. Some of the catechists in particularly trying circumstances have endured physical or moral hardship and suffering in order to bear witness to religious freedom or to defend it. They have thus testified by their own lives that the relationship of man to God and the freedom to profess this relationship publicly are at the very foundation of peace. Yes, the catechists of Africa have truly been, and are, heralds of peace!

Trusting that this motivation will be admired by all men and women of good will in Africa and in the whole world, on this the ninth day of May, 1980, in the city of Kumasi, in the nation of Ghana, I, John Paul II, bestow on the catechists here present the honor of the John XXIII International Peace Prize, for the glory of the heavenly Father from whom all good things come (cf. Jas. 1:17), in memory of my predecessor John XXIII, and as an encouragement to all, especially the youth of Africa, that they may persevere in the ways of peace.

The peace of the Lord be with you always!

ORIGINAL EXPRESSIONS OF FAITH DERIVING FROM DIFFERENT CULTURES

On May 9, after the awarding of the John XXIII International Peace Prize, John Paul II received the homage of the King of the Ashanti, Otombuo Opoku Ware II Asantehene, and of his entire court. Later he went to the minor seminary of Kumasi about 1:30, where he met the bishops of Ghana and delivered the following address.

Venerable and dear brothers in our Lord Jesus Christ,

1. My coming among you today is intimately linked to Christ and His Gospel. I have come to share with you and the whole Catholic Church in Ghana the joy of your centenary celebrations. Together we praise the grace of God that initiated and sustained the full process of evangelization in your midst: missionaries were sent to preach the word of God to your ancestors; these people heard the message of salvation; they believed and called upon Him in whom they put their faith, confessing with their lips that Jesus is Lord and believing in their hearts that God raised Him from the dead (cf. Rom. 10:9). Through the sacraments your people came to share in the death and resurrection of Christ and were grafted into

the vital organic unity of the Church. Generous missionary congregations realized the need for workers in the vineyard of the Lord, and conversions were made through divine grace. In 1935, the first two Ghanaian priests were ordained, and in 1950, the hierarchy was established. And today there are two metropolitan sees and seven dioceses. The Church is thus fully implanted in Ghana, but her mission is not yet complete. By reason of their full membership in the Body of Christ, Ghanaian Catholics are called to be workers for evangelization in a Church that is, by her nature, missionary in her totality (cf. *Ad gentes*, no. 35). Only in accepting their own responsibility for the spread of the Gospel do the Catholic people fulfill the vocation to which they are called.

SPIRIT OF CATHOLIC UNITY

2. This great ecclesial reality of an evangelized and evangelizing Church in Ghana, which explains the depth of our joy today, is celebrated in a spirit of Catholic unity. It is a unity that belongs to your individual local Churches: priests, religious and laity united with the bishop, who presides in love and service, and who is called to be an example to everyone in humility and holiness of life. This Catholic unity is further manifested in the solidarity of the sons and daughters of this country with the missionaries, who continue to give their fraternal service—deeply appreciated and very necessary—for the benefit of each local Church, under the direction of an autochthonous pastor.

The unity of this centenary celebration is likewise the unity of all the bishops of this country with the entire college of bishops united with the successor of Peter, and intent on proclaiming the one Gospel of Christ and ensuring the enactment of Catholic unity in the Eucharistic Sacrifice, which is at one and the same time the expression of the worship of an individual community and of the universal Church. This is a special motive of joy for me as I celebrate with you your centenary celebrations. I wish to assure you of my gratitude for everything you have done, as pastors of local Churches, to preserve unity, you who likewise share responsibility for the Church throughout the world. Your fidelity and zeal are themselves an effective contribution to the spread of the kingdom.

INCULTURATION OF THE GOSPEL

3. Be assured that all your efforts to proclaim the Gospel directly and indirectly are a great credit to the Church. On my part I am close to you in all the joys and disappointments, the challenges and hopes of your ministry of the word, and in your sacramental ministry. I am close to you in all your concrete pastoral initiatives, in everything that brings the message of salvation into the lives of the people. A reflection on the essential and constitutional patrimony of the Catholic Faith, which is identical for all people of all places and times, is a great help to the pastors of the Church as they ponder the requirements of the "inculturation" of the Gospel in the life of the people. You are familiar with what Paul VI called "the task of assimilating the essence of the Gospel message and of transposing it, without the slightest betrayal of its essential truth, into the language that these particular people understand"

(*Evangelii nuntiandi,* no. 63). He singled out as subject to certain adaptations the areas of liturgical expression, catechesis, theological formulation, secondary ecclesial structures, and ministries. As local pastors you are eminently fitted for this work, because you are sons of the people to whom you are sent with the message of faith; in addition, in your episcopal ordination you have received the same "governing Spirit" who was communicated to Jesus and by Him to His Apostles for the building up of His Church. This work is of God. It is an activity of the living Body of Christ; it is a requirement of the Church as a truly universal means of salvation.

And so with serenity and confidence and with profound openness towards the universal Church, the bishops must carry on the task of inculturation of the Gospel for the good of each people, precisely so that Christ may be communicated to every man, woman and child. In this process, cultures themselves must be uplifted, transformed and permeated by Christ's original message of divine truth, without harming what is noble in them. Hence worthy African traditions are to be preserved. Moreover, in accordance with the full truth of the Gospels and in harmony with the magisterium of the Church, living and dynamic African Christian traditions are to be consolidated.

As you pursue this work in close union with the Apostolic See and the entire Church, you are strengthened in knowing that the responsibility for this activity is shared also by your brother bishops throughout the world. This is an important consequence of the doctrine of collegiality, in which every bishop shares responsibility for the rest of the

Church; by the same token, his own Church in which by divine right he exercises ordinary jurisdiction is also the object of a common episcopal responsibility in the two dimensions of making the Gospel incarnate in the local Church: 1) preserving unaltered the content of the Catholic Faith and maintaining ecclesial unity throughout the world; and 2) bringing forth from cultures original expressions of Christian life, celebration and thought, whereby the Gospel is brought into the heart of peoples and their cultures.

Venerable brothers, your people are called to the highest ideals and to the most lofty virtues. In this saving power Christ is present in the humanity of Africa, or as I have already said during my visit to this continent: "Christ, in the members of His Body, is Himself African."

FOSTER VOCATIONS

4. There are many individual aspects of your apostolate that are worthy of special mention and support. Of particular importance for the future of your local Churches is every effort that is made to foster vocations to the priesthood and religious life. The faithful are called to share responsibility for this dimension of the Church; they exercise this responsibility by esteem and respect for these vocations and by helping to create the sound spiritual atmosphere of Christian families and other communities in which a vocation can develop and can persevere. Vigilance is needed on the part of priests to detect the signs of a vocation. Above all, the effectiveness of all these human efforts is linked to the prayer of the Church and to the witness of priests and religious.

When your people see priests and religious living a life of authentic celibacy in intimacy with Christ, when they perceive the human fulfillment that comes from the total giving of oneself in the service of the Gospel, when they observe the joy that comes from bearing witness to Christ—then the priesthood and the religious life are attractive vocations for youth, who will then more easily hear Christ's personal invitation to them: Come, follow Me!

Another dimension that I would like to stress in this regard is the missionary dimension of your Church with regard to the needs of sister Churches on the African continent and beyond. I understand your concern about the need of your own Christian communities to be guided by priests chosen by God from among their own people. But the Church is missionary by nature. And let us always remember that God will never fail to bless those who give with generosity. The promotion of missionary vocations—either in the framework of the *Fidei donum* formula or through membership in international missionary societies— will in its turn incite the local community to greater confidence in God's grace and to a deeper awareness of faith. It will open hearts to God's love.

WOMEN IN THE CHURCH

5. I know that you are committed to the advancement of the role of women in the Church and in society. It is an expression of this same concern to promote women's vocations to the religious life. African women have willingly been bearers of life and guardians of family values. Similarly, the consecration of women in radical self-giving to the Lord in chastity,

obedience, and poverty constitutes an important way of bringing to your local Churches the life of Christ and an awareness of a larger human community and a divine communion. This requires of course that they be carefully formed, theologically and spiritually, so that they can assume their rightful place as workers for evangelization, exemplifying the true meaning of religious life in an African context, and thus enriching the whole Church.

YOUR SPECIAL MISSION

6. In the beautiful celebration in the stadium and by honoring the catechists, I have already expressed my esteem for them, as well as my thoughts on the value of this institution for the Church—its value for the future as for the past. I shall not expand this point further except to repeat the words I addressed to the bishops in my apostolic exhortation: "Dearly beloved brothers, you have here a special mission within your Churches: you are beyond all others the ones primarily responsible for catechesis. ...You can be sure that if catechesis is done well in your local Churches, everything else will be easier to do" (*Catechesi tradendae*, no. 63).

MEDIA OPPORTUNITIES

7. In this context I would draw attention to a special aspect of the apostolate: the question of the media. All over the world the communications media offer special opportunities for the spread of the Gospel and for the useful presentation of information from the viewpoint of charity and truth. Ghana and all Africa are no exception. Through your interest and

When your people see priests and religious living a life of authentic celibacy in intimacy with Christ, when they perceive the human fulfillment that comes from the total giving of oneself in the service of the Gospel, when they observe the joy that comes from bearing witness to Christ —then the priesthood and the religious life are attractive vocations for youth, who will then more easily hear Christ's personal invitation to them: Come, follow Me!

collaboration may the mass media truly perform their providential role at the service of humanity. For the Church these are splendid instruments to preach the message of Christ, as from the housetops (cf. Mt. 10:27). Be assured of my admiration for your efforts to utilize these means as often as possible. In this regard, you deserve great praise for setting up *The Standard,* which I pray will ever assist you in the task of evangelization.

WORK OF DEVELOPMENT

8. Linked with evangelization is the work of development, which must continue to go on in Africa. In imitation of Christ, who was sensitive to the uplifting of humanity in all its aspects, the Church works for the total well-being of man. The laity have a distinctive part to play in the area of development; they have also been given a special charism in order to bring the presence of the serving Christ into all areas of human affairs. The human being asking to be uplifted from poverty and want is the same person in need of redemption and eternal life. Likewise the entire Church must serve development by offering to the world her total vision of man, and by proclaiming ceaselessly the pre-eminence of spiritual values (cf. Address to the United Nations, October 2, 1979, no. 14). Providence has endowed your people with an innate understanding of this fact. Only by being sensitive to every need can the Church continue to render her many services, but one of her most effective contributions to progress will be to point out that the goal of personal development is found only in a transcendent humanism, which is attained by union with Christ (cf. *Populorum progressio,* no. 16).

LEAD BY EXAMPLE

9. There are many other aspects to our pastoral ministry and we cannot now speak about all of them. But as bishops let us call our people constantly to conversion of life, and by our example let us lead the way. The importance of the sacraments of Penance or Reconciliation and of the Eucharist cannot be over-emphasized. In both of these we are the ministers of God's mercy and His love. At the same time, as bishops we are called to bear a consistent witness to Christ the High Priest and Pontiff of salvation by being signs of holiness in His Church. A difficult task? Yes, brothers. But this is our vocation, and the Holy Spirit is upon us. Moreover, the effectiveness of our pastoral ministry depends on our holiness of life. Let us not be afraid, for the Mother of Jesus is with us. She is in our midst today and always. And we are strong through her prayers and safe in her care. *Regina Caeli laetare, alleluia!*

THROUGH OUR MINISTRY THE GIFT OF SALVATION

After his meeting with the bishops of Ghana, the Holy Father then met, in the seminary chapel, the visiting bishops from the neighboring countries. Among these was Cardinal Ignatius Dominic Ekandem, Archbishop of Ikot Ekpene (Nigeria). The Pope addressed them as follows:

My dear brother bishops,

1. It is a joy for me to be with you today. You have come from your respective dioceses, and I from Rome, and all of us have assembled here in the name of our Lord Jesus Christ. We truly feel His presence in our midst. Indeed, we have come to Ghana to celebrate His Gospel, to celebrate the centenary of the implantation of His Church in this region. Our thoughts are turned therefore to the great reality of evangelization. This is very natural for us, since we are the successors of the Twelve and, like them, are called to be servants of the Gospel, proclaiming Jesus Christ and His message of Redemption.

Our ministry makes many demands on us. The effective preaching of the Gospel, which is "the power of God for salvation to everyone who has faith" (Rom. 1:16), requires our constant effort in going out to the

People of God with a deep understanding of their culture, their pastoral needs and the pressures put upon them by the modern world. Evangelization requires farsighted planning on our part, the utilization of the proper means and the full collaboration of the local Churches. But I wish to limit myself today to a brief consideration on the content of evangelization, on what Paul VI called its "foundation and center" and what he described as being "a clear proclamation that in Jesus Christ, the Son of God made man, who died and rose from the dead, salvation is offered to all men as a gift of God's grace and mercy" (*Evangelii nuntiandi*, no. 38).

2. As bishops we must reflect not only on our duty, but also on the immense privilege it is to bring this fundamental message of salvation to the people. This is the nature of our divine mission, this explains our human fulfillment: to proclaim salvation in Jesus Christ. What a wonderful ministry it is to preach a Gospel of redemption in Jesus, to explain to our people how they have been chosen by God the Father to live in Christ Jesus, how the Father "rescued us from the power of darkness and brought us into the kingdom of his beloved Son. Through him we have redemption, the forgiveness of our sins" (Col. 1:14).

3. Christ's gift of salvation gives rise to our sacramental ministry and to all our efforts to build up the communion of the Church, a redeemed community living the new life of Christ. Because our message is the message of salvation, it is also a constant invitation to our people to respond to God's gift, to live a life worthy of the calling that they have received (cf. Eph. 4:1). The message of salvation brings with it an invitation to our people to praise God for His goodness, to

rejoice in His gift, to forgive others just as they themselves have been forgiven, and to love others just as they themselves have been loved.

God gives this great gift of salvation through His Church, through our ministry. In accordance with God's will, let us go forward in our evangelizing activities, announcing with perseverance the Good News of salvation, and proclaiming explicitly: "It is in Christ and through his blood that we have been redeemed and our sins forgiven, so immeasurably generous is God's favor to us." This proclamation is fundamental to all our moral doctrine, to our social teaching, to our pastoral concern for the poor. It is the basis of our pastoral ministry to the needy, the suffering and those in prison. It is fundamental to everything we do, to our whole episcopal ministry.

Dear brothers: Praised be Jesus Christ, who has called us to proclaim His salvation and who sustains us by His love. May He keep us strong in joy, persevering in prayer together with His Mother Mary, and united to the end.

Praised be Jesus Christ.

TO BE LIKE JESUS THE PRIEST

On Friday afternoon, May 9, the Holy Father delivered the following address to 150 seminarians assembled in the seminary garden. Later he went to Kumasi Airport and returned to Accra by plane.

Dear seminarians,

1. I am always happy to talk to young men who are preparing for the priesthood. Today I am particularly happy to meet you in your own country.

2. Even though you are young, you are able by your lives to teach the world a great lesson. What is this lesson? It is the lesson of *faith*. Your lives show that you believe in Jesus Christ and that you want to follow Him. You accept Him as God, as the Son of God who took on a human nature, who became man, and who became your brother and mine. You believe that He died on the cross, and became your Savior and mine. And you believe that He rose from the dead, and made it possible for you and me and everybody to live forever. This is the Jesus whom you have come to know and love, the Jesus in whom you have put your faith.

3. Yes, you believe in the Person of Jesus, and you also believe that His grace is strong—that it can overcome sin. You believe that Jesus can give you the grace to follow Him, to come after Him, to be like

Him. And that is what you want to do: to be like Jesus the priest—to spread the Good News that Jesus brought, to tell the world about salvation, and to give people the bread of eternal life.

4. So faith in Jesus is important for you now and in the future. Your life as a seminarian depends on faith; faith is the foundation of the life of every priest. Faith means accepting Jesus into your lives, taking His message into your hearts, obeying His commandments. It also means being filled with the joy and love of Jesus. And the more this happens, the more you will be able to show Jesus to the world—the Jesus who lives in you and who wants to work through you.

When you live by faith and follow Christ's commandments, you are able to give a dynamic example to other young people. You are able to show by your lives and by the example of your Christian joy that Jesus' love is important—important for you in your vocation, and important for all your brothers and sisters who are trying to discover the fullness of their humanity. Living in this way, you can see that you have already begun the task of communicating Christ, of bringing Him to your friends and to the other youth of Ghana.

5. At the same time your fidelity to Christ, your courage to say *yes* to your special vocation, your faith in the power of Jesus to sustain you in His love during your whole life is a strong support for other young people of your age who have heard the call of the Good Shepherd and want to follow it faithfully. You know how much your country and all Africa needs priests—workers in the Lord's harvest. Remember the words of Jesus: ''...lift up your eyes, and see how the fields are white for the harvest'' (Jn. 4:35). *And*

pray for vocations, pray for perseverance in your own vocation, pray that the Church in Africa will have the strength and fervor to supply the priests that Christ needs to preach His Gospel and to carry His message of salvation throughout this continent.

6. Dear seminarians: stay close to Jesus through prayer and the Holy Eucharist. And so by the way you live, let everybody know that you really do have faith, that you really believe in our Lord Jesus Christ.

And stay close also to our Blessed Mother Mary and to her Immaculate Heart. When Mary said *yes* to the angel, the mystery of Redemption took shape beneath her heart. This pure heart of Mary was the inspiration for many of the missionaries who brought the word of God to the African people. And for the Church today this heart of Mary continues to express the mystery of the Mother in Redemption (cf. *Redemptor hominis,* no. 22).

In the name of Jesus, I bless you all. And I commend you and your families and friends to Mary, who is the Mother of us all.

ONLY A TRULY HUMAN WORLD CAN BE STRONG AND PEACEFUL

On his return to the Nunciature in Accra on Friday evening, May 9, John Paul II received the members of the Diplomatic Corps accredited to the Republic of Ghana. After an address by their Doyen, the Ambassador of the Ivory Coast, the Holy Father spoke to them as follows.

Your Excellencies,
Ladies and gentlemen,

1. Meeting the heads of Mission and the Diplomatic Corps in this capital city of Accra gives me great pleasure. I feel honored by the courtesy which you extend to me by your presence here, and I wish to thank His Excellency, the Dean, and the Diplomatic Corps for the kindness shown me. After a week in Africa—such a short time yet one filled with indelible memories—I wish to share with you a few of the impressions and concerns which I have experienced in my first contact with the African continent.

When I came to Africa at the invitation of the civil authorities and of my brother bishops, I did so as the head of the Catholic Church. But I also came as a humble servant entrusted by God's providence with a mission to all mankind: the mission of proclaiming the dignity and fundamental equality of all human beings and their right to live in a world of justice and peace, of brotherhood and solidarity.

2. The purpose of my journey is, in the first place, religious and spiritual. I wish to confirm my brother bishops, the clergy, religious and laity in their faith in God the Creator and Father, and in the one Lord Jesus Christ. I wish also to celebrate the common faith and charity that unites us, to rejoice with them in the communion that binds us all together in one family, in the Mystical Body of Christ. I bring to them the greeting of the Apostle Paul: "All the Churches of Christ greet you" (Rom. 16:16). My coming to the Church in Africa is meant to be a witnessing to the universality of the Church and a rejoicing in the richness of its various expressions. For "in the mind of the Lord, the Church is universal by vocation and mission, but when she puts down her roots in a variety of cultural, social and human terrains, she takes on different external expressions and appearances in each part of the world" (*Evangelii nuntiandi*, no. 62).

By virtue of her mission and nature, the Church is not tied to any given form of culture, or to any political, economic, or social system. By her very universality, she can enter into communion with various cultures and realities, creating a mutual enrichment (cf. *Gaudium et spes*, no. 58). By virtue of that same universality she can also create a very close bond between diverse human communities and nations, provided that they acknowledge and respect her right to freedom in the carrying out of her specific mission.

3. Here I feel that we have a common mission. As individual diplomats you are mandated to represent and foster the interests of your respective states. As a group, you are also bearers of a mission that transcends regional and national boundaries, for it is also

part of your mission to foster better understanding among people, closer collaboration on a worldwide scale—in a word, to be the promoters of the unity of the whole world. It is the greatness of your task to be the builders of international peace and justice in an age that is a witness at the same time to growing interdependence and to the stronger affirmation of each nation's own identity and dignity. Yours is a noble, even if difficult, task: while serving your own nation, you are also the artisans of the common good of the whole human family, working together to save the earth for humanity, to ensure that the world's riches reach all human beings, including our brothers and sisters who are now excluded by social injustice. As diplomats, you are involved in the establishing of a new order of international relations based on the fundamental and inescapable demands of justice and peace. And those of you here present who represent international or regional organizations are also engaged—though by different methods and means—in the process of concentrating the efforts of all nations on building a just and fraternal world.

4. I am sure that your experience in different parts of the world as diplomats or international servants, together with the familiarity that you have acquired of the African scene, has created in you a keen awareness of the major problems that face humanity today—especially the global issues arising from the economic and social disparities that exist in the world community. When I spoke to the Thirty-fourth General Assembly of the United Nations Organization, I was able to draw attention to this fundamental problem when I said: "It is no secret that the abyss separating the minority of the excessively rich from

the multitude of the destitute is a very grave symptom in the life of any society. This must also be said with even greater insistence with regard to the abyss separating countries and regions of the earth'' (no. 18).

It is a great contradiction of our day and age that these glaring disparities can exist, and that the gap which separates rich and poor countries, or rich and poor continents, is still widening rather than decreasing, at a time when peoples have become more aware than ever before of their interdependence. Is it not a sad fact that the efforts—so worthwhile in themselves—of the international organizations and of the different nations in bilateral and multilateral initiatives have not been able to draw the poorer countries out of the vicious circle of poverty and underdevelopment? Why is it then that these efforts have not produced better and more lasting results? Why have they not given hope to the developing countries—the hope that their own resources, fraternal aid, and especially the hard work of their people would enable them to chart their own development course and satisfy their essential needs?

5. I am convinced that we all agree that the only way to eliminate inequalities is through the coordinated cooperation of all the countries in a spirit of true partnership. In this context, much has been said and written about the importance of revitalizing what has been called the North-South dialogue. Without accepting an over-simplified view of a world divided into a rich North and a poor South, one must concede that this distinction has a certain foundation in fact, since Northern countries generally control the world's industry and economy. The Holy See cannot but encourage every initiative that aims at looking honestly

at this situation, and at achieving an agreement among all parties on the necessary action to be taken. But at the same time, I would ask the question: Why is it that such initiatives encounter such difficulty and fail to achieve tangible and lasting results? The answer is to be found primarily, not in the economic or monetary spheres, but in an area of much deeper dimensions—in the domain of moral and spiritual imperatives. New insights and a fundamental change in attitude are called for.

The difficult and controversial subjects which divide richer and poorer nations cannot be faced as long as an attitude of prejudice persists; these subjects must be approached in a spirit of trust and mutual openness, in a spirit of honest evaluation of reality and in a generous willingness to share.

Above all, the examination of the North-South problems must be made with a renewed conviction that no solution can be found unless it is rooted in the truth about man. The complete truth about man is the necessary condition for people to live together harmoniously and to come to an agreement on solutions that fully respect the dignity of all human beings.

6. Your presence here in an African capital, ladies and gentlemen, is of great significance for your countries and for the organizations that you represent. But it is also very meaningful for the country that offers you its hospitality, for all Africa, and for the whole world. This is a lofty vision but it is also the necessary condition for success in your endeavors to bring about better and more just relations between peoples and nations. Each diplomatic community is in a way a proving ground where you test your own attitudes and insights against a vision of the world

where man is central to all history and to all progress. My message to you, therefore—the message of one who is aware of his mission as a servant of God and a defender of man—is this: only a world that is truly human can be a world that is peaceful and strong.

Thank you.

GUARD THE HUMAN VALUES, THE GLORY OF YOUR PEOPLE

Pope John Paul II left Ghana early on Saturday morning, May 10. Before boarding the Air Afrique *plane that was to bring him to Ouagadougou, capital of Upper Volta, he delivered the following address to the ecclesiastical and civil authorities who had come to bid him farewell.*

Dear friends in Ghana,

1. The journeys of the Pope to the different continents and countries of the world all have one characteristic in common: the visits are always too short! Perhaps too short for you, but certainly too short for me! I would have loved to spend more time with you, to travel through your country from north to south, from east to west, to be with you in your homes, to visit your children in their schools, to accompany you to your fields or to the river, and to listen to your songs. But so many more of your African brothers and sisters are waiting for me.

The two days that I have spent with you have been days of great joy and spiritual consolation for me. I shall forever cherish in my memory and in my heart the impressions of this happy occasion. I shall remember your friendly people and courteous authorities, the smiling faces of your children and the wisdom of your elders.

I shall above all carry with me the image of a people that wants to be faithful to its own cultural heritage, and at the same time move forward in peace, and in truth—which is the power of peace—towards a more just situation through constant material, social and moral progress.

2. My gratitude for the hospitality shown by this land and its people to the head of the Catholic Church, who is the servant of humanity, will be expressed in fervent prayer for each one of you and for your entire nation. I shall ask God, who is all-powerful and good, who created all things and without whom no life can exist, to guide and strengthen this nation in the pursuit of true happiness for all its citizens. Because we are all children of one and the same heavenly Father, created to His image and likeness (cf. Gen. 1:26), every human being, every Ghanaian has a fundamental right to the conditions that are in keeping with his or her dignity. I shall raise my prayer to God that Ghana may achieve true progress through the development of all the natural and human resources with which it has been blessed, and that it will benefit from the will of the international community to create throughout the world and the African continent just and equitable relations in all fields of human endeavor. I shall pray especially that the continuing development of Ghana will be achieved while safeguarding the authentic human values which have been, up to the present, the glory of your people: hospitality, magnanimity, respect for the elders, a sense of community, and reference to God in all your relations.

3. My deep gratitude goes to His Excellency, the President of Ghana, for his courteous and warm

welcome, which I would be most happy to reciprocate in the Vatican. I thank the authorities and all who
have given so much of their time and effort to prepare
this visit and to make it such a rewarding experience
for me. I express my cordial appreciation also to the
journalists and to all the people of the media, through
whom I was able to reach out to a vast audience, telling all Ghanaians that the Pope holds them in his
heart; at the same time the world was able to come
into close contact with the warm and noble people of
this land.

I cannot take leave of this hospitable country
without addressing a special word of thanks to you,
the bishops and the whole Catholic community, for
everything you have done to give me this unforgettable welcome, but also, and even more, for what you
are: true Ghanaians and true Christians. Be "firm in
your faith" (1 Pt. 5:9). Always remember that you
have been baptized in Christ Jesus, and that, therefore,
beyond any differences of ethnic origin, education or
position, "you are all one in Christ Jesus" (Gal. 3:28).

Goodbye now! Thank you, and may God bless
this beloved land of Ghana!

FOLLOWING THOSE
WHO BROUGHT YOU
THE GOSPEL

About 9:30 on Saturday morning, May 10, John Paul II arrived at Ouagadougou Airport in Upper Volta. Present to welcome him were the Archbishop of Ouagadougou, Cardinal Paul Zoungrana, the bishops of Upper Volta, the Apostolic Pro-Nuncio, Most Reverend Justo Mullor Garcia, the President of the Republic of Upper Volta, H. E. Sangoulé Lamizana, the Diplomatic Corps, and numerous religious, civil and military authorities. The Holy Father delivered to them the following discourse.

It is with great joy in my heart that I arrive here, in Upper Volta, and greet with respect and harmony of feelings His Excellency, the President of the Republic, as well as the high authorities who have come to receive me. They have just bidden me welcome with such deep cordiality, which also expresses, I know, the sentiments of the whole nation of Upper Volta and which touches me very much.

With what joy, I repeat, I accepted the delicate invitation of the government of Upper Volta, which has understood so well the purely spiritual purpose of my journey in Africa, and which made it possible, consequently, to organize this all too brief visit to its capital.

I desire, therefore, that my first words should be to express, with my gratitude, my fervent wishes to almighty God for this country and its industrious and noble people, for those who bear responsibility for it, and for all its citizens.

I greet all believers. Not only Christians, but those who have in common with them belief in the one merciful God, who wish to submit their lives to the Almighty in the Islamic religion, or who are animated by religious sentiments according to their ancestral traditions.

You will allow me to greet with special affection, and in the first place in the person of my brother, Cardinal Paul Zoungrana, and my brothers the bishops of this country, all my Catholic sons and daughters. I have come for you! Before returning to His Father on the day of His ascension, our Lord commanded His Apostles: "Go all over the world to bring the Good News!" Many centuries passed before your dear country received the Gospel, and already, in less than a century, the seed has become a great tree. Now the successor of St. Peter follows in the steps of those who brought you the Gospel, the sons of the great Cardinal Lavigerie, the indefatigable bishops such as Bishop Thevenoud, whom so many of you remember with emotion. And I now meet the heads of your diocesan Churches and successors of the Apostles dedicated entirely like them to the service of the Lord, sons of Upper Volta, who receive me in their country, in your country.

To the people of Upper Volta, to its President, to the members of its government and to the representatives of the Church who have come to welcome me so warmly, I express again my thanks and my cordial greeting. I know too that many people have come from Togo; to all of them, my very warm and cordial greeting. Thank you and greetings to all! May the Lord, almighty God, heap His blessings upon you all!

TO SPEAK
THE LANGUAGE
OF THE HEART

After his reception at Ouagadougou Airport the Holy Father drove in an open car to the President's residence, where he was officially welcomed by the Head of State. In reply to President Lamizana's address, His Holiness spoke as follows:

Mr. President,

1. As soon as I arrived, just now, I wished to express publicly my joy in responding to the invitation, such a cordial one, that had been addressed to me, both by Your Excellency in the name of the Republic of Upper Volta, and by the bishops of the country. On the occasion of this meeting with the highest authorities of the state, allow me to repeat to them my sentiments of deep gratitude, and present to them my respectful greeting.

I am proud and happy to be able to come and visit the people of Upper Volta in their own country. I come to them like a brother who, for this very reason, wishes to know them better in order to be still closer to them. My words are meant to be words of love and peace for everyone, for Christians, and also for those who belong to the ancestral religions or to the large Islamic community of the country. We have religious values in common. We must, therefore, with all the more reason, respect one another, and recognize each one as having the right to profess his faith freely. This applies reciprocally for each of us. I come consequently as a man of God, to speak to everyone the *language of the heart,* which all the inhabitants can understand if they listen to it. At this level, there is no difference between men, all formed by the hand of the Creator, all called to live in brotherhood, to help one another, and to seek spiritual values.

So my thought and my affection go at this moment to one and all of the inhabitants of Upper Volta, the young as well as the old and wise, families, parents, the poor, the sick, the workers of the country—whether they are at home or abroad—who cooperate in development in spite of so many natural difficulties. I greet them in the persons of those who have the task of guiding them, with awareness of their great mission. To all, I renew the good wishes that my predecessor Pope Paul VI addressed to them on many occasions, and in particular when Your Excellency paid him the honor of a visit to the Vatican, some years ago (cf. *L'Osservatore Romano,* English edition, July 5, 1973). I will recall personally my satisfaction at having been able to converse, on last July 13, with His Excellency, the Prime Minister of the Republic.

2. If preceding stages of this pastoral journey have already offered the opportunity of tackling certain more specific problems of the African continent or of the place in the world which belongs to the peculiar genius of the latter, my essential concern has been their religious and moral dimension, and the desire to dialogue in the name of man taken in his integrality (cf. my *Address to the XXXIV General Assembly of the United Nations Organization,* no. 5, October 2, 1979).

The Catholic Church does not intend in any way, therefore, to interfere with the specific responsibilities of the rulers. She likes to remember, however, that, in the spirit of her Founder, the concept of power is inseparable from the concept of service, and that, in a way, all power being received from above, it must be exercised according to God (cf. Jn. 19:11). Such is the concern that animates her when she dedicates herself, for example, to works of education, in order to make her contribution, also, to the formation of those who will have to take over the development and the future of their country: to prepare men and women inspired by the ideal of true public service, honest, disinterested and concerned about the common good of the population.

In this field, the Church in Upper Volta has already collaborated loyally in the progress of the country. It continues to do so today as far as its possibilities permit, convinced of the importance of this task. I do not doubt that its catechetical teaching is open, moreover, to life as a whole, so as to form in depth the man of the future, in the service of his country and of the most noble ideals.

3. In the same way, it asks only to be present wherever it can help the dignity of man, of the citizen, with poor means but with the generosity of heart ready to share. May she persevere in this enthusiasm, which, eighty years after the beginning of evangelization, has never weakened, urging it ever to take new initiatives, in respect for consciences and in loyalty to the civil authority. I have full confidence in the bishops of the country and in my dear collaborator, Cardinal Paul Zoungrana, to remain faithful to this line inspired by the sense of true brotherhood.

4. It is certain that, nourished by a common desire for dialogue, relations between the Holy See and the Republic of Upper Volta will continue to be strengthened in the future. It is my very dear wish, which I am anxious to communicate to Your Excellency and to all who hear us. Let this stage of my journey bear witness to it, with the joy I feel at spending this day in Ouagadougou, in the midst of the dear people of Upper Volta! Thank you for your hospitality, Mr. President. Thank you for your welcome and for so much consideration for my humble person.

APPEAL
FOR SAHEL

On May 10, John Paul II left the President's residence and then drove to the cathedral where he celebrated Mass in the nearby square for a congregation of many thousands of the faithful. During his homily he made an appeal for the drought-stricken people of the Sahel region of Upper Volta.

Dear brothers and sisters in Christ,

1. "When the poor and needy seek water...I the Lord will answer them,...I will make the wilderness a pool of water..." (Is. 41:17-18). "The water that I shall give him will become in him a spring of water welling up to eternal life" (Jn. 4:14).

That is the lesson contained in the word of God which we have just heard; that is the lesson that the Lord gives us!

I am the living water, the Lord said further; I am the spring of water that gives life. To draw from this spring you have come here, this morning, to listen to the word of God proposed to you by him whom divine Providence has chosen to be the Head of His Church, to be, like St. Peter, His spokesman among all the faithful, in union with the bishops, the successors of the Apostles.

It is with deep emotion that I look at you, my brothers and my sisters of the Church which is in Upper Volta. It is a desire of my heart that is realized today: to come and bear witness alongside you, in your own country, to the love of God our Father and His Son Jesus Christ, to His love for each of you. Should it not fill our hearts with great joy, to be able to say, to be able to proclaim: God loves me! Yes, God loves you, wherever you may be: in your cities, your villages and your families, in the market-place and along the paths; God loves you elsewhere and always!

Your presence here bears witness also to your affection for the Church which brings you this message of love. When I look at you, my heart is filled with pride, for I know that you have accepted the message of love with joy and gratitude; for I know that you are attached to the Church and that you want to be witnesses to the Gospel with generosity and courage.

2. My stay among you will be short, too short for me, for I would have liked to meet you everywhere, in your parishes, your schools and your houses; too short for you, for I know that many people who would have liked to come are unable to be here this morning, those who live far away, those who are sick or suffering, those who have to work, and those who are still too small! To all those who are not present, I say: the Pope greets you and blesses you!

I greet also with affection my brother, Cardinal Paul Zoungrana, who was one of the first three priests of your country and who is now the great and faithful pastor of this archdiocese of Ouagadougou. I greet with him my brothers in the episcopate, as well as my brothers and sisters in all their dioceses: Ouagadougou, Koupéla, Bobo-Dioulasso, Diébougou, Fada N'Gourma, Kaya, Koudougou, Nouna-Dédougou and Ouahigouya!

I would like to greet you one by one, my brothers in the priesthood, priests whom the people of Upper

Volta have generously given to the Lord, and priests who have come from afar in the service of the Gospel among you. All of you, men and women religious and catechists, who dedicate yourselves devotedly to your task of evangelization; and you, Christian women: on you, too, there rests a great part of the future and its hopes for the Church and for your people; mothers of families and girls, who are or will be responsible with your husbands for the formation of your children. I greet the elders, the fathers of families who work hard for their dear ones, the men, the boys and the children. I greet you all, and also those of you who have come in such large numbers from Togo, I greet you in the name of the love that unites us in one Church, in God's large family!

3. In the Gospel that we listened to together, Jesus spoke to us of thirst and water. He had stopped near a well, a deep well, which the patriarch Jacob had dug with great effort for his family and for his flocks. It was there that Jesus met a woman of Samaria. She came to draw the water necessary for household needs. She needed water for her thirst, but, without knowing it, she was even thirstier for truth, for the certainty of having, in spite of her sins, a place in God's love. She was thirsty for the word of Jesus and for this life of the soul that He alone can give us.

We are all, like this woman, thirsty for the truth that comes from God. Truth about ourselves, about the meaning of our life, about what we can and must do, straightway, wherever we may be, to respond to what God expects of each one of us, to be really part of His family and live as children of God. I know your difficulties and the extreme poverty of so many of you, so numerous, and also your generosity in service of the Lord, and that is why, to you who are sons of God through your Baptism and membership of the Church, I can recall His words: "Seek first the kingdom of God and his righteousness" (Mt. 6:33)! Yes, that is the essential thing for us Christians!

4. Nevertheless, meditating on the Gospel, we cannot forget that, if the people of Samaria went home bearing in their hearts the word of salvation, the water that springs for eternal life, they also continued to come and draw the water necessary for the life of their bodies. Men are thirsty for love, for brotherly charity, but there are also whole peoples who are thirsty for the water necessary for their life, in special circumstances which are present in my mind, now that I am among you, in this land of Upper Volta, in this area of Sahel. If the problem of the progressive advance of the desert arises also in other regions of the globe, the sufferings of the people of Sahel which the world has witnessed, invite me to speak of it here.

From the beginning, God entrusted to man the nature He had created. It glorifies God to make creation serve human advancement, integral and in solidarity, and thus to permit man to reach his full spiritual dimension. Man must endeavor, therefore, to respect it and to discover its laws in order to ensure the service of man. Great progress has been made in the field of ecology, great efforts have been carried out. But a great deal remains to be done, to educate men to respect nature, preserve it and improve it, and also to reduce or prevent the consequences of what are called "natural" catastrophes.

It is then that human solidarity must be manifested to come to the help of the victims and the countries which cannot cope at once with so many urgent needs, and the economy of which may be ruined. It is a question of international justice, especially with regard to countries that are too often overtaken by these disasters, whereas others are in geographical or climatic conditions which must, in comparison, be called privileged. It is also a question of charity for all those who consider that every man and woman is a brother and a sister whose sufferings must be borne and alleviated by everyone. Solidarity, in justice and charity, must know no frontiers or limits.

5. From here, from Ouagadougou, the center of one of these countries that can be called the countries of thirst, allow me, therefore, to make a solemn appeal to all, in Africa and beyond this continent, not to close their eyes to what has happened and is happening in the region of Sahel.

I cannot give an account of the history and the details of this tragedy: they are in all your memories anyhow. It would be necessary to recall at least the time taken to become aware of the drama brought on by a persistent drought, then the movement of solidarity which spread at all levels, local, national, regional and international. A great deal was done by the citizens and governments of the countries concerned as well as by the various international institutions. The Church also played an important part. Her action was supported and followed attentively by your bishops and by Pope Paul VI who, distressed from the beginning by the extent of the catastrophe, did not spare his appeals and his support, in particular through the pontifical council *Cor Unum,* whose president, dear Cardinal Bernardin Gantin, I am happy to greet here. He kindly agreed to leave his native Africa and his archdiocese of Cotonou, in Benin, to come and work with the Pope, in Rome. Today, wherefore, let us thank all those who dedicated themselves, all those who came to the help of their brothers in need. May they hear the Lord say to them one day: "I was thirsty and you gave me drink" (Mt. 25:35)! Through them, in fact, God gave the answer that we listened to in the reading of this Mass: "I will not forsake them" (Is. 41:17).

6. And yet, how many victims for whom help came too late! How many young people whose development has been stunted or compromised! Even now the danger has not been averted. From the beginning of these tragic events which constitute the drama of Sahel, the conditions of the future were studied in your region on the intergovernmental plane with the help of the United Nations, plans were drawn up to combat the drought, its causes and its consequences, to envisage effective remedies such as irrigation, the drilling of wells, afforestation, the construction of granaries, the introduction of varied crops and other measures.

But the needs are immense if it is desired to stop the advance of the desert and even gradually drive it further back, if it is desired that every man, every woman and every child in Sahel will have sufficient water and food, and a future more and more worthy of a human being.

7. That is why, from this place, from this capital of Upper Volta, I launch a solemn appeal to the whole world. I, John Paul II, Bishop of Rome and Successor of Peter, raise my suppliant voice, because I cannot be silent when my brothers and sisters are threatened. I become here the voice of those who have no voice, the voice of the innocent who died because they lacked

water and bread; the voice of fathers and mothers who saw their children die without understanding, or who will always see in their children the aftereffects of the hunger they suffered; the voice of the generations to come, who must no longer live with this terrible threat weighing upon their lives. I launch an appeal to everyone!

Let us not wait until the drought returns, terrible and devastating! Let us not wait for the sand to bring death again! Let us not allow the future of this people to remain jeopardized forever! The solidarity shown in the past has proved, through its extent and efficacy, that it is possible to listen only to the voice of justice and charity, and not that of selfishness, individual and collective.

Listen to my appeal!

You, international organizations, I beg you to continue the remarkable work already carried out, and to speed up the persevering implementation of the programs of action already drawn up. You, heads of state, I beg you to contribute generous aid to the countries of Sahel, in order that a new effort, a large-scale and sustained one, may remedy even more effectively the drama of drought. You nongovernmental organizations, I beg you to redouble your efforts: bring forth a movement of personal generosity, of men, women and children, in order that everyone may know that the fruit of their sacrifices really serves the purpose of ensuring the lives and the future prospects of their brothers and sisters. I beg you, men of science and technicians, research institutes, to direct your work towards the search for new means to combat desertification. Would not science progress just as much if it were put in the service of man's life? It can and must have other goals than the pursuit of new means of death, creators of new deserts, or even the satisfaction of artificial needs created by publicity. That is why I beg you, too, you who work in the media of social communication, journalists of the press, radio and television: speak of this problem according to its true dimension, that of the human person weakened and mutilated. Without seeking useless effects, show possible solutions, what has been done and what remains to be done. Is it not a noble task, the one that permits you to awaken generosity and good will? Listen, all of you, I beg you, listen to these voices of Sahel and of all the countries that are victims of drought, without any exception. And I say to all of you: "God will pay you back!"

8. But I also wish to address particularly your Catholic brothers in the world, those in the most privileged countries. Let them meditate on the well-known saying of St. Vincent de Paul, one of the heroes of charity and love of the poor. When he was asked in the evening of his life what else he could have done for his neighbor, he replied: "Even more." It is the glory of Christian charity, of this love we have for one another and which is spread in our hearts by the Holy Spirit, to want to do "more and more." That is why I say to you: now, those who are hungry and thirsty in the world are at your door! Modern means make it possible to help them. You must not rely only on national and international political responsibilities. Beyond the universal duty of solidarity, it is your faith that must lead you to examine your real possibilities, to examine, personally and in the family, if what is too often called necessary is not actually superfluous. It is the Lord who invites us to do more.

9. To everyone, I express my confidence. It is based on this love of the Lord that unites us, on our participation, in the immensity of the world, in His one sacrifice, since we all partake of the one bread, and we share the same cup (cf. 1 Cor. 10:17). May the Lord, to whom we are going to pray together and who is going to come among us sacramentally in order that we may receive Him, make us progress in His love and cause the water of eternal life to gush in all hearts! Amen.

MEANING OF VOCATIONS IN THE DIVINE PLAN

After the Mass in Ouagadougou on Saturday morning, May 10, the Holy Father then met the bishops of Upper Volta led by Cardinal Paul Zoungrana, Archbishop of Ouagadougou, and by the President of the Episcopal Conference of Upper Volta and of Niger, Most Reverend Dieudonné Yougbare, Bishop of Koupéla. His Holiness addressed them as follows.

Dear brothers in the episcopate,

1. In the course of this journey of mine in your African land, I never tire of expressing my joy at meeting, too rapidly alas, these men and women who are the Church in your countries, the kingdom of God which takes root and grows among you.

This joy becomes even greater when I meet the bishops, the spiritual leaders of the new people, my brothers in the episcopate. I am particularly happy, as I said, to return in this way dear Cardinal Zoungrana's visit, who was the first African Cardinal who came to see me in Krakow. We have just time, dear brothers, to recall some thoughts which are close to my heart and yours.

The first one is our unity in collegiality. You live it among yourselves; we live it together, linking the Church which is in Upper Volta with the life and evangelical concerns of the universal Church. Collegiality is a structural element of the Church, a way of government of the episcopate, to which our age, following an important teaching of the Second Vatican Council, rightly attaches particular importance. The fact of putting it into practice well, as you certainly experience every day, is a great support for our pastoral action, and also a great hope for the growth of its effectiveness. But it is on spiritual and theological reasons, in the first place, that we must build our episcopal collaboration, the source of our ministry being the person of the Lord.

2. I encourage you, therefore, to continue to work to found your unity and that of your presbyterium really in Christ. The presbyterium consists of different elements; try to ensure that its diversity may always be a source of mutual enrichment, not of division or rivalry. For this purpose remain yourselves very close to your priests, very much present in their difficult life. Your words and your example will be able to direct more and more towards the service of the People of God the minds and the wills of those who have generously dedicated themselves to this mission.

Your dioceses, too, are varied, with different apostolic forces. Together you must face up to the common tasks and the sectors in greatest need. This spirit of solidarity must also extend outside your frontiers, particularly in the framework of the regional episcopal conference of West Africa, of which Your Eminence is president, and even in the framework of the S.C.E.A.M., for the whole of Africa and Madagascar. You have to become your own missionaries to an ever increasing extent.

3. That brings me to share with you two concerns of prime importance for evangelization and for the Christian fervor of your Church in Upper Volta. I wish to speak of your concern for vocations, and also for an apostolate based on the specifically African sense of the family.

In addition to the "missionaries," the incomparable service of whom, always so precious as a testimony of the universal Church, is recognized by everyone, you have the joy of having numerous priests, men and women religious, and seminarians of Upper Volta, as well as large numbers of catechists. The mission of the Church would require even more. It is an important part of your ministry to see to the awakening and guidance of priestly and religious vocations, through a thorough formation, which has stood the test of experience in the Church, and which is well integrated in the African reality. We must never tire of explaining the deep meaning of this vocation in God's plan. To offer oneself to follow Christ in all availability, in the exclusive service of His kingdom, to dedicate one's strength and love to Him in celibacy, is a grace that the Church, and therefore the African Churches, cannot lack today.

By these priests, or religious, Christians will be helped to make progress in personal awareness of their own vocation. Among them, the catechists, whom I am anxious to encourage through you, set a magnificent example of a Christian lay vocation put in the service of the Church's mission. Paul VI had made a point of decorating, five years ago, the centenarian Simon Zerbo, the first catechist of Upper Volta and a pioneer of faith in your country.

4. For this mission you have been making, for several years, a pastoral effort aimed at showing that the Church is really the family of God, in which each one has his place, in which each one is understood and loved. In this way, I hope together with you, your Christian communities will benefit from a deep element of structuralization, which will also constitute a concrete testimony of the Gospel, and even an appeal to non-Christians. In this conception of the family, stress is also laid on the connection between a fundamental reality and the Gospel revelation and one of the moral values characteristic of the civilization of your people.

5. There are many other questions which could be considered. I have just dealt with the very serious one of the drought in Sahel, which must bring forth a more real, more concerted and more persevering solidarity in the whole world. I am also thinking of the fact that many of your fellow countrymen are followers of Islam. The two principal religious communities, Catholic and Muslim, must therefore continue their efforts to esteem one another, respecting on both sides, what religious freedom, rightly understood, requires, and to collaborate when it is a question of meeting the human needs of the populations and their common good.

6. With you, dear brothers, I am full of hope, in spite of the difficulties, and I know your deep attachment to the Holy See and the universal Church. The Lord did not promise us a life and a ministry free of trials. He simply assured us that He had overcome the forces of evil at work in man. That is why we must always keep in mind the words He spoke on sending the Apostles on their mission after His resurrection:

''Do not be afraid.... I am with you always, to the close of the age.'' How better could I express my encouragement to you? The efforts you make incessantly in the Lord's service will yield their fruit. May the Lord bless each of you, and all those in your hearts, priests, men and women religious and the faithful, one and all of your dioceses!

YOUR COMMUNITIES
LIKE THE FAMILY
OF GOD

In the early afternoon of Saturday, May 10, John Paul II left Upper Volta en route to the Ivory Coast—the last stage of his African pilgrimage. Awaiting him at Ouagadougou airport to bid him farewell were the President of Upper Volta, ecclesiastical and civil authorities, and a large gathering of people. Before boarding the plane the Holy Father gave the following address.

1. Already it is time for departure, the end of this too short stay among you, in your country of Upper Volta, which is now even dearer to my heart. Although I must leave it, rest assured that you will all remain in my thoughts, those I have met and those who were unable to come. To the latter, dear sons and daughters of Upper Volta, you will transmit the encouragement and good wishes of the Pope, who asks the Lord Jesus to bless you all, even in the most distant of your villages, in the humblest of your homes.

2. Here is the last instruction that I leave with you. It sums up the message that I wished to make heard during this journey in your African countries, so well prepared to understand it by their rich tradition on the significance of the family and the sense of hospitality. I take up again for this purpose the teaching of St. Peter, the first Pope, to whom the Lord entrusted His Church, and whose Successor I am among

you today. He reminded the faithful: become the "spiritual house" of God, for you are "God's own people" (cf. 1 Pt. 2:5-9). In the same sense, the Second Vatican Council recalled many times that the Church is the house of God in which His family lives (cf. *Lumen gentium,* no. 6) and that all men have to become aware that they form one family, and that they are all called to belong to God's family (cf. *ibid.,* no. 51). This truth is at the basis of the mission, that is, the effort to make known to all men salvation, God's love for us and its requirements (cf. *Ad gentes,* no. 1).

So I say to you: follow faithfully the guidelines given by your bishops, my brothers in the episcopate, in order that your communities may become more and more, here in Upper Volta, the family of God. May your way of life be inspired by this deep truth. And I will indicate three points.

First, he who is really a member of the family is not afraid to put himself in the service of His Father: so be concerned about vocations. Young men and women, be generous in answering God's call if He asks you to follow Him in chastity, poverty and service to make His family increase, thanks to your efforts. I am thinking particularly also of catechists, whose dedication is so necessary for the progress of the Gospel. Parents, be generous in engendering and supporting the vocations necessary for the life of the Church in Upper Volta, and in the first place by your example of the Christian life.

Second, he who is a member of the family of God also wishes everyone to discover the same happiness. In your turn, be missionaries of your own country by being witnesses of God's love for all its inhabitants.

Third, for the same reason, because they wish to be witnesses of God's love for his family, Catholics of Upper Volta must always be active and loyal members of their national community, which also forms a large family. Your people is divided, in fact, between various religious beliefs: traditional, Muslim and Christian. This situation, which is for you an additional call to exemplary behavior, must not prevent, and does not prevent, I know, neighborly relations such as the collaboration of all in the service of local and national development, always in mutual and reciprocal respect.

That is why I am happy to greet once more the whole people of Upper Volta, whose warm and moving welcome I appreciated so much. I sincerely thank His Excellency, the President of the Republic, and all the civil authorities for the delicate way in which they made this unforgettable meeting possible. I thank all the members of the press, for the coverage they have given to my words, and all those who have become and will become the echo of my voice. And finally I thank all the inhabitants of Upper Volta without exception, and all their brothers from Togo, who joined them. To all those who have come at the cost of so much trouble and fatigue, I know, I say: thank you.

If I am obliged to go away, you know very well that our Lord does not leave you, that He remains with you always. In His name, I bless you again with all my heart.

RICH IN PROMISE

On arriving at Abidjan Airport on Saturday afternoon, May 10, John Paul II was welcomed by Archbishop Bernard Yago of Abidjan, President of the Episcopal Conference of the Ivory Coast, and by all the bishops of the country, by the Apostolic Nuncio, Archbishop Justo Mullor Garcia, by the President of the Republic, His Excellency Felix Houphuët-Boigny, by many ecclesiastical and civil authorities, and by a huge concourse of people. After an address of welcome by the President of the Ivory Coast, the Holy Father replied as follows:

Mr. President,
Your Excellencies,
Dear brothers and sisters of the Ivory Coast,

God bless the Ivory Coast! Reaching your land, I tell you of my joy, my very great joy, in visiting this country. I was waiting for this moment. The opportunity has been given to me. God be praised! It is with the Ivory Coast that I am going to end my first journey in Africa.

I can spend only two days here, and outside the capital, my meetings will be few and short. But I would like to assure straightway all the men and women of the towns and villages, of the Ivory Coast, of my esteem, my affection and my most cordial good wishes.

In the first place I thank the authorities of this country, the head of the state and the Catholic hierarchy, for their eager invitation and their dedication in organizing this stay in the best possible way. And I thank you all already for the warmth of your welcome which touches me deeply.

I greet joyfully this promising country, in the heart of West Africa. I know that its citizens are hospitable, tolerant, respectful of human life and freedom. When today they establish wide contacts with other civilizations, which fascinate them with their technical progress, they bring within them many traditional human values which they have cultivated on their own soil, springing from their traditions and, to a certain extent in the last century, also from the Gospel.

I greet indeed my Catholic brothers and sons, since I have come above all as Pastor of the universal Church. They form here a community important because of its number, and even more perhaps because of its dynamism. I greet the nine bishops of the Ivory Coast, its priests—I will shortly have the joy of concelebrating with those most recently ordained—its sisters, all the faithful. I will take care not to forget the many missionaries who, particularly since 1895, have carried out admirable work in this country, out of love for Christ and the inhabitants of the Ivory Coast, and who continue it in the service of their brothers, in a happy and fruitful collaboration.

I greet the other Christians and believers: they know as we do that the concept of God is inseparable from the human heart.

On the civil plane, I greet all those responsible for the common good and experts of every category, including the foreigners who are cooperating with them; they have undertaken to accelerate the development of the country, of all its resources, and at the same time to give to youth an adequate education. I hope that this work will redound to the complete human progress, not only the technical, but also moral and spiritual, of the inhabitants as a whole.

I greet all the workers of this country, both rural workers and those in the towns, and I have a special thought for the many migrants from neighboring countries, who have come to join the workers of the Ivory Coast.

I greet specially the young and students, to whom I will devote a long meeting.

My thought and my prayers go out to all the families of this country, and particularly where there are people who are suffering: the sick, the handicapped and the old, all those who know physical or moral distress. They always have a special place in my affection. I will get in touch with those suffering from leprosy.

I come here, in fact, as a messenger of peace. Christ, whom I serve as successor of His first Apostles, blessed peacemakers. I come to receive the testimony of everything beautiful and brotherly that is being done in this country and in this Church. I come to encourage it, and if possible to bring the enthusiasm which comes from our Faith, in order that a civilization worthy of men, who are sons of God, may be constructed. The unity of all, this will be the theme of the Mass that will gather us together this evening.

God bless you, may He reward you for welcoming the Pope in this way! May He bless the whole Ivory Coast!

I come here, in fact, as a messenger of peace. Christ, whom I serve as Successor of His first Apostles, blessed peacemakers. I come to receive the testimony of everything beautiful and brotherly that is being done in this country and in this Church. I come to encourage it, and if possible to bring the enthusiasm which comes from our Faith.

WE MUST MEET THE REAL NEEDS OF HUMANITY

After President Houphuët-Boigny's welcoming address at Abidjan Airport, on May 10, John Paul II drove to the Nunciature. In the evening he visited the President, whom he addressed as follows.

Mr. President,

1. On last February 2, receiving members of the communities of the different African nations residing in Rome, who had been presented to me by the ambassador of the Ivory Coast, I had the joy to announce to them a journey in the near future to "honor and encourage the whole of Africa" *(L'Osservatore Romano*, English edition, February 11, 1980). The Lord has permitted the realization of a very dear wish. And now this journey ends with the Ivory Coast stage, very courteously proposed by Your Excellency at the same time as by my brothers the bishops. At this memorable moment, before the people of the Ivory Coast here present, through those to whom has been given the mandate of guiding it, I wish to express my deep gratitude for the warm and friendly welcome I have been given.

Solemnity and perfect organization do not exclude simplicity or spontaneity. Allow me in the first place, therefore, to open my heart to the population of this country, which you offer me the happiness of visiting. I greet it with affection. How could it feel far in any way from the Pope, even though he will not be able to go to every province, to every town, to every family to bring his words of blessing? Yes, I really wish to greet all the women and all the men of the Ivory Coast. Some of them, Christians, have already been to Rome, to pray at the tombs of Peter and Paul. Others, who do not share the same Faith, have also had the opportunity to go to the center of the Christian world. I come in these days to make my own pilgrimage to the African land, long sanctified by the preaching of the Word of God.

CONCERN FOR THE COMMON GOOD

2. Your Excellency will allow me to tell you of my admiration for this people which on the threshold of the third millennium, capable of assuming its destiny itself, endeavors to unite in a happy and fitting synthesis the possibilities with which Providence has provided it, the traditional genius inherited from its ancestors and concern for the common good. The task, which the rulers of the republic are tackling tenaciously, is not an easy one. It is a question of creating an orderly whole, in which none of the best products of the past are denied, while drawing at the same time from the modern world what can help to elevate man, his dignity, his honor. There is no real development or real human or social progress outside that. Nor justice. There would be the risk of constructing a facade, something fragile, therefore, in which many inequalities would be found, not to mention the inequality within man himself as a result of which more importance is attached to the pursuit of super-

ficial things that are seen than to the pursuit of the essential things that constitute his hidden strength. There is a great danger, in fact, of wanting just to copy or import what is being done elsewhere, for the mere reason that it comes from so-called "advanced" countries: but advanced towards what? What claim have they to be considered advanced? Has not Africa too, more perhaps than other continents which were formerly in control of it, the sense of interior things called to determine man's life? How I would like to contribute to defend it from invasions of every kind, views of man and of society that are one-sided or materialistic, and which threaten Africa's way towards a really human and African development!

Dealing with this question, the Second Vatican Council measured its whole complexity. It noted, in fact, that "many of our contemporaries are prevented by this complex situation from recognizing permanent values and duly applying them to recent discoveries. As a result they hover between hope and anxiety and wonder uneasily about the present course of events. It is a situation that challenges men to reply; they cannot escape" (Gaudium et spes, no. 4).

This problem is not peculiar to Africa, far from it. And yet, I do not think I am mistaken to suppose that it frequently gives the statesmen of this great continent food for thought; that is perhaps the most fundamental problem they have to cope with, they who, by their choices, by the directions they are led to take when drawing up development plans, lay the foundations of the future of their respective peoples.

Wisdom is needed, much wisdom and clear-sightedness also, to carry out the necessary adaptations according to experience. The reputation that Your

Excellency has acquired in the matter, in your country as well as on the international level, gives reason for confidence with regard to the future of the people of the Ivory Coast.

MAN'S REAL RICHES

3. Quoting a passage from the texts of the Council, I recalled a moment ago the permanent values which constitute man's real riches. Consideration of these values and, if we may use the term, their implementation seem to me to be a safeguard against everything that is, in our times, artificial or the consequence of taking the easy way out. They alone lead man to build on rock (cf. Mt. 7:24-25). Examples could be multiplied, taken from the same conciliar constitution which wished to judge by the light of God's plan the experiences of our contemporaries, and connect them with the divine source.

I consider this subject so important that I dealt with it at length in New York, before the XXXIV General Assembly of the United Nations Organization. It can be summed up in a pithy formula: the pre-eminence of spiritual and moral values over material or economic ones. "The pre-eminence of the values of the spirit"—I said then—"defines the proper sense of earthly material goods and the way to use them...." It is also a contributing factor "to ensuring that material development, technical development, and the development of civilization are at the service of what constitutes man. This means enabling man to have full access to truth, to moral development, and to the complete possibility of enjoying the goods of culture which he has inherited, and of increasing them by his own creativity" (no. 14).

We must continue, therefore, to reflect and work along these lines if we wish to meet the real needs of mankind and particularly the real needs of the African, who is in the act of acquiring the dimension that is due to him on the world scale. Africa is still in search of herself to some extent. She has in her hand the keys to her future. I hope that she will study deeply this fundamental subject so that spiritual and moral values will impress an indelible character on her, the only one worthy of her.

SPIRITUAL MISSION

4. The Church, on her part, has no direct competence in the political or economic field. She intends to remain faithful to her spiritual mission, and fully respects the specific responsibilities of rulers. The moral support she can offer to those in charge of the earthly city is explained and justified, by the will to serve man, reminding him of what constitutes his greatness, or awakening him to realities that transcend this world. I express particular satisfaction here at the help she gives in the Ivory Coast, through her presence in schools and in intellectual circles, to the great national enterprise of education and formation, which has already succeeded in ensuring the population of a cultural level that is enviable for more than one reason. But her help aims mainly at the conscience of the man and woman of the Ivory Coast, to show them their dignity and to help them to make good use of it. Her help would also like to facilitate a real justice, with greater concern for the poor, the emarginated, humble people, migrants, in a word, those who are often abandoned. Is not the sense of

God also the sense of man, of one's neighbor? Does it not imply honesty, the integrity of citizens, the determination to share with the underprivileged, rather than the race for money or honors? In this way, being concerned with the fate of the populations, the Church intends to work effectively for the advancement of the inhabitants of the Ivory Coast, and she hopes to contribute her stone to the more and more solid construction of the Ivory Coast homeland.

BEST WISHES TO ALL

5. I wish with all my heart, Mr. President, for the success of the effort to which all your fellow countrymen are called, thanking you once more for your kindness, and presenting my respectful greetings to all the high personalities that surround us, and praying fervently for the people of the Ivory Coast. God grant that this stay may be a fruitful one and meet the hopes that we have set on it!

THE CHURCH:
VISIBLE SIGN
OF COMMUNION

After visiting the President of the Ivory Coast on May 10, John Paul II went to Abidjan Stadium where he concelebrated Mass with the nine local bishops. The following is the text of the homily which he preached.

Dear brothers and sisters,

Let us give thanks to God, who has called us to form one Church, in His Son Jesus Christ.

1. The prophet Ezekiel already proclaimed this great mystery, thinking in the first place of the Israelites of his time, scattered among the nations. But, "through the Church," the call was extended to sons of all the nations, who were called pagans. And we have dared, as St. Paul, the Apostle of the Gentiles, says "to approach God trustfully," "through the way of faith in Christ"—the same faith. Yes, "the one God and Father of us all" gathers us, from wherever we come, with all the riches of our own history, in the family of the Church. He pours pure water on us— "one baptism"—and we are then "purified of all our stains." He gives us "a new heart," a heart sensitive to His love, "a heart of flesh." He puts His Spirit, "one Spirit," in us. He permits us "to walk according to his law, and to follow his ways." It is thus that the same Body of Christ is constructed throughout the uni-

verse, with different members, who have each received their qualities, their share of grace, their duties in the Church.

This deep unity, through the multiform variety of peoples and races, is our joy and our strength. We must also make our conscious and generous contribution, in order to realize, in maturity, the fullness of Christ.

So I invite you, dear brothers and sisters, to traverse with me the various concentric circles of this unity: at the level of Christ first of all, at the level of the universal Church and her Pastor, at the level of the Church which is in the Ivory Coast and of your diocese, at the level of each of your parish communities, with the influence that radiates from them for the unity of those around us.

THE SPIRIT AND THE RISEN CHRIST

2. Yes, our unity is not only or primarily an exterior unity, like that of a social body with its organizational structures. It is a mystery, as the Second Vatican Council stressed at the beginning of the Constitution *Lumen gentium* (no. 4). We form "a people brought into unity from the unity of the Father, the Son and the Holy Spirit."

The Holy Spirit "dwells in the Church and in the hearts of the faithful," "guiding the Church in the way of all truth" and "unifying her in communion and in the works of ministry," "He bestows upon her the various hierarchic and charismatic gifts," and in this way directs her. By the power of the Gospel, He rejuvenates and renews the Church constantly, and leads her to perfect union with her Spouse, Christ (cf. *ibid.*). Thus the Holy Spirit unfolds in the Church "the unfathomable riches of Christ," and turns her aspiration towards Christ and His Father (cf. Rev. 22:17).

The risen Christ, indeed, lives for all eternity at the side of His Father who made Him Lord of the universe and Head of the Church which is His Mystical Body (cf. Phil. 2:11; Col. 1:18). Through the Holy Spirit, He communicates His life to those who believe in Him, being born again of water and the Spirit (cf. Jn. 3:5), who are united with Him through prayer, the sacraments, and a life in conformity with His love. He is the invisible Head of the Church, it is He who sustains her (cf. *Lumen gentium,* no. 8). He is the good Shepherd who gathers the scattered children of God and makes them a kingdom of priests for His Father (Rev. 1:6).

You know all this well, dear friends, but I am reminding you of it to exhort you to turn constantly to Christ, to pray to Him even better—in the community, in the family, and also personally—to re-read His word. A Church is living, united and strong only when its members have an interior life, a spiritual life, that is, a life connected with the Spirit of God, a life of prayer. That is the heart of the Church. That is where the most intimate communion is established, which is the source of all the others. Your life, your unity is at first "hid with Christ in God" (cf. Col. 3:3).

UNITED WITH THE UNIVERSAL CHURCH

3. But this grace of Christ reached you and is constantly given to you by the visible Church, which is the "Body" of Christ, the "sacrament" of Christ, the

sign which makes communion visible and actualizes it. Unity is manifested around him who, in each diocese, has been constituted pastor, bishop. For the Church as a whole, it is manifested around the Bishop of Rome, the Pope who is "the perpetual and visible source and foundation of the unity both of the bishops and of the whole company of the faithful" (*Lumen gentium*, no. 23). And now this is being realized this evening, before your eyes. What grace for us all!

Every bishop of the Catholic Church is a successor of the Apostles. He is connected with the Apostles by an unbroken line of ordinations. I am the Successor of the apostle Peter, in the See of Rome. Now you have heard, in the Gospel, Peter's marvelous profession of faith: "You are the Christ, the Son of the living God." And the answer of Jesus: "On this rock I will build my Church.... I will give you the keys of the kingdom of heaven" (Mt. 16:16-19). And later, Christ added: "Strengthen your brethren" (Lk. 22:32); "Feed my lambs...tend my sheep" (Jn. 21:15-17). Such is also the faith of the Pope, which I solemnly professed when I inaugurated my ministry in Rome; and such is also the mission with which the Lord has charged me, in spite of my unworthiness: to strengthen you in the Faith and in unity.

Every local Church, like the one you form here, must always remain united with the universal Church, through the visible sign of communion with Peter's successor. For there is only one Church of Jesus Christ, which is like a great tree, on which you have been grafted, like the Christians of Rome, like the Christians of Poland. The branch cannot live if cut off from the tree, nor the vine shoot apart from the vine. You live participating in the great vital stream that makes the whole tree live. But your graft will permit the Church to experience a new flowering, to have new fruits. The Pope rejoices at this. He rejoices at the springtime of the Church which is in the Ivory Coast.

INTENSIFYING UNITY

4. I come now to your diocesan communities, of Abidjan or the other dioceses. There, too, your bishops know the necessity of intensifying the unity that links them with one another, at the level, for example, of pastoral collaboration for the whole country.

In each diocese, which can be called the "particular Church," there must be great unity around the bishop who is its leader in the way of the Gospel, that is, its pastor and father. Unity of Faith, of course; unity of prayer; unity of brotherly sentiments; unity of pastoral efforts. And this in a great diversity of indispensable and complementary functions. You have heard St. Paul speak of "apostles," "prophets," "evangelists," "pastors," "teachers," "saints" (Eph. 4:11-12); today, the list of ministries, services and charisms could be developed. Let every Christian know, then, in this Church, that he is responsible at his level, and that if he does not give what he should, the Church will feel the lack.

NEED FOR PRIESTS

5. My first thought goes to the priests, proclaimers of the Gospel, dispensers of God's mysteries, spiritual guides presiding over unity, in their different offices: parish priests and assistants, teachers, chaplains.... How happy I am to concelebrate with the young priests who received the sacred powers by the laying

on of hands not long ago! How I hope that many inhabitants of the Ivory Coast will hear the same call! The harvest is plentiful! Oh, all of you, my brothers, sustain priestly vocations, so that your Church will no longer lack priests, holy priests. The Church of tomorrow will have to depend on them. But also the missionaries who have come from far away have still a great role in this country, a role that is indispensable at present, because of the highly appreciated service they render and as witnesses of the universal Church; they are fully members of your Church. All priests are called to form the one presbyterium around the bishop, in humility and brotherly support. There would be room, too, for the ministry of deacons alongside the priests.

What good fortune, moreover, to benefit from the example and help of other consecrated souls, men and women religious, indigenous or missionaries, who call forth so much confidence among the people, because chastity, poverty and obedience make them incomparable witnesses of love of Christ and His Gospel, fully available to everyone.

Let catechists, well informed, continue their role as educators in the Faith, and let animators of small communities in the districts know that, without them, an important relay would be lacking. I am thinking also of the responsibility of fathers and mothers of families; is not every Christian home, as it were, "a domestic sanctuary of the Church"? (Decree *Apostolicam actuositatem,* no. 11) I take the liberty of stressing here the special role of mothers. Woman has the marvelous mission of giving life, bearing unborn life, and, in Africa, she continues for a long time to carry her child so tenderly and to nurse it so devotedly! Let her not forget either to open the hearts of her children to the love of God, to the life of Christ: it is an initial education that can hardly be replaced. There are many other services in the Christian community: educational services, services of medical and social mutual aid. And the young also have a part in them.

6. But how to maintain unity of prayer, unity of charity, pastoral unity among all? It is the special role of the parish, with its Church and its team of pastors, linked with the religious and lay leaders. The parish must welcome everyone: there are no real "strangers" in a family of Christians! I am thinking in particular of migrant workers or of experts from other countries who must receive and give their share of Christian life. One Body, one Spirit, as St. Paul said.

UNITY OF CHRIST

7. Dear friends, unity does not stop here. We wish further to promote it with all those who, without professing our Catholic Faith in its entirety or without preserving communion under Peter's Successor, have been baptized and bear the noble name of Christians. The Holy Spirit stirs up in all disciples of Christ the desire and the action which aim at unity such as Christ willed it, in truth and charity (cf. *Lumen gentium,* no. 15). The plan of salvation includes, with us, also those who worship the one God or those who in shadows and images seek the unknown God with a sincere heart (cf. *ibid.,* no. 16). Thus, while bearing witness to our own faith, we are animated by sentiments of esteem and brotherly dialogue for everyone.

8. Finally, the disciples of Christ and Christian communities must be a leaven of unity, agents of brotherly rapprochement, for all the inhabitants of this country, whether Africans or non-Africans. The Ivory Coast and its capital are going through a rapid social revolution, in which urban concentration, family uprooting, the search for a roof and a job, but also, for some people, unsuspected possibilities of technical success, of getting rich quickly, with temptations of personal profit, sometimes invested elsewhere, of exploitation of man, of the underling, of the native or migrant worker, yes, all that may, as alas in other so-called "advanced" countries, sorely try solidarity, justice, the hope of the humble, peace and also the religious sentiment. It is necessary to avoid it at all costs—I say so out of love for you, out of love for this country and those in charge of it—that the opportunity offered to the Ivory Coast and its workers by development today should be lost, that the gap between rich and poor should grow dangerously, as the gap between rich countries and poor countries is growing, that civilization should fail to materialize. Under these conditions, care for the poor, the abandoned, the sense of the common good of all and of fairness must dwell especially in the hearts of Christians. Happy Christians, happy Christian communities, if other men of good will find in them an example of unity and a source of brotherhood. The recent Council did not hesitate to say that the Catholic unity of the People of God "prefigures and promotes universal peace" *(Lumen gentium,* no. 13).

That is, dear brothers and sisters, the dynamism of the unity of our Church at all levels, from Rome to your village or to your district. As the Vicar of Christ,

I am happy to be in your midst to strengthen this hope. The project is a splendid one. The way will be long and difficult; it calls for sacrifices—Jesus warned us so in the Gospel. But His grace is at work among you, His Spirit is in you. And as the Blessed Virgin lent herself to it in a marvelous way, she who conceived Christ from the Holy Spirit and who is also Mother of the Church, we pray to her especially to prepare our hearts for it. Now, this Eucharist will make present the Sacrifice of Christ, who overcame barriers of separation (cf. Eph. 2:14), to unite all the children of God and to give them access, together, to the God of love.

Lord, strengthen the unity of your Church.
Amen. Alleluia!

SIGN OF THE CONSTRUCTION OF THE KINGDOM OF GOD

Early on Sunday morning, May 11, John Paul II traveled by helicopter to an industrial area of Abidjan known as the "Plateau." He blessed the foundation stone of the cathedral which is to be erected there; he then signed the parchment which was sealed and enclosed in the foundation stone. On the same occasion he also blessed the foundation stone of another church to be erected, one dedicated to Our Lady of Africa. During the ceremony the Holy Father delivered the following address.

1. I thank Archbishop Bernard Yago, my dear brother in the episcopate, for his fine words, and I join in his joy for this liturgical ceremony. How could we fail, in fact, dear brothers and sisters who are listening to me, to let our joy burst forth before the spiritual reality manifested in this way, and to recall for a moment with you its deep meaning? I am going to bless the foundation stones of the future cathedral of Abidjan and of a church which will be dedicated to Our Lady of Africa.

Now, the Church is the house of God. Yes, all Christian life is based on this marvelous supernatural reality, which must always be studied, always be meditated upon, and which St. John expressed in this simple sentence: "The Word became flesh and dwelt among us" (Jn. 1:14). Yes, the Lord was born, suffered, died and rose again in order that the Christian may really be a son of God. This supernatural truth must determine the Christian's life always and everywhere. How? I take up here again the teaching of St. Peter's first letter: "Like living stones be yourselves built into a spiritual house" (1 Pt. 2:5). The Church, the new Jerusalem of which the Gospel and the liturgy speak, is constructed in our lives, within us!

NOT SOLELY SPIRITUAL

2. Yet the Church, the house of God, is not solely spiritual. The human roots of our Catholic communities, as manifested and expressed in the construction of churches, and in particular of this cathedral, closely depend on the Incarnation, on this coming of God in our humanity, on the fact that God became like us and that He willed to meet us through our concrete ways of life!

The church is the place in which the Christian people gathers, it is also the place where the Lord is really present: present in the celebration of Holy Mass, present in the Blessed Sacrament. The church is the place in which the Christian is born to divine life through Baptism, finds forgiveness of his sins through the sacrament of Penance, and enters into communion with the Lord and with his brothers in the Eucharist.

However humble may be the churches you build, see how great is the spiritual reality they manifest! They are the sign of the construction of the kingdom of God in you, in your country! Among all the churches of a diocese, the cathedral, your cathedral, which will soon rise here, has a very particular meaning. Just as the basilica of St. John Lateran, the cathedral of the Pope, of the bishop of Rome, is called for this reason "Head and Mother of all the churches," so the cathedral of the diocese is called "mother of the churches" of the diocese. It is so because it is the church of the bishop, of the head of the diocese, of the successor of the Apostles to whom Christ entrusted the task and care of evangelization. So you will love this new cathedral, which will be dedicated to St. Paul, the missionary Apostle par excellence! Love all your churches too! Love your bishops and all the priests who enable you to be born and grow in divine life!

OUR LADY OF AFRICA

3. It is not without difficulty or effort that the kingdom of God grows in us! Nor is it without difficulty that churches are built. I know that your hearts are set on them, in spite of urgent matters of every kind, and what sacrifices you make to build them. Those who are surprised that churches should be built instead of dedicating all resources to the improvement of material life, have lost the sense of spiritual realities; they do not understand the meaning of the Lord's words: "Man shall not live by bread alone" (Mt. 4.4). But we are well aware that the stone church that is constructed with great effort is the sign of the one that is built up in the community!

I am particularly happy to bless also, at the same time as the foundation stone of your future cathedral, the foundation stone of the church that will be built under the patronage of Our Lady of Africa.

A deeply enlightening meeting! On the one hand, the Apostle of the Gentiles, who lived only to proclaim the Gospel, and on the other the Blessed Virgin, who kept in her heart all the mysteries of her Son's life, and who remains, for all time and for the whole Church, as we will commemorate again in a few days, the example of ardent prayer while waiting for the coming of the Holy Spirit.

It was not, therefore, without very deep spiritual reasons that the first missionaries who came to your countries dedicated the field of their apostolate to the Immaculate Heart of Mary as soon as they arrived. This heart is, in fact, the symbol of divine closeness, of God's love for our poor humanity and of the love it can give Him in return through faithfulness to His grace. The devotion of these missionaries to the Virgin, their confidence in her, were therefore closely linked with the accomplishment of their apostolic mission: to make Christ, "born of the Virgin Mary," known and loved.

That is why, venerated brothers, dear sons and daughters, I feel deep spiritual joy in renewing in a way, among you and in your name, the act of those who had come, their hearts full of love for God and for their African brothers, to bring the Gospel of salvation. Entrusting Africa to the Blessed Virgin, we place it under the protection of the Mother of the Savior. How could our hope be deceived? How could she fail, when you invoke her fervently in this church and in all the churches of your country, to lead you towards her divine Son, towards the fullness of His love?

May the Lord bless you! May He bless all builders of the Church, spiritual and material! May He give His grace and His peace to all those who seek Him and who come to meet Him in these sacred buildings! Amen!

THE WORLD NEEDS
GOSPEL WITNESSES

On May 11, the Holy Father's second engagement was at the Church of Notre Dame de Treichville, where he met a large gathering of priests, men and women religious, and the laity. He spoke to them as follows:

Dear brothers and sisters in Christ,

Your magnificent gathering enables me, once more, to measure the vitality of the Church in the Ivory Coast. Thank you for having come in such large numbers and so eager to advance along the ways of the kingdom of God and to help others to approach it!

I address the same pressing and trusting encouragement to all: be what you must be before the Lord who has called you, and in the eyes of the world which needs your evangelical witness! And be so in the vocation which belongs specifically to each one. It is a question of faithfulness to the Lord, of loyalty to yourselves, of respect for others, of ecclesial solidarity.

You have given a great deal to the Church and your country. Give them even more.

TO PRIESTS

To you, dear sons who have received the incomparable grace of priestly ordination, I express in the first place my deep happiness to know that you live in unity among yourselves, whether you are sons of the people of the Ivory Coast or have come from other countries, and in trusting collaboration with your bishops. May the cry of Christ's heart, "May they be one," always resound in your own heart! The credibility of the Gospel and the effectiveness of apostolic work depend largely on the unity of the pastors, called to form one presbyterium, whatever the post and the responsibilities of each one may be.

At this moment, so moving for me and for you, I would like above all to strengthen in you an absolutely essential conviction: Christ has made you His own (cf. Phil. 3:12-14) and has specially conformed you to Himself through the priestly character, to serve the Church and the men of today by dedicating all your physical and spiritual strength to them. The mystery of the priesthood is not determined by sociological analyses, wherever they may come from. It is in the Church, with the leaders of the Church, that it is possible to study deeply and live this gift of the Lord Jesus. I beg you: have faith in your priesthood!

I hasten to add another encouragement, which is also of essential importance. May Christ be, as it were, the breath of your daily life! Your everyday faithfulness and your radiating influence call for this. Develop even more your brotherhood among priests, in your parish teams, your meetings for apostolic reflection and concerted action, and even more so in your times of prayer and retreat. These two dimensions, with the Lord and among yourselves, will be the bulwark of your priestly celibacy and the guarantee of its fruitfulness. Live this evangelical renunciation of fatherhood in the flesh in the constant perspective of the spiritual fatherhood which fills the hearts of priests completely dedicated to their people. Live these requirements and these joys in the spirit of apostles of all times.

TO MEN AND WOMEN RELIGIOUS

I am particularly happy to be able to express to you in person my affection and the great hope I set in the testimony of your evangelical life.

My deep wish for you, monks and enclosed nuns who live the mystery of Christ worshiping the Father in the name of mankind, is that the year of Saint Benedict, proposed to the whole Church, may stimulate your fervor, spread the influence of your monasteries, and bring forth new and strong contemplative vocations. To brothers and sisters who collaborate with their whole soul in the direct tasks of evangelization, I express my admiration and gratitude which is also that of the Church. How many parish centers, Catholic domestic training, chaplaincies of high schools, hostels for the young, dispensaries, reception places for migrants, benefit from your talents and from the treasure of your faith and charity! Through you, dear brothers and sisters, Christ scours the towns and villages of Africa today and proclaims the Good News to their inhabitants. Such a mission calls for very deep union with the Lord, nourished regularly by special periods of silence and prayer. Such a mission also requires that, in the legitimate diversity of the spiritual families to which you belong, you should remain very united and very willing to cooperate for the credibility of the Gospel. This real spiritual dynamism and this realistic concerted action in the apostolate, can certainly awaken in the young the call you heard yourselves: "Come, and follow me."

Finally, remember constantly that the foundation of your unity is Christ in person. You have all given Him voluntarily the dominion and use of all that you are, of all that you have, in order to intimate that He is the ultimate purpose, the fullness of every human creature, and to bear witness to that through your multiple activities. Your religious life is in a word the mystery of Christ in you and the mystery of your poor life in Him. That must be more and more clear. Christian communities need your witness so much! The world, even unbelieving, dimly expects of you an ideal of life. So your three religious vows are not lessons given to others, but signs capable of opening them up to values that abide. May your poverty be also a sharing with the poorest! May your obedience be an appeal to be less self-centered, to humility! May your chastity, lived in the greatest faithfulness, be a revelation of universal love, of God's own tenderness!

TO THE LAITY

To you, dear Christian laity, I express my confidence and gratitude for everything you have done and will do further—together with the episcopate and the clergy of the Ivory Coast—on the plane of evangelization. You are living today, in your towns and villages, like the first Christian communities, according to the Acts of the Apostles and St. Paul's epistles, which speak to us of so many Christian lay people in the service of the Gospel.

You all know, too, that the recent Second Vatican Council highlighted the resources that every lay person has because of his place in the Body of Christ, the Church, through his baptism and confirmation. The time has come to unite more and more all the forces of the People of God around the pastors whom the Holy Spirit has given you.

I rejoice deeply in the excellent work of lay catechists as well as in the existence of apostolic movements offered to the young and adults for their formation and as a support of their Christian commitments. I hope that these movements will always be adapted, always flourishing. I would like to revive your apostolic flame by encouraging you on three points which seem to me very important. Evangelize your own lives, be always in a state of conversion if you really want to take part in the evangelization of the world; the others need your experience of the Christian life. Reserve times for retreat and revision of life.

Be very attentive to those around you, out of charity and always with respect. In your parishes which remain the vital centers of your Christian life, in your little district communities, in your scholastic or professional environments, open your minds and your hearts to the problems, the sufferings, the plans, the joys of those men and women who need to confide in you, to find in you moral and spiritual support.

At your meetings between members of apostolic movements, check your common faithfulness to the Lord who has called you to work for the salvation of your brothers. Look squarely at the concrete situation lived by the people of your district, your region, your country, in all their positive aspects, and, alas, in their dehumanizing aspects. All together precisely, discern with wisdom the action to be undertaken or continued at the religious level and at the human level for the evangelization of Africans and for the integral advancement of their persons in respect for the cultural values of Africa.

Be of good cheer and confident! The light and the power of the Spirit of Pentecost have always been given in abundance to intrepid workers of the Gospel.

PROCLAIM UNCEASINGLY THE WORD OF SALVATION

After his meeting with the various groups in the church of Notre Dame de Treichville on May 11, the Holy Father then went to the Catholic Institute for West Africa (I.C.A.O.) where he met the visiting bishops from the neighboring countries and addressed them as follows:

Dear brothers in the episcopate,

Great is my joy to meet you here, in this Catholic Institute for West Africa, which bears high witness to the effective collaboration of the episcopates of the whole region.

Too rapid, like all my visits, alas, my short stay here gives me, however, and will leave with me, an extremely comforting impression. Serious work, I know, is being carried out here I earnestly encourage all the bishops on whom this institute depends to continue to be full of solicitude in order to ensure it fresh adherents, so that its future may be as fruitful as the present permits us to hope.

In a moment I am going to bless the first stone of the building that will house the Secretariat of the Regional Episcopal Conference of French-speaking

West Africa. That, too, is a new symbol of your will to work together, for the sake of efficiency, and to bear witness better to the spirit of unity that animates you.

To you all, dear brothers, who have in many cases undertaken a long journey to come and greet me during my journey in Africa, in the Ivory Coast, my thanks for your presence. Thank you for the warm hospitality given me in these pastoral visits. My joy is great, I repeat, at seeing myself welcomed in this way and surrounded by so many bishops in order to manifest together the unity of the Church. Receive all my fervent and brotherly encouragement for the apostolic work you courageously assume. For the service of God, we must bear the weight of the day and the heat! So continue unceasingly to proclaim the word of salvation, this Gospel which was solemnly entrusted to us at our episcopal ordination!

Take my warm and deep encouragement also to all your dioceses, to everyone: to the priests whom I love so much, to men and women religious, to all the faithful, and particularly to those who are unhappy, to the sick, to those who are suffering. Take the Pope's affection and blessing to them all.

MAY THE VIRGIN MARY WATCH OVER THE YOUNG CHURCHES

At midday on Sunday, May 11, the Holy Father delivered the following short address before the recitation of the "Regina Caeli" from the chapel of the Nunciature at Abidjan. It was broadcasted by Vatican Radio to the whole of Africa and to Europe.

Dear brothers and sisters in Christ, who hear me directly or over the radio,

It is the time to honor the Virgin Mary with the recitation of the Regina Caeli! I would like this Marian praise to be for you as for me a very fervent *thank you* to her whom the Church has venerated from its foundation as the very holy Mother of Christ the Redeemer, to her whom the Church—the Mystical Body of Jesus—also considers as its Mother.

For ten days, I have been the amazed and often overwhelmed witness of the vitality of the young African Churches! Christ's promise. "I am with you always, to the close of the age" kept coming into my mind in the course of my pastoral visits!

I invite the whole Church, and particularly the Churches with a long Christian past, to consider their young sister-Churches with esteem and trust, in a fruitful dialogue. The hunger for the word of God; the spontaneity of prayer and of the religious sense; the joy and pride of belonging to the Church; the hospitable welcome; the sense of responsibility of bishops and priests; the generosity of sisters; the apostolic ardor of catechists; the solidarity of Christian communities; the brotherly mutual aid, courageous and disinterested, that priests, sisters and the laity from other Churches continue to bring, and many other encouraging signs, invite us to give thanks to God and can stimulate our zeal, our faith and our charity.

These Churches were connected up with the universal Church by missionary pioneers animated by great faith. They are now yielding their own fruit, which has the savor of Africa and the authenticity of Christianity, and they are letting others benefit from their witness. They also need brotherly mutual aid to meet their immense human and spiritual needs. May these exchanges take place in the spirit of communion which characterizes the Church.

In paschal joy, let us contemplate the Virgin Mary beside her glorified Son, and let us pray to her for one another.

May she watch over these Churches which we entrust to her! May she obtain for them constantly the light and the power of the Holy Spirit!

THE IMMENSE FIELD OF EVANGELIZATION

Shortly after noon on May 11, John Paul II met the Ivory Coast bishops in the Nunciature and addressed them as follows.

Beloved Brothers in the episcopate,

Since last night, we have been meeting in the midst of your people. Now, we have at our disposal some time which will be rather a family talk. We are a family party!

I do not forget that your nine dioceses are rather different as regards the implantation of the Church. I will speak of the situation as a whole.

1. In the first place, I rejoice with you in the vitality of the Church in the Ivory Coast, and I give thanks to God for it. There have certainly been favorable exterior conditions: peace, the hospitable and tolerant character of the inhabitants, an innate religious sense as is often found in Africa. But we owe it above all to remarkable men of faith, to the zeal of the pioneers that the missionaries were, to numerous and persevering initiatives on their part. We owe it today to you yourselves, dear Brothers, whose courageous and far-seeing dedication I know. You have created an excellent atmosphere of collaboration between the African clergy and the numerous foreign priests and religious who, thank God, continue their mutual aid. You are also trying to make your laity become aware

of their responsibilities on the apostolic and material plane. While continuing in your concern for a really worthy liturgy and Christian life, you do not omit to cope with the many pastoral problems that arise.

SOME PASTORAL PROBLEMS

2. I take the liberty of stressing some of these problems, not to provide solutions which are the object of your reflection and concerted action, but to manifest to you the interest I take in your episcopal ministry.

I am thinking for example of the large towns of Abidjan and Bouaké, where a considerable number of newcomers have arrived from the country and also immigrants from neighboring countries: how to make the Church present in these new districts and these new environments? There are poor people of all kinds, the uprooted, the humble people to whom we owe a special presence and solicitude, like Christ. There is also an elite, the executives, who need a deeper Christian reflection at the level of their culture and their responsibilities, in the first place in order not to remain on the fringe of the Church, and also to take part in a more harmonious development of the country. For there is a social justice to be promoted, with regard to privileges of fortunes or power, too great inequalities, temptations of excessive enrichment, sometimes of corruption, as you yourselves say. The Church must help leaders not to transpose to your country certain Western patterns of life, which tend to establish persons and families in materialism, individualism and practical atheism, and to abandon the underprivileged.

You are also concerned about the multitude of the young and of students. In the framework of parishes and schools, they merit a specialized apostolate and particularly a catechesis for which the help of their elders would certainly be welcome. You have done a great deal for Catholic schools, in a country which should not have known the nasty whiffs of Western laicism, and you are right. The stake of student youth is a very great one; if only we could put at their disposal the chaplains they would need!

Catechists remain the indispensable collaborators of evangelization, and you are rightly concerned to give them an initial and continuous formation, suited to the needs of the various communities and the various environments. I have often spoken about this in the course of my journey. It is also necessary to train educators, priests, sisters and lay people, who will engage in more thorough religious studies, taking their African culture into account. Evangelization will greatly benefit from their qualified service on the theological and apostolic plane. I know the excellent work that is being carried out here by the Catholic Institute of West Africa, which I have just visited. It is also a blessing for you.

The family apostolate is particularly important; I am aware of the difficult problems it raises. I spoke about them in Kinshasa. It is up to you, to you bishops, to solve them in concerted action, maintaining the conviction that, on the basis of the Gospel, according to the centuries-old experience of the Church expressed by the universal Magisterium and thanks to a patient formation of future spouses, it is possible for African couples to live, with particular intensity, the mystery of the covenant, of which God's covenant with His people, the covenant of Jesus Christ with His Church, remains the source and the symbol. Deep and lasting blessings will spring from these Christian families, for the faith of the young and vocations as well.

Your Catholic communities must also establish adequate relations with other Christian communities, with the Muslims and with other religious groups. But, above all, you have still an immense field of evangelization before you: those who remain available for the proclamation of the Gospel, in the villages and towns. There is a specifically missionary apostolate to be carried out here.

DEFINE PASTORAL PLANS TOGETHER

3. All that has its value, its importance, and it is very difficult for me to indicate to you priorities in these sectors of the apostolate. However, I think that you must, without neglecting anything, define pastoral plans together in order that efforts may converge on what is essential, in precise directions, and stick to them with perseverance.

On my part, I would like just to confirm your convictions on some fundamental attitudes.

In the first place with regard to your episcopal ministry. You know its requirements better than anyone. St. Paul warned us that to be ministers of Christ, with our eyes fixed on the Gospel, is to expose ourselves to misunderstanding and tribulations. As one of your proverbs says: "The tree by the side of the path receives blows from all those who pass." But I wish you also great spiritual consolations. Remain spiritual leaders who are at the same time fathers for their people, in the manner of Christ who serves. Be free with regard to all secular power, while recognizing its sphere of competence and its specific responsibility. Continue to call forth wide collaboration on the part of your priests and your laity, to examine problems, and associate them with your decisions. Above all, maintain close union and real collaboration with one another, as also with the bishops of West Africa. O yes, live closely united in the unfailing solidarity among yourselves and with the Holy See; this is your strength.

I lay stress especially on your priests, your born collaborators, whether they were born in the Ivory Coast or have come from afar. They form the same presbyterium, the same family. They are sometimes scattered, in a difficult apostolate. They need particularly to feel your support, your closeness, your friendly presence, your appreciation of their work, your encouragement for a worthy and generous priestly life. And that will also stimulate vocations.

For I greatly encourage the care you dedicate to bringing forth priestly and religious vocations, to providing young and older seminarians with a formation that gives them a taste for the Gospel, a solid faith, and the desire to meet Christ's call and serve the Church in a disinterested way, with regard to all the needs of the Christian communities and also of evangelization. Paul VI had said in Uganda in 1969: "You are your own missionaries." It is more and more necessary for you. The step has already taken place at the level of the episcopate; it must be prepared at the level of priests, even if, as I hope, you will still have at your disposal for a long time to come priests put at your service by other Churches or religious congregations. Finally, I will go even further along this "missionary" way: it is your entire Church that must become missionary, priests, sisters and laity, and the communities themselves, through the welcome, the witness and explicit proclamation, among those who still do not know the Gospel, in this country and in others.

4. These attitudes, as well as the different pastoral works to be promoted, must not make us lose sight of what is essential, dear brothers: the presence of Christ among us, acting with us and through us, to the extent to which we refer to Him our lives, our cares, our hopes, in constant prayer. Help all your collaborators to keep kindled within them this flame of spiritual life, this love of God without which we would be only clanging cymbals. Precisely at the moment when your Ivory Coast society is in rapid economic and cultural expansion, with all the opportunities, but also the temptations to materialism which this involves, it is a question of ensuring to this civilization a soul. Only spiritual beings will be able to bear it along in a deeply Christian direction which is at the same time deeply African. May our Lady open our hearts to the Spirit of her Son! Receive my affectionate blessing.

CHRIST CALLS YOU TO CONSTRUCT A NEW SOCIETY

In the afternoon of May 11, John Paul II travelled by helicopter from Abidjan to Yamoussoukro. On his arrival there he concelebrated Mass with thirteen young priests for the student youth of the country. The celebration was held in the largest square of Yamoussoukro, which by presidential decree of May 10 is now known as John Paul II Square. It was estimated that more than 200,000 were present. During the Mass the Holy Father preached the following homily.

Dear students, boys and girls,

1. How can I thank you for having come in such large numbers, so joyful and trusting, around the Father and Head of the Catholic Church? I hope and I ask God that this meeting may be a moment of deep communion of our hearts and minds, an unforgettable moment for me and a decisive one for you.

Your problems and aspirations as Ivory Coast students have come to my knowledge. They make me both happy and moved. It is, therefore, young people, in a concrete setting and bearers of great human and Christian hopes, that I address with perfect confidence. The Liturgy of the Word which has just ended has certainly contributed to putting your souls in a state of receptiveness. These three readings constitute an ideal framework for the demanding meditation we shall make shortly.

The Church, of which you are members through the sacraments of Baptism and Confirmation—I shall have, moreover, the joy of conferring the latter on some of you—is a Church that has been open, since her foundation, to all men and all cultures; a Church assured of a glorious conclusion through the humiliations and persecutions inflicted upon her in the course of history; a Church mysteriously animated by the Spirit of Pentecost and eager to reveal to men their inalienable dignity and their vocation as "members of God's family," creatures inhabited by God, Father, Son and Spirit. How bracing it is to breathe this atmosphere of a Church always young and resolute!

Your bishops have recently addressed to you, but also to your parents and those in charge of you, a letter intended to diagnose the dangers that threaten youth and bring about, in its ranks as well as among adults, a generous spiritual outburst. Many of you are very conscious of the difficulties and miseries affecting the environments of the young. Without generalizing, they are not afraid to call a spade a spade and to question their elders, referring to the famous words of the prophet Ezekiel: "The fathers have eaten sour grapes, and the children's teeth are set on edge" (Ezek. 18:2).

A CALL TO PERSONAL CONVERSION

2. Today, on my part, I would like to convince you of a truth of common sense but of fundamental importance, which applies to every man and every society that is suffering physically or morally: namely, that a sick person cannot get better unless he himself takes the necessary remedies. That is what

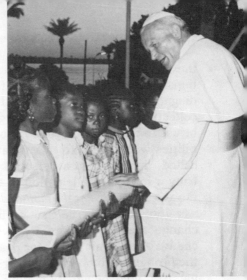

Allow me, further, to stress a very important aspect of your human, intellectual and technical preparation for your future tasks. It is also part of your duties. Preserve carefully your African roots. Safeguard the values of your culture. You know them and are proud of them: respect for life, family solidarity and support for relatives, respect for the old, the sense of hospitality, etc.

the apostle St. James wished to make the first Christians understand (cf. Jas. 1:23-26). What is the use of diagnosing the disease in the mirror of individual and collective conscience, if we forget it immediately or refuse to treat it? Everyone in society bears responsibilities with regard to this situation and each one is called, therefore, to a personal conversion which is truly a form of participation in the evangelization of the world (cf. *Evangelii nuntiandi,* nos. 21, 41). But I ask you: is it not true that if all the young agree to change their own lives, the whole of society will change? Why wait longer for ready-made solutions to the problems from which you are suffering? Your dynamism, your imagination, your faith, are capable of moving mountains!

Let us look together, calmly and realistically at the ways that will lead you towards the society of which you are dreaming: a society built on truth, justice, brotherhood, peace; a society worthy of man and in conformity with God's plan. These ways are inescapably those of your ardent preparation for your responsibilities tomorrow and those of a true spiritual awakening.

Young people of the Ivory Coast, find again together the courage to live! The men who cause history to advance, at the humblest or at the highest level, are those who remain convinced of man's vocation: the vocation of a searcher, of one who strives vigorously, and of a builder. What is your conception of man? It is a fundamental question, because the answer will determine your future and the future of your country, because it is your duty to make a success of your lives.

YOU ARE A PRIVILEGED YOUTH

3. You have, indeed, obligations towards the national community. The past generations carry you invisibly. It is they who enable you to have access to studies and a culture destined to make you the executives of a young nation. The people count on you. Forgive them for considering you privileged persons. You really are privileged, at least on the plane of the distribution of cultural goods. How many young people of your age, in your country and in the world, are at work and are contributing already, as workers or farmers, to the production and economic success of their country! Others, alas, are unemployed, without a trade, and sometimes without hope. Others again have not and will not have the chance to have access to schooling of quality. You have a duty of solidarity towards all. And they have the right to be demanding with regard to you. Dear young people, do you want to be the thinkers, the technicians, the leaders that your country and Africa need? Avoid like the plague carelessness and the easy way out. Be indulgent to others and severe with regard to yourselves! Be men!

PRESERVE ROOTS AND SAFEGUARD VALUES

4. Allow me, further, to stress a very important aspect of your human, intellectual and technical preparation for your future tasks. It is also part of your duties. Preserve carefully your African roots. Safeguard the values of your culture. You know them and are proud of them: respect for life, family solidarity and support for relatives, respect for the old, the sense of hospitality, judicious preservation of tradi-

tions, the taste for feasts and symbols, attachment to dialogue and palaver to settle differences. All that is a real treasure from which you can and must draw something new for the building up of your country, on an original and typically African model, made up of harmony between the values of its cultural past and the most acceptable elements of modern civilization. On this precise plane, remain very vigilant, with regard to models of society which are based on the selfish pursuit of individual happiness and on the god of money, or on the class struggle and violent means. All materialism is a source of degradation for man and of enslavement of social life.

LOOK WITH NEW EYES TOWARDS JESUS

5. Let us go even further in clear vision of the road to take or to continue. Who is your God? Without ignoring any of the difficulties that the social and cultural changes of our time cause all believers, but also thinking of all those who struggle to keep the faith, I venture to say concisely and insistently: Look up! Look with new eyes towards Jesus Christ! I take the liberty of asking you in a friendly way: have you read the letter I wrote last year to all Christians about Christ the Redeemer? In the wake of the Popes who preceded me, Paul VI especially, I endeavored to ward off the temptation and error of modern man and modern societies to exclude God and to put an end to the expression of the religious sentiment.

The death of God in men's hearts and lives is the death of man. I wrote in that letter: "The man who wishes to understand himself thoroughly—and not just in accordance with immediate, partial, often superficial, and even illusory standards and measures of his being—must with his unrest, uncertainty and even his weakness and sinfulness, with his life and death, draw near to Christ. He must, so to speak, enter into Him with all his own self, he must 'appropriate' and assimilate the whole of the reality of the Incarnation and Redemption in order to find himself. If this profound process takes place within him, he then bears fruit not only of adoration of God but also of deep wonder at himself. How precious must man be in the eyes of the Creator, if he 'gained so great a Redeemer,' and if God 'gave his only Son' in order that man 'should not perish but have eternal life!' " *(Redemptor hominis,* no. 10) Yes, beloved young people, Jesus Christ is not a kidnapper of men, but a Savior. And He wants to free you, to make you, one and all, saviors in the student world of today as in the professions and important responsibilities that you will assume tomorrow.

FAITH IS TRULY A GIFT FROM GOD

6. So stop thinking to yourself or saying out loud that the Christian faith is good only for children and simple people. If it still appears to be so, it is because adolescents and adults have seriously neglected to make their faith grow at the same rate as their human development. Faith is not a pretty garment for childhood days. Faith is a gift from God, a stream of light and power that comes from Him, and must enlighten and give dynamic impulse to all sectors of life, in proportion as it takes root in responsibilities. Make up your minds, and persuade your friends and fellow students to adopt the means of a personal religious formation worthy of the name. Take advantage of the

chaplains and animators placed at your disposal. With them, train yourselves to make a synthesis between your human knowledge and your faith, between your African culture and modernity, between your role as citizens and your Christian vocation. Celebrate your faith and learn to pray together.

You will find again in this way the sense of the Church which is communion in the same Lord among believers, who then go out into the midst of their brothers and sisters to love them and serve them in the way of Christ. You have a vital need of integration in Christian, brotherly and dynamic communities. Frequent them assiduously. Inspire them with the breath of your youth. Build them, if they do not exist. In this way your temptation to go and seek elsewhere —in esoteric groups—what Christianity brings you fully, will disappear.

APOSTOLIC COMMITMENT

7. Logically, the personal and community deepening of faith of which we have just spoken, must lead you to concrete apostolic commitments. Many of you are already on this way, and I congratulate you. Young people of the Ivory Coast, today Christ calls you through His representative on earth. He calls you exactly as He called Peter and Andrew, James and John and the other Apostles. He calls you to construct His Church, to build a new society. Come in crowds! Take your place in your Christian communities. Offer loyally your time and your talents, your heart and your faith to animate liturgical celebrations, to take part in the immense amount of catechetical work among children, adolescents and even adults, and to

be integrated in the numerous services for the benefit of the poorest, illiterates, the handicapped, the isolated, refugees and migrants, to animate your student movements, to work with the authorities for the defence and promotion of the human person. Truly, the workyard is immense and stirring for young people who feel overflowing with life.

It seems to me the very moment to address those young people who are going to receive the sacrament of Confirmation, precisely in order to enter a new stage of their baptismal life: the stage of active service in the immense workyard of the evangelization of the world. The laying on of hands and the anointing with the holy chrism will really and effectively signify the plenary coming of the Holy Spirit into the very depth of your person, at the crossroads, in a way, of your human faculties of intelligence in search of truth and freedom, in pursuit of an ideal. Your Confirmation today is your Pentecost for life! Realize the seriousness and grandeur of this sacrament.

What will be your lifestyle from now on? That of the Apostles when they came out of the Upper Room! That of Christians of every era, energetically faithful to prayer, to deepening of, and bearing witness to, faith, to the breaking of the eucharistic bread, to service of one's neighbor and especially of the poorest (cf. Acts 2:42-47). Young confirmed persons of today or yesterday, advance all of you along the ways of life as fervent witnesses of Pentecost, an inexhaustible source of youth and dynamism for the Church and for the world.

Expect to meet sometimes with opposition, contempt, mockery. True disciples are not above the Master. Their crosses are like the passion and cross of

Christ: a mysterious source of fruitfulness. This paradox of suffering offered and fruitful has been confirmed for twenty centuries by the history of the Church.

Allow me finally to assure you that such apostolic commitments prepare you not only to bear your heavy responsibilities in the future, but also to found solid homes, without which a nation cannot hold out long; and what is more, Christian homes, which are so many basic cells of the ecclesial community. There are commitments which will lead some of you towards complete donation to Christ, in the priest-hood or religious life. The dioceses of the Ivory Coast, like all the dioceses of Africa, have the right to rely on your generous response to the call that the Lord cer-tainly makes many of you hear: "Come, and follow me."

A flash in the pan, this celebration? A flash in the pan, this meditation? The liturgical texts of this sixth Sunday of Easter affirm the contrary. The Gospel of John assures us that the Holy Spirit dwells in the lov-ing and faithful hearts of the disciples of Christ. His role is to refresh their memory as believers, to enlight-en them in depth, to help them to solve the problems of their time, in the peace and hope of the new world conjured up in the reading from Revelation.

May this same Holy Spirit unite us all and dedi-cate us all to the service of God our Father and of men our brothers, through Christ, in Christ, and with Christ! Amen.

GREAT MYSTERY OF SOLIDARITY IN SUFFERING

After the Mass at Yamoussoukro, the Holy Father returned to Abidjan by helicopter. On his arrival in the Nunciature about 11:00 p.m. he met a group of Polish immigrants with whom he remained for about half an hour.

Next morning, May 12, after celebrating Mass in the Nunciature, John Paul II met President Felix Houphouët-Boigny. Afterwards he went by helicopter to the leprosarium of Adzope. The Pope's meeting with the lepers was his last engagement in Africa, and perhaps the most moving. He visited the "Raoul Folloreau" National Institute for Leprosy founded in 1971. After greeting all the patients suffering from the disease, and also the medical and religious staff, he spoke to them as follows.

Dear friends,

1. I come to pay you a visit, and in the first place to greet you, one and all, with respect, with affection.

It is the Bishop of Rome who comes to you, that is, the spiritual Head of the Catholic community of Rome. But he has at the same time the task of being the center of unity among Christians of the whole world, of being their Pastor, like the shepherds of flocks who do not forget any lamb. In this leper hospital, not all are Catholics; I respect their religious sentiments, their way of addressing God, according to their conscience. For no one is dispensed from turning towards God, and how can we forget Him in times

389

of affliction? But I think I have a good word for everyone. For Christ Jesus, the Son of God, whom I serve and represent among you, stopped with predilection before human suffering, disease, infirmity and, above all, infirmity which sets one somewhat apart from others, such as leprosy, and which thus creates a double suffering.

Certainly, He came for everyone, in order that everyone, big and small, rich or poor, the just and sinners, may know that the kingdom of God was open to them, that the love of God was upon them, that the life of God was destined for them, by means of faith and conversion. The Pope also addresses the whole people and, if he meets especially the spiritual and civil leaders, it is because their responsibilities are wider, for the good of a large number. But I should fail in my mission if I did not pass considerable time with those that Jesus loved particularly, because of their misery, because they needed comfort, relief, cure and hope. So I wanted my last visit in Africa to be for you. And through you, I visit in spirit and embrace all the other lepers and sick people of this country, and of the whole of Africa.

2. Thanks to medicine, thanks to the zeal of admirable pioneers, thanks to the daily dedication of numerous men and women nurses, of friends of every kind who help you, among whom there are many religious, thanks also to the civil leaders who have promoted the assumption of this responsibility, it has been possible to improve your fate; not only your health, but your environment, often permitting you to live, as it were, in a village, as if in a family. Now leprosy is no longer so frightening as before, especially if it is detected and treated quite early. I join you in

But I should fail in my mission if I did not pass considerable time with those that Jesus loved particularly, because of their misery, because they needed comfort, relief, cure and hope. So I wanted my last visit in Africa to be for you. And through you, I visit in spirit and embrace all the other lepers and sick people of this country, and of the whole of Africa.

thanking all these friends of lepers, who dedicate their lives to you. Without knowing it, perhaps, or without believing it, they are doing exactly what Christ asked. May God sustain them and reward them!

3. But I am sure too that they receive consolation from you. Not only because you love them, but because they admire your patience, your serenity, your courage, the solidarity that unites you, the family sense that you maintain. For you are not just in the care of others; you take charge of yourselves, you do everything you can to live, to walk, to work, with poor means, with the handicapped limbs that the disease leaves you. This hope is beautiful. I am moved by it myself. This desire to live pleases God, and I hope that you will develop it. You are, it could be said, your own doctors.

4. But I do not come just to give you this human encouragement. I come to confirm what priests, sisters and Christian laity have probably said to you already: in your misery, God loves you. This disease does not correspond to His plan of love. And you yourselves are in no way to blame. Do not look upon it as a fatality. Look upon it just as a trial. The Christ we worship Himself underwent a trial, that of the cross, a trial that disfigured Him, and that without any fault of His own. He put Himself in the hands of God, His Father. He turned towards Him to ask for deliverance too. But He accepted; He offered. And His suffering became for countless men, for you, for me, a cause of salvation, forgiveness, grace and life.

This solidarity in suffering is a great mystery. It is the heart of our religion. Those who are Christians understand my language. Your suffering, accepted, borne with patience and love of others, offered to God, becomes a source of grace, for you for whom the Lord has His paradise in store, and for many others. You can also pray for me, and for all those who entrust their misery to me.

May God help you! May God give you peace!

5. I now turn towards those among you who have opened their souls to faith in Jesus Christ the Savior and who are going to receive Baptism and Confirmation after a long preparation. What grace! They are going to become visibly members of the family of Christians, the Church. After renouncing the devil and his allurements and proclaiming their faith, they, too, are going to receive, like us, with forgiveness of their sins, the life of Christ, in order to participate in His sacrifice and His resurrection. Love of God will be spread in their hearts by the Holy Spirit. They will be able to receive as nourishment the holy Bread that is the Body of Christ. God, the Father, Son and Holy Spirit, will dwell in them. They will become in their turn witnesses to Christ's love for their suffering brothers.

God bless you, dear sons and daughters! May He bless all the inhabitants of this leper hospital! May He bless all your brothers who are suffering from leprosy as well as their families, their friends and those who assist them!

FAREWELL, AFRICA! I TAKE WITH ME ALL YOU HAVE REVEALED

After visiting the leprosarium, the Holy Father travelled by helicopter to Abidjan Airport. Present to greet him before his departure for Rome were the President of the Republic, Felix Houphouët-Boigny, Archbishop Bernard Yago and all the bishops of the Ivory Coast, and an immense gathering of people. Before boarding the Air Afrique DC-10 that would bring him to Rome, the Holy Father made the following speech of farewell in the VIP lounge.

At the end of my visit to the Republic of the Ivory Coast, it is with a grateful heart that I address you, Mr. President, for the last time, and, through you, the whole people of the Ivory Coast. Thank you, yes, thank you for your really unforgettable welcome, for the warmth of our meetings, and for the fervent and friendly atmosphere that has marked all contacts. Thank you for having understood the special character I wished to give to this stay, in keeping with my spiritual mission of universal service. Thank you for your joy. Mine has been even greater. I feel the honor you have done me. I appreciate also your efforts to give your guest a hospitality worthy of the Ivory Coast and of Africa. I will always remember all that, I promise you.

In particular, I thank the authorities for the honor they have done me in naming after me a street of the city of Abidjan and the Great Square of Yamoussoukro. It is a delicate gesture which I hope will contribute not only to keeping alive the memory of my visit but, above all, of my esteem and affection for all the people of the Ivory Coast.

Moreover, I rejoice at having had the opportunity to bless the foundation stone of the cathedral of Abidjan and of the church of Our Lady of Africa. A personal bond is thus established between the Pope and these two churches. I dare to hope that all those who pray therein, will not forget to pray also for the universal Church...and for me!

The journey outside of the capital which I undertook yesterday in order to meet the youth of this country, has been for me an experience of joy and an hour of hope for the future of this dear country.

2. To Most Reverend Bernard Yago, my brother bishops and all the Catholics of the country, now that it is necessary to bid them farewell, may I confide a certain incipient nostalgia? That of having seen living communities, full of enthusiasm and imagination, and of having to leave them now. Imagination is a virtue that is given too little consideration. But you are able to give proof of it in order to find, in the context that is yours, suitable ways of evangelization. In this way you set an example that could serve to encourage other episcopal Conferences and other local Churches.

That creates for you at the same time a kind of moral obligation, in the name of the solidarity of members of the Body of Christ, which is that everyone, the clergy, men and women religious, the laity, should try to purify their witness further in order to make it more and more in conformity with what the Lord expects. I express to you my hope at the same time as my deep satisfaction.

3. Farewell now, Africa, this continent which I love so much already and which I had been longing, since my election to Peter's See, to discover and traverse. Farewell to the peoples that have received me, and to all the others to whom I should like so much, one day, if Providence permits, to bring my affection personally. I have learned a great many things during this journey. You cannot know how instructive it has been. In my turn I would like to leave to Africans a message which has sprung from my heart, which has been meditated upon before God, and which is demanding because it comes from a friend for friends.

Africa struck me as being a vast workyard, from all points of view, with its promises and also, perhaps, its risks. Wherever you go, you admire a considerable undertaking in favor of development and of raising the standard of living, in favor of the progress of man and society. There is a long way to go. Methods can be different and turn out to be more or less suitable. But the desire to advance is undeniable. Already, considerable results have been obtained. Education is spreading, diseases that used to be fatal are overcome, new techniques are started, success is beginning to be achieved in the struggle against certain natural obstacles. The value of the riches peculiar to the African soul is also being felt more, and that arouses pride. Parallelly, accession to national sovereignty and respect for it seem to be the object of everyone's aspirations.

There is here an important heritage, which must absolutely be safeguarded and promoted harmoniously. It is not easy to control this seething life, to make sure that its living forces are used for true development. There is a great temptation in fact to demolish instead of constructing, to acquire at a high price arms for populations that need bread, to want to seize power—even by setting some ethnical groups against others, in bloody and fratricidal struggles —whereas the poor are longing for peace, or else to succumb to the intoxication of profit for the benefit of a privileged class.

Do not get caught up, dear African brothers and sisters, in this disastrous mechanism, which has really nothing to do with your dignity as creatures of God, or with what you are capable of. You have not to imitate certain foreign models, based on contempt of man or on interest. You have not to run after artificial needs which will give you an illusory freedom or which will lead you to individualism, whereas the community aspiration is so strong in you. Nor have you to delude yourselves about the virtues of ideologies which hold out bright prospects of complete happiness, always postponed to tomorrow.

Be yourselves. I assure you, you can; you who are so proud of your possibilities, give the world the proof that you are capable of solving your own problems yourselves, with the humanitarian, economic and cultural assistance which is still useful for you and which is only justice, but taking care to turn all that in the right direction.

A personal and social morality is necessary if you wish to succeed in this. Honesty, the sense of work, of service, of the common good, the deep sense of life in society, or the sense of life itself, these are words or expressions that appeal to you already. I hope that you will always seek their concrete and loyal application, as I hope that my Catholic sons and daughters will put them better into practice themselves and help people to discover their significance.

4. I came to Africa in particular to commemorate the centenary of evangelization in several countries. They are anniversaries charged with hope, the hope of a new lease of life to undertake a new stage. This applies, moreover, to all the countries I visited. You are the Church in Africa. What an honor, and also what a responsibility! You are the whole Church and at the same time, you are a part of the universal Church, rather like the Gospel which belongs to everyone and is also addressed to everyone. Rather like Jesus Christ Himself who, having become incarnate within a people, lives His Incarnation with each people, for He came for everyone, He belongs to everyone, He is the marvelous gift of the Father to the whole of mankind. I really believe and I profess that He came for Africans, to raise and save the African soul, which is also waiting for salvation, to show it its beauty but also to enrich it from within, to preach to it eternal life with God. He came for Africans as for all men, that is to say, for the same reason, and He is not alien to any national sentiment, to any mentality, inviting His disciples, from whatever continent they may come, to live the admirable exchange of faith and charity with one another.

Like Him, I would like to say to you, on this day, with all the love that fills my heart: the Pope is the servant of all men, the Pope feels at home in Africa!

Farewell, Africa! I take with me all that you have so generously given me and all that you have revealed to me in the course of this journey. May God bless you in each of your children, and may He let you enjoy peace and prosperity!

Like Jesus, I would like to say to you, on this day, with all the love that fills my heart: the Pope is the servant of all men, the Pope feels at home in Africa!

COLLABORATION OF JOURNALISTS FOR THE SPREAD OF THE TRUTH

During his return flight to Rome on May 12, John Paul II went to the part of the plane reserved for the journalists and the others of the communications media who had accompanied him on his journey. After answering their questions for quite a while, he then expressed his thanks to them, speaking first in French and then in English.

I am anxious to express my hearty thanks to the journalists, and all agents of social communication, the press, radio and television. In the first place to those who have accompanied me throughout this journey, with a patience worthy of Africa, in the sun, at the cost of a great deal of fatigue. That is part of your profession, but I am aware of your merits. I thank also those who, on the spot, in Africa, did their work of reporting, recording and disseminating, all the more so because the program was a very heavy one, for them as for me! Finally, I thank the people of the mass media who, in other countries, reported this journey, and gave it appropriate coverage, for readers and listeners.

I know that many other important events were taking place in the world, and they were not absent from my thought and my prayer. But Africa also deserved, and had deserved for a long time, this place of honor. It is sometimes apart from the great discussions and confrontations of world policy; yet it, too, has great human problems to solve, and its efforts deserve to be encouraged. The Church has also a great vitality to unfold.

But I will not insist on the meaning of my journey. It is up to you to define it, from many addresses and deeds, by just telling the truth, what you have seen and heard. It is difficult sometimes for non-Africans to avoid projecting on this continent and its inhabitants judgments and interpretations that are far from African realities, from the African soul, from its aspirations and its reactions.

I have often used the word "witnesses" for Christians. Be good witnesses. And once more, thank you for your collaboration.

UNIQUE AND PROFOUND PASTORAL EXPERIENCE

On his return to Rome at about 8:00 p.m. on May 12, John Paul II was welcomed by the Prime Minister, Honorable Francesco Cossiga, and by numerous Cardinals and ecclesiastical and civil authorities.

In reply to the Prime Minister's greetings the Holy Father spoke as follows.

LAUS DEO!

This brief ejaculation, which rises spontaneously to my lips after my journey in the African continent, is intended to express the deep feeling of gratitude and honor to the Lord, that I now feel in my soul, thinking of the many meetings, the moving spectacles of faith, the extraordinary pastoral hopes, which I experienced daily in the span, short though it was, of ten days. I must really thank the Lord with all my heart for having given me once more the opportunity of getting to know, close at hand, choice portions of His undivided Church, bringing to the beloved brothers and sons who live in the lands I visited that comfort that I must give them according to the mandate received from Christ (cf. Lk. 22:32: *Confirma fratres tuos!*). In my turn—according to that admirable law of exchange, intrinsic in ecclesial communion—I have drawn reasons for comfort for my ministry.

I was able to enjoy, in fact, deep joy at bringing the word of the Lord to those peoples as the missionaries did a hundred years ago; and this joy was increased by being able to see the maturity which those Churches have reached, in spite of their relatively recent foundation. Their testimony of faith and their love for the whole Church of Christ, scattered all over the world, gave me deep comfort. Nor can I pass over in silence the deep impression made on me by the vitality of that continent, which preserves intact a good many fundamental moral values, such as those of hospitality, the family, the community sense, life as a precious gift, which is always given a generous and happy welcome.

When, at the general audience on last March 26, I announced the official communication of the journey, which now is happily concluded, I wished to point out its apostolic character, and I said that it was only the intention of fulfilling my mission as pastor that prompted the journey. In consistency with that announcement, I can now state that my visit was really such. I approached so many souls; I was able to realize the living conditions of so many peoples; I was able to see to my deep satisfaction—on the basis of a "test" that was, I would say, vast and representative enough—the magnificent work that was done in the past and which is still being continued for the increase of the kingdom of God. Africa is nurtured on the Gospel of our Lord Jesus Christ, it is dedicated to the glory of His Name, it is open to the breath of His Spirit. LAUS DEO!

My thanks turn, then, to all those who, in each of the six countries that I visited, arranged, with exquisite delicacy, the most fitting and carefully planned reception. I wish therefore to name all the civil and religious authorities of those countries, and in particular my brother bishops, of whom I admired both their individual activity and their collegial work within the episcopal conferences, the priests and religious, men and women missionaries, exponents and members of Catholic lay movements, Christian families, and all the faithful. What they did for me, what they showed me with their deeds, their words and their attention, will remain indelibly imprinted on my memory as a sign and stimulus of sincere gratitude. Africa has a great future before it; my wish for that immense continent is that it will be able to continue with increasing achievements along the way of peace, industry, and solidarity at home and abroad.

I must finally thank each of you present here. Mr. President of the Council of Ministers, I am very grateful to you for the respectful words you addressed to me at the moment when I set foot again on the beloved and always hospitable soil of Italy. And to you, brother Cardinals and Bishops, Your Excellencies, the Ambassadors of the countries accredited to the Holy See, Mr. Mayor of Rome, I wish to say that I consider your coming here as a cordial support of the initiative of my journey, and its aims; I know that you have also prayed for its success. Therefore, I have more than one reason to thank you publicly and call upon you, also, to direct this sentiment with me to Him who is the generous Giver of every good and who alone can give the necessary increase to human enterprises (cf. 1 Cor. 3:6-7).

LAUS DEO!

In Africa I approached so many souls,...and I was able to see to my deep satisfaction...the magnificent work that was done in the past and which is still being continued for the increase of the kingdom of God. Africa is nurtured on the Gospel of our Lord Jesus Christ, it is dedicated to the glory of His name, it is open to the breath of His Spirit.

JOY OF COMMUNION
IN CHRIST'S
ONE CHURCH

At the beginning of the general audience on May 14, the Holy Father spoke briefly, as follows, about his journey to Africa.

I cannot begin today's meeting without manifesting my deep gratitude to God, who guided my steps along the ways of Africa. In the course of ten days He permitted me to visit six different countries of the African continent, thereby granting me the opportunity to live, together with so many brothers and sisters of ours in the Faith, the joy of spiritual communion in the one Church of Christ and at the same time to share with so many new societies, which are opening to life, the joy of their young independence and sovereignty.

For all that I express the deepest gratitude to God and to Christ, the Redeemer of man and of the world and, at the same time, the Lord, crucified and risen, of the history of mankind. I also express deep thanks to all those in the African continent, who welcomed me as pastor and, at the same time, as father and brother. They were bishops, priests, religious sisters and brothers; they were lay people: men and women, young people and children. They were heads of state and authorities, and also representatives of ancient tribal traditions. They were married couples and families. They were Catholics and Christians, as well as Moslems and followers of the traditional African religions, in which there is also a core of the original revelation.

Thanks to this visit I was able to meet, even though briefly, those dear populations, to enjoy their spiritual youth, to pay tribute to their beautiful cultural traditions and at the same time to the many successes they have obtained.

I wish to return to the subject of the pilgrimage in the African continent next week and perhaps also on other occasions. These words today are only a first expression, dictated by an urgent need of the heart and by a deep sense of gratitude.

VITALITY OF THE CHURCH IN AFRICA DUE TO THE MISSIONARIES' LABORS

On Sunday, May 18, Pope John Paul II was sixty years old. A huge crowd was present in St. Peter's Square at noon to wish him a happy birthday. He said that he did not regard himself as one year older, but rather as one year younger—because he was one year nearer to death, and therefore to the new birth.

He asked his hearers to pray for his parents, for those who had been killed in the crush in Kinshasa before his Mass two weeks before, and also for the faithful in Czechoslovakia.

1. In this common prayer of ours in honor of the Queen of heaven and Mother of the risen Christ, I wish, in the first place, that we should unite with every parish, every community of the People of God, and every missionary station of the African continent, which I had the joy of visiting at the beginning of this month. In the course of that pilgrimage I met a great many crowds, gathered in some centers. Only a few times was it possible for me to arrive at a normal mission station. However, I am fully aware that precisely in those places, around a priest—sometimes already African, often still a missionary—with the help of the local sisters and catechists, the very structure of the Faith and the sacramental life of the Church in Africa

is being constructed. There the sons and daughters of the black continent gather round a teacher and apostle, around Christ's priest; and the Lord Himself is in their midst.

Today, the first Sunday after the return from my pilgrimage, I wish to unite myself in a particular way, in paschal joy and in the prayer of the *Regina Caeli*, with all those communities, living cells of the Church, which is developing in the whole African continent, to which I renew with particular intensity of feeling my greeting and my good wishes.

2. At the same time, with the same prayer I turn in another direction. I am induced to do so by the memory of St. John of Nepomucene, a priest and martyr, a son of the Czechoslovakian nation, who is venerated by the Church precisely in these days of May.

Therefore, in memory of this saint, I commend to the prayer of all of you gathered here—and of all those who are listening to me—our brothers and sisters in the Faith who belong to that nation and live in that country. Owing to my origin, they are particularly close to my heart; from the beginning of history they have been the kindred and neighbors of the Poles, and it was from them that my country of origin received Christianity a thousand years ago.

Let us pray, therefore, that believers in Christ may distinguish themselves in modern Czechoslovakia for their consistency in confessing Christ and that they may enjoy full religious freedom in every field of life and activity, including also the possibility of living normally the priestly and religious vocations, which the Lord does not fail to bestow on so many brothers of ours in those lands. Doing so, we are praying at the same time likewise for the good of society and the state, which also depends on respect for the rights of all citizens.

I entrust this supplication to our Lady, who is greatly venerated in that nation, while I renew to the whole Czechoslovakian people, with special intensity of feelings, the expression of my deep and sincere affection and most fervent wishes for the social and civil progress of the country.

3. This Sunday is also the fourteenth World Day of Social Communications. In view of the importance that the mass media have in the life of the Church for the proclamation of the Gospel to modern man, I wished to dedicate a special message to this celebration, which was published a few days ago, as you know. The theme submitted to common reflection this year is: "The role of social communications and the tasks of the family." Everyone can see how important and how delicate the subject is. The Pope's wish is that Christians and all men of goodwill will do their utmost so that, on the one hand, operators of social communications will feel committed to publicizing what helps to strengthen the foundations of the institution of the family and to promote a healthy process of formation in the young, and on the other hand, families will be able to use with discernment the various means of communication in harmony with the requirements, the duties and the rights of all their members.

Let there not be lacking a special, fervent prayer on the part of everyone for this purpose.

APOSTOLIC JOURNEYS
IMPLEMENT VATICAN II

On Wednesday, May 21, the general audience began at 5:30 p.m. in St. Peter's Square, and it was about 9:00 p.m. when the Holy Father left the Square. The following is the text of his address.

1. Today I wish to speak of Africa, of my ten day pilgrimage in that continent. I do so, in the first place, to meet a need of my heart, and also—at least in a provisional draft—the requirements of a first balance-sheet. It would be difficult, indeed, to think of a full settlement of the debt which I contracted, for this visit, towards so many men, as well as societies and Churches in Africa. It would be all the more difficult to "narrate" in an address, a comparatively short one, this event, or rather the whole series of events that took place, so eloquent and full of manifold content. It is a subject that must return again and again and bear fruit for a long time to come.

Right from the first days of my pastoral service in the Roman See of St. Peter, I felt a deep need to approach the black continent. Therefore I accepted with joy, first of all, the invitation from the Episcopate of Zaire, an invitation connected with the first centenary of evangelization in that country. Subsequently, another similar invitation arrived from the Episcopate of Ghana, where, likewise, the beginning of the evangelizing mission of the Church goes back to the year 1880.

However, alongside these invitations, justified by a special anniversary, there soon appeared others from different African countries. They came from the various episcopates and also from representatives of the civil authorities. There were so many of them that it was impossible to accept them all during this first journey. Although the ten day itinerary included, in addition to Zaire and Ghana, also Congo-Brazzaville, Kenya, Upper Volta and the Ivory Coast, this is only a part of the task which I have to carry out and which, with God's help, I wish to accomplish. I consider it, in fact, my pastoral duty.

MISSIONARY AWARENESS

2. The above-mentioned events can be considered in different ways, just as it is possible to evaluate differently all this way of exercising the pastoral service of the Bishop of Rome in the universal Church. However, the fact remains that John XXIII already foresaw such possibilities, ánd Paul VI carried them out on a vast scale. That is certainly connected also with the development of the modern media of communication—but, above all, it is connected with the new missionary awareness of the Church. We owe this awareness to the Second Vatican Council, which showed, to its deepest roots, the theological significance of the truth that the Church is continually in a state of mission (*in statu missionis*). It cannot be otherwise, since there constantly remains in her the mission, that is, the apostolic mandate of Christ, the

Son of God, and the invisible mission of the Holy
Spirit, who is given by the Father to the Church and
by means of the Church to men and to peoples, thanks
to the crucified and risen Christ.

It can be said, therefore, that after Vatican II it is
not possible to carry out any service in the Church, unless in the sense of the missionary awareness formed
in this way. This has become, in a way, a fundamental
dimension of the living faith of every Christian, a way
of life of every parish, of every religious congregation
and of the various communities. It has become an
essential characteristic of every "particular" Church,
that is, of every diocese. Therefore, it has also become
a specific and appropriate way of carrying out the
pastoral mission of the Bishop of Rome. It seems that
after the Second Vatican Council he cannot accomplish his service in any other way but by going
out towards men, therefore towards peoples and nations, in the spirit of the words—so clear—of Christ
who ordered the Apostles to go all over the world and
"make disciples of all nations, baptizing them in the
name of the Father and of the Son and of the Holy
Spirit" (Mt. 28:18).

VATICAN II GIVES ADDED INCENTIVE

3. The doctrine of the Second Vatican Council
constituted the most adequate preparation for the
Pope's pilgrimage in Africa, almost an indispensable
"manual." It can be said, at the same time, that this
same journey or pilgrimage is nothing but the implementation, that is, the introduction into practical
life, of the doctrine of Vatican II. That might, perhaps,
surprise some people, but it is precisely so. The doc-

trine of the Council is not, in fact, a collection of abstract concepts and formulas on the subject of the Church, but is a deep and global teaching on the life of the Church. This life of the Church is a mission in which, through the history of every man and, at the same time, through the history of nations and generations, the eternal mystery of God's love revealed in Christ is developed and realized. The African continent is an immense area in which this dynamic process is carried out with special expressiveness. The soul of Africa deserves the remark that Tertullian, himself an African, once made about it, namely, that it is *naturaliter christiana*. In any case, it is a deeply religious soul in the layers, still vast, of its traditional religious spirit, sensitive to the sacred dimension of the whole being, convinced of the existence of God and of His influence on creation, open to what is beyond that which is earthly and beyond the grave.

Although only a part of the inhabitants of the black continent (of whom thirteen percent are Catholics) have accepted the Gospel, there is, however, a great readiness to accept it; and the enthusiasm of the faith and the vitality of the Church is also significant. It can be said that all this—both the internal mission of the Church, and ecumenism, and also the influence of Islamism and the range, still vast and perhaps prevalent, of the traditional religion, or animism—can be rightly understood only with the help of the teaching of the Council in the Dogmatic Constitution on the Church, *Lumen gentium,* and in particular, in the chapter on the People of God. Here the individual members of this people were defined in relation to the eternal salvific will of God, Creator and Father, and to the reality of the Redemption and mediation of Christ, which do not exclude anyone, and also, finally, in relation to the mysterious action of the Holy Spirit, which penetrates human hearts and consciences.

THE CHURCH IS MISSIONARY

4. Having before our eyes this rich and differentiated image that the Council has portrayed, we move among the men and peoples of Africa not only with deep awareness of the mission, but also with the particular hope of salvation, which—if it is also accomplished outside the visible Church—is carried out, however, through Christ operating in the Church. That explains also, perhaps, that unusual relationship established with a pilgrim, who did not represent any temporal power, but came exclusively in Christ's name, to bear witness to His infinite love of men, of every man and all men—even those who do not yet know Him and have not yet fully accepted His Gospel together with the sacramental ministry of the Church.

At the same time, this great and yet differentiated meeting bears witness to how enormous the missionary task of the Church still is in this promising continent. Although, in the individual countries, most of the episcopates consist of black bishops, yet not only a large part of the clergy and of the personnel engaged in evangelization are still made up of men and women missionaries but also requests for them continue to be numerous, perhaps more numerous, indeed, than ever. The most vigilant pastors—sons of the black continent—often speak of it, adding that there has arrived a special hour of Africa in the history of evangelization and that really "the harvest is plentiful" (Mt. 9:37). How admirable, therefore, are for example those white bishops who, after making way for their African successors, continue to work as missionaries in the normal everyday apostolate of those Churches! How much their example should attract others!

5. In this concise description, I still owe the last word to the young African societies, which have recently become independent, to the new sovereign states of that continent. The Church attributes great importance to them—as the Constitution *Gaudium et spes*, for example, bears witness—guided by motives that are not political, but first and foremost ethical, in character. I tried everywhere, therefore, to manifest the joy deriving from the fact that, thanks to the sovereignty of African societies, the natural rights of the nation are fulfilled; living and developing autonomously, it realizes its innate dignity, its own culture, and can serve other societies more fully, by means of the fruit of its mature activity. The Church, which tries on her side in the various continents to help the development of nations and societies, rejoices in what she has already been able to do in this field in the African continent, and wishes also in the future to serve the young nations of the black continent with all dedication and love.

I think that my first pilgrimage in African countries has given this reality the due and indispensable expression. Therefore, I express once more my gratitude to God Himself, who directed my steps to those countries—and also to all those who, in different ways, helped me to carry out this task.

God bless Africa: all its sons and its daughters!

God bless Africa: all its sons and daughters!

INDEX

politics 44, 126, 215
poor, the 102, 108, 208, 311f., 357
Pope 75, 134, 185, 261, 274, 353, 379;
    see also *Bishop of Rome, Successor of Peter, Vicar of Christ*
  pastoral service of 412
poverty 45, 196
  religious 83, 298, 355
  vow of 79
power 93, 209
prayer 37, 82, 101, 123, 220, 260, 285,
    307, 352, 387
  apostolate of cloistered religious 81
  life of 352
  for vocations 222
  of Christ 270
  power of 242
  strength of Church 352
preaching 235
prejudices 78, 265
presbyterium 38f., 126, 333, 355
press 330, 334; see also *communication, social; media*
priest(s) 26, 35, 37ff., 59ff., 68f., 76,
    98, 101f., 108, 122ff., 148, 157,
    161, 167, 181, 222, 246, 250, 296f.,
    333f., 354f., 363, 408f.
  ministry of 121
  seminary training of 245
priesthood 18, 37, 98, 123, 127, 129f.,
    196, 222, 244, 257, 276, 297, 305f.,
    364f., 388
progress 45ff., 53, 57, 93, 104, 112,
    118, 128, 153, 209, 267, 315, 321,
    345
prosperity 26, 165
prudence 64, 102
purity 37

races 76
racism 91
radio 330
rapprochement 357
realism 53
reconciliation, ministry of 126
Redeemer 51; see also *Jesus Christ*
Redemption 66, 150, 174
Redemptor hominis 384-385
refugees 206f.
religion 30, 111, 204

religious 37, 60, 76ff., 81, 102, 108,
    125, 127, 129, 244, 250, 257, 259,
    282, 297, 334, 355; see also *life, consecrated*
  cloistered 81, 219
  men and women 26, 38, 61, 69, 121,
    148, 157, 167, 181ff., 196, 221,
    365f.
religious life 77, 297f., 388
renunciation 53
research 113
respect 53
responsibility(ies) 210, 214
  of citizens 215
  pastoral 61
  political 202
  social 56, 382
resurrection 140
retreats 57, 83
revolution, social 357
rich, the 311f.
rights 104, 126, 134, 204, 254
  human 30, 90, 93, 203, 205f., 232
  inalienable 153
  of citizens 215
  of man 57
  of nations 416
Rome 18, 402
rosary, the 136, 138, 169, 177f.

sacrament(s) 54, 82, 98, 101, 125f.,
    159, 276, 292
sacrifice 40, 124, 358
Sahel 323, 327ff.
salvation 28, 33, 40, 132f., 156, 159,
    213f., 274, 303, 392
  message of 242
  plan of 356
Samaritan woman 20
sanctification 53
sanctity 102
schools 72
  Catholic 375
  centers of culture 215
science(s) 111, 113ff., 329
Scripture 123, 269; see also *Bible, Word of God*
Second Vatican Council see *Vatican Council II*

Daughters of St. Paul

IN MASSACHUSETTS
    50 St. Paul's Ave. Jamaica Plain, Boston, MA 02130;
       617-522-8911; 617-522-0875;
    172 Tremont Street, Boston, MA 02111; 617-426-5464;
       617-426-4230
IN NEW YORK
    78 Fort Place, Staten Island, NY 10301; 212-447-5071
    59 East 43rd Street, New York, NY 10017; 212-986-7580
    7 State Street, New York, NY 10004; 212-447-5071
    625 East 187th Street, Bronx, NY 10458; 212-584-0440
    525 Main Street, Buffalo, NY 14203; 716-847-6044
IN NEW JERSEY
    Hudson Mall — Route 440 and Communipaw Ave.,
      Jersey City, NJ 07304; 201-433-7740
IN CONNECTICUT
    202 Fairfield Ave., Bridgeport, CT 06604; 203-335-9913
IN OHIO
    2105 Ontario St. (at Prospect Ave.), Cleveland, OH 44115; 216-621-9427
    25 E. Eighth Street, Cincinnati, OH 45202; 513-721-4838
IN PENNSYLVANIA
    1719 Chestnut Street, Philadelphia, PA 19103; 215-568-2638
IN FLORIDA
    2700 Biscayne Blvd., Miami, FL 33137; 305-573-1618
IN LOUISIANA
    4403 Veterans Memorial Blvd., Metairie, LA 70002; 504-887-7631;
      504-887-0113
    1800 South Acadian Thruway, P.O. Box 2028, Baton Rouge, LA 70821
      504-343-4057; 504-343-3814
IN MISSOURI
    1001 Pine Street (at North 10th), St. Louis, MO 63101; 314-621-0346;
      314-231-1034
IN ILLINOIS
    172 North Michigan Ave., Chicago, IL 60601; 312-346-4228
IN TEXAS
    114 Main Plaza, San Antonio, TX 78205; 512-224-8101
IN CALIFORNIA
    1570 Fifth Avenue, San Diego, CA 92101; 714-232-1442
    46 Geary Street, San Francisco, CA 94108; 415-781-5180
IN HAWAII
    1143 Bishop Street, Honolulu, HI 96813; 808-521-2731
IN ALASKA
    750 West 5th Avenue, Anchorage AK 99501; 907-272-8183
IN CANADA
    3022 Dufferin Street, Toronto 395, Ontario, Canada
IN ENGLAND
    57, Kensington Church Street, London W. 8, England
IN AUSTRALIA
    58 Abbotsford Rd., Homebush, N.S.W., Sydney 2140, Australia